DAI-UY

To
JOSEPH

WITH EVERY
BEST WISH

DAI-UY

DAI-UY

LT. COL. JAMES E. BEHNKE, USA/RET

Behnke Books

© 1992 Lt. Col. James Behnke, USA/RET

First Edition
First printing, October 1992

Published by
Behnke Books
P.O. Box 888
Bisbee, Arizona 85603

Typographics and design by
Taylor Desktop Publishing
Bisbee, Arizona

ISBN 0-9633545-0-7
LCCCN 92-073231

INTRODUCTION

This book is dedicated to Dai Uy Duong and the men of the 33rd Ranger Battalion, who never once cried out in pain, "who fought with bravery that was terrible to see," and who, when they could touch the face of death in the jungle, took one step forward.

"This poor man cried and the Lord heard him and delivered him out of all his troubles."

— *Psalm 34:6*

CHAPTER 1

I looked around the inside of the cabin of the 707 jet at friends and fellow officers that I had gone to school with in the MATA course. They were all young Captains in fresh, starched khakis. Only a few hours before we had been in Honolulu. Upon arrival there we had decided to have an impromptu party. We drank as many Mai Thais as fast as we could while the plane refueled and then climbed back on again for the final leg to Saigon.

The first part of our flight from Honolulu was a carry over from the party; lots of laughing and giggling and all the guys waving at the pretty stewardesses on the World Airways charter flight. But as we approached Saigon the mood changed. The exhilaration of the Mai Thais had worn off long ago. Perhaps the somber look on their faces reflected their tiredness from the long eighteen hour journey across the Pacific. But in all our hearts we knew what was bothering each of us. In a few minutes we would be landing in Saigon. The "rubber was going to meet the road" very quickly now, and there was no turning back.

When we had volunteered for the job as an Advisor in Vietnam (and we were all volunteers), it was just a little war. Oh, yes, a little rifle fire here and there, but in the main, a good job living overseas in the Orient with an exciting opportunity to live and work with the Vietnamese people. Sure, there was a chance of being shot at or wounded, but in the main nothing really terrible. A good "rabbit hunt," really. However, in the last two months the situation in "Nam" had changed dramatically. Advisors were being killed like flies. Word had filtered back to us at the Military Advisor and Training Assistance Course (MATA) at Fort Bragg and we knew what we were in for. 1964 would be a tough year.

I looked out of my window at the lush, green rice fields of South Vietnam below. Green jungle stretched off to the far right and ahead was the air strip. Then I heard the wheels screech as the plane jolted and the engines reversed gushing out a cacophony of sounds. It seemed like an endless ride as the plane taxied to the hanger area. The engines had barely died down when the front door popped open and an Air Force Sergeant entered. I didn't like him from the start. He came on too officious, and barked orders about getting off the plane and getting onto a bus. I moved up to the front of the cabin. The heat hit me like a blast furnace. It was hot in Vietnam. I walked down the ramp and across to the bus. I noticed that there were thick wire screens on the bus windows. When the bus was loaded, we traveled down the runway and then through the streets of Tan Son Nhut Air Force Base and finally out the main gate.

About this time, the Air Force Sergeant stood up in the front and announced to all of us in a very dramatic way that the purpose of the screens on the windows was to keep the VC from throwing grenades into the bus as we traveled on our way to the hotel. I was sure that there was a remote possibility that something like that could happen. But from my own knowledge of the situation, Saigon was at that time a pretty safe town and the announcement from this Sergeant just sort of came across as a "look at me, I'm the John Wayne of the United States Air Force" facade. I shrugged it off. We continued to travel through town. The excitement built as I looked around the streets. Whenever the bus stopped, waiting for a traffic light, hundreds of people on bicycles would pull up alongside the window. Others rode on motorcycles, or motocyclos (the three wheeled motorcycle where the driver rides behind and the people ride up front), and there were lots of extremely small cars. Then the light would change, and everybody would gun their engine. Clouds of gasoline smoke and oil fumes would rise into the air as we lurched

2

forward, heading for the Chinese section of Saigon and our hotel.

It was late afternoon before we finally got to our rooms. About six of my friends from the MATA course gathered with me in the hallway, and we decided to go out and eat together that night in a Chinese restaurant. We also agreed to carry pistols. But, before taking a bath and getting ready for the night's activities, I decided to go back out onto the streets again to try my luck with the Vietnamese language. I was really looking forward to speaking Vietnamese, because I had worked very hard in the MATA course to learn the language, and had graduated second in a class of over one hundred students. I could speak it fairly well, although not fluently. So I walked out of the front entrance of the hotel and onto the street, and tried my luck with an individual standing in front of a shop. I began talking to him in Vietnamese, but all I got back was a blank stare. Whenever I walked, no matter what I said or no matter what I asked (such as, "how much?" or "what time is it?" or "where is a restaurant?"), all I got was this dumb look. It wasn't until I got back to my hotel that I realized that I was in the Chinatown section of Saigon, and the people there spoke Chinese and not Vietnamese. So I had a good laugh on myself.

It was time to get ready to go out with troops. After a refreshing shower, I put on my civilian trousers and began slipping a belt through the loops. But when I got over to the right side of my trousers, I took out my pistol holster and strapped it on then cinched it up tight. Then I stuck my loaded .38 caliber pistol into the empty holster, put on a large Hawaiian shirt, letting it hang out over my trousers, and checked in the mirror. It looked pretty good. Nobody could see the pistol. No bulges. The Hawaiian shirt covered it beautifully. Then I walked down into the lobby and met the guys. We didn't have to walk far. We had only walked about three-quarters of a block when we ran into a Chinese restaurant. We could see through the window that it looked pretty nice so we went inside. A Chinese man came up to meet us and took us to the back. All six of us sat around a table. It was just like eating in a Chinese restaurant back home. We had wanton soup, rice, beef with peppers, and sweet and sour pork. All of those dishes were washed down by a delicious beer called "Biere Larue." It was a local beer made in Saigon. This beer came in a large dark brown bottle and was very, very watered down. It wasn't powerful at all. It sort of tasted like half Budweiser and half water. After the meal we went back to the hotel. It was then that I ran into a Sergeant that had worked for me previously in Italy. He was in the Military Police and had been stationed in Saigon for six months already. It was good to see him. We sat down and talked for over a half hour about the good old days in Italy, where I used to run a Military Police Platoon. Later, I asked him about changing money. He said it was illegal to go out on the streets and change on the black market. On the other hand, he said that the open rate in Hong Kong was ten times what they were paying in Saigon. It didn't take him long to tell me that everybody in Saigon was changing their money in various shops in Cholon (Chinatown). The way it worked was like this: you went into a shop, bought something cheap (like a handkerchief for fifty cents), and then gave the shop owner a twenty dollar bill. The man in turn gave you $19.50 in Vietnamese change back...but at the Hong Kong rate. It was just a way of getting around the extremely low, and artificially set, government rate. If somebody was watching you, you were simply "getting your change back." So I decided to try it out.

I walked out of the hotel and down the street. About half a block down, I noticed a shop that sold shoulder holsters. Since I needed a shoulder holster for my pistol I went in and bought one. It only cost three dollars, I gave him a twenty dollar bill. He in turn gave me a whole bunch of Vietnamese money back. When I got back to my hotel room, I counted it out. Sure enough, he had given me the Hong Kong rate in exchange.

It was now late. I lay down on the bed, listening to the window air conditioning unit grind away on my first night in Vietnam. I wondered what the rest would be like.

Day two: time to get our assignments. We walked outside the hotel. The street was bustling with bicycles, and motorcycles belching out their black fumes. Motoyclos

4

pedaled by with their passengers seated up front. There were buses, big trucks, lots of sounds, lots of traffic. Our military taxi showed up and we rode over to the Military Assistance and Advisory Group (MAAG) Headquarters. They brought us into a large room and seated us around a rather long, expensive looking, dark wood table. The whole room was decorated very nicely, not military at all. It contained stuffed chairs like those you would find in a corporate board room. We all took our places around the table, looking anxiously at one another and wondering where we were going to end up. We all knew there were only two types of jobs available. One was to be assigned to the local forces as a village advisor, working with the people and showing them how to organize the defense of their own village. The other option was to be assigned to a combat infantry battalion of the Vietnamese Regular Army. Vietnamese infantry battalions were commanded by Captains, and accordingly had an American Captain as an Advisor. A Captain was called "Dai Uy" in the Vietnamese language (pronounced "Dye We").

Suddenly the G-1, a Lieutenant Colonel, walked in. We all stood up. He told us to be seated, and that the assignments would now be handed out. One of the first things he told us was that a Captain Lynch, an Advisor to a Ranger battalion, had just been killed by a sniper. He "got it" very close to Saigon. He was departing Saigon as part of a convoy, and somehow a sniper picked him out of all the vehicles in that line and shot him. I heard he was hit in the head and died instantly. I had known him before in Germany. Why the G-1 had announced this right off the bat, I don't know, except to imply that there was now a vacancy in that Battalion. I looked around at the rest of the guys in the room. Not a one of them was wearing a Ranger tab. I was the only one "Ranger qualified" in the room so I knew I was going to get that assignment. This is where it all hits home in a military career. You want to be the very best, you want to be the finest soldier possible, you volunteer to go to Ranger School, and then suddenly you have to put it into practice. The "chickens all come home to roost." The man in front of you has been killed and it's time for you to step forward and take his

5

place. I was a little bit scared, because it had all now caught up with me. Everyone around the table knew that the situation in Vietnam was going very badly. The Viet Cong had taken the offensive. They were fighting large scale battles. Vietnamese Army units were being hit hard every day and many American Advisors were turning up missing or captured. There were many wounded, many dead. But, oddly enough, I didn't get Lynch's battalion. The G-1 had something else in mind and assigned me to the 35th Ranger Battalion in Phuc Vinh.

Immediately after the meeting, we all ran up to a large map on the wall that pin-pointed the location of all the battalions in Vietnam. I noticed that Phuc Vinh was way north of Saigon, and separated by miles and miles of trackless jungle. Somebody told me that the road to this city was impassable, held by the enemy. They said the only way to get there was to fly in. I was very apprehensive about that. Nothing like being surrounded by fifty thousand "screaming meemies." But the next day brought yet another change. They had now assigned me to the 33rd Ranger Battalion in Tay Ninh. Tomorrow I would fly out and replace a Captain Ramsey.

After the meeting we all moved over to the supply shed to draw jungle fatigues. They were really great; very light weight with large pockets, very comfortable and designed to withstand the heat. If you did get them wet, they would dry out in a hurry. I was also issued a pair of jungle boots. They came with a very hard rubber sole, and a foot pad like Dr. Scholl's; only the foot pad was made out of metal. You inserted it inside your boot to stop panji stakes (sharpened bamboo spikes hidden on the trail designed to pierce through your foot when you step on them). The top part of the boot was made out of canvas so that it too would dry out in a hurry. Of course, I was also issued a weapon. It was a carbine (a short barrel rifle). I asked for an M-1 carbine rather than an M-2. The M-2 carbine only fired on full automatic. I wanted the type that would fire each time you pulled the trigger. It held thirty rounds (bullets), and I knew I could pull the trigger thirty times in a big hurry, if I had to. Holding the trigger down on a fully automatic M-2 only wasted ammunition, and shot

6

up thirty rounds faster than you could blink your eye. Then suddenly, you would find yourself without any ammo. That was not for me.

We got off early that afternoon, so we all went back to the hotel, and later made plans to eat out again that night. I slipped on my newly purchased shoulder holster, stuck in my .38 caliber Smith and Wesson "Combat Masterpiece," put on a large shirt, and walked out the door. We hired a couple of small Peugot taxis and went downtown, ending up at a French restaurant. I had "Cordon Bleu," along with some french fries and tossed salad. Of course, French wine was served with the meal. After supper, we all decided to take a motocyclo home from the restaurant. (The motocyclo is a 3 wheel motor cycle. One wheel is in the back and the other two wheels are up front. Mounted between the two front wheels is a seat, not unlike a sofa that can hold two or three people. The only problem is, you are the bumper.) So away we went. We hired a total of three and raced around town, each encouraging his own driver to beat the other guy. We laughed ourselves silly. Finally, we made it back to Cholon, and got ready for the next day.

Day three: I woke up sick as a dog. It was the French food. I had terrible stomach cramps. Not only was my stomach severely upset, but about every ten minutes I felt a sharp pain in my intestines. It came and went. I knew I had eaten something bad the night before, so I got out my tetracycline tablets. All the Advisors had been issued these. Tetracycline was a new "wonder drug," a type of penicillin. It killed all sorts of bacteria. The Army had to buy them from a pharmaceutical company in Italy because the FDA had not approved them yet. They issued them to all the Advisors because out in the field they would have to be their own doctor. I popped one in my mouth and took another one four hours later. By three o'clock in the afternoon, the shooting pains were gone.

It was time for me to leave for my assignment. A military taxi took me out to III Corps Headquarters in Binh Hoa. There, a helicopter was waiting for me, blades turning slowly. I got out, ran over and jumped on. I heard the engine whine and pick up speed. I saw the pilot pull up on the collective stick, with his left arm as we started to lift off. At the same time, he pushed forward with his right hand on the stick located between his knees, and the nose tilted forward, and we started moving forward. As we gained speed we started climbing. The next thing I knew we were above the little houses of Binh Hoa. Some had red tile roofs, others were just covered with sheet metal. Off to my right, through the open door, I could see Binh Hoa Air Force Base with its long concrete runway. I could see fighters, AIE's, coming in and out, practicing landings; I knew that our Air Force Advisors were over there teaching them how to fly. Then we headed north for Tay Ninh. It was a beautiful, bright, clear day. We left the city of Binh Hoa behind and passed over the Vietnamese countryside. No jungle yet, just big wide expanses of rice paddies below. We traveled on for about 30 minutes. Occasionally I could see a village here and there.

We then flew over what was probably Viet Cong territory. The government might exercise some control over these hamlets during the day but the Viet Cong controlled them at night. The people were sympathetic to the Viet Cong, because they knew they would have to "answer to them" at night if anything went wrong during the day. Down below, I saw a man working in a field. He looked up and waved his hat. Later on, we saw another man walking along a dike near a clump of trees. Suddenly he surreptitiously moved over to the trees. We were flying along at 1200 feet, but I could see him clearly. He slid up alongside the trunk of one of the trees and took off his hat, a pith helmet. He was definitely trying to hide from us. I wondered what he was up to. Maybe he thought we were a gunship and would dive down and shoot him for no reason.

As we approached Tay Ninh, I looked off to my left. I saw white smoke and artillery shells exploding. As the artillery impacted, it emitted a sudden bright flash of orange and then black smoke billowed up into the air. Somebody over there was in a fire fight. I put on my earphones so I could talk to the pilot. He told me that it was my unit over there. The 33rd was locked in a fire fight at that very moment. I tried to be brave, but I was a little

8

scared. I told him it would be all right for him to take me over there and let me join them on the ground. I said it with bravado, but deep down in my heart I knew I wasn't all that anxious to go. I was scared and wondered what my first reaction to combat might be. He replied, however that he couldn't do that. He had to take me over to the Senior Advisor first. As we approached Tay Ninh, I could see a huge cathedral off to my right. But it wasn't Catholic. It belonged to the Cao Dai religion, the religion of Tay Ninh Province. We circled and came in. As we approached I heard the crack of a rifle. It was a sniper firing at the chopper, but he didn't hit us. I found out later that he was a bad shot, and fired at every aircraft that came in. One time he fired on some gunships (attack helicopters), and naturally they got mad at him and wanted to "take him out," but Colonel Tansey, the Senior Advisor, wouldn't let them. He told them, "He's the best damn sniper we ever had." He hadn't hit a thing in over a year. If the gunships knocked him out, the Viet Cong would probably replace him with someone who was a good shot. So everybody just tolerated him.

We landed on the strip. I got out. There was a jeep waiting for me. We passed by an old fort off the end of the runway. You could see the firing ports in the walls where French soldiers used to stick their old bolt action rifles out and fire at the enemy. The fort today was really a series of offices and barracks encased in a wall. Just past the fort, we turned left and headed down a street. There were many nice homes along this street. At the end of the street on the left I spotted a beautiful home, two stories tall with a white cement wall around it. It was the Advisors compound, and my home for the next four months.

I arrived at the Compound and met Lieutenant Colonel Tansey. His job was to coordinate the activities of all the Advisors in Tay Ninh Province. The 33rd Ranger Battalion that I was to join had two Advisors; a Captain named John Ramsey (whom I was to replace) and a Lt. Jerry White who was the Assistant Advisor. Colonel Tansey also served as an Advisor to the Province Chief, a Vietnamese Brigadier General who also happened to be a high ranking member of the local Cao Dai religion. The Cao Dai religion was found only in Tay Ninh, and was the official religion of the Province. There were other Americans there, too: one was a Major, the executive officer who took care of the meals, ordering all the logistical supplies, ammo resupply, etc. Then there was an artillery unit of the Fifth Division, and they had an Advisor, too. Finally, there was an American who served as an Advisor to the Regional Forces (the local village defense forces). Some of his independent companies were stationed in really remote outposts. One of these outposts was located across a river, and on the far side of the river at that. There were about 100 men over there. There wasn't much anybody could do for them if they got into trouble, because the bridge had been blown between us and them.

Later they showed me my room. It reminded me of the interior of a French home. It was a large room with a high ceiling and had white walls. An Army cot stood in the corner. Overhead a ceiling fan rotated slowly. Part of my monthly fee included room service. There was a little boy who came around and made the beds. He had a little sister, and the two of them cleaned and dusted. They were so cute. They even shined my shoes, if that needed to be done, and washed my clothes, too. Of course we tipped them extra for that. The monthly rent also included meals. Our food was purchased out of the commissary in Saigon, and was flown to us once a week in an Army Caribou aircraft.

Later, at supper that night, I was introduced to another American, Captain Howard Shook of the United States Air Force. Captain Shook flew a small airplane called the L-19, and his job was to spot the enemy from the air, then dive down, fire marking rockets at them and bring in fighter aircraft to destroy them. I met Captain Ramsey, too, the man I was to replace. John was a little shorter than me, a wiry looking guy, and real tough. I liked that in a professional soldier. There didn't appear to be an ounce of fear in him. On the other hand I mused maybe his tough personality would clash with mine and we wouldn't get along. I hoped we would get along, because it would be very important for the good of the battalion. But I could tell right from the start that I was the "new kid on the block," and John didn't want me there. The problem was that John had wanted to stay a full year with the battalion. Most Advisors didn't last that long. They either got killed or wounded in the first six months. If they did last longer than that, they were usually transferred back to safe jobs in Saigon. John had been out there nine months when he got wounded. He had been on a convoy that had come under attack along a highway. When he stopped his vehicle to get out and fire back, a sniper shot him in the foot. At this point, he should have been transferred from the Ranger battalion, but he volunteered to go back and did go back. So he wanted to make it a whole year. But later, the Army decided that John had been there long enough, and had decided to put me in. Needless to say, John did not want me there, taking his place the last three months. I felt this resentment strongly. Also, John and Lt. White were close. Very close. They had been through a lot together; life and death every day. Now here I came, a guy who had never been fired at before in his whole life. I felt the resentment from both sides.

The next day after breakfast John said, "Let's go out and meet the Dai Uy." He wanted to introduce me to the man that I would be advising. (That would be my job; to observe the battalion and to make suggestions for improvement to the Vietnamese Commander.) So we hopped in a jeep. John sat up front. At that time I also met my new jeep driver. His name was Tau. He always had a big grin on his face and looked like a wonderful, mischievous character. Every time he started the jeep he would say "Bool sheet," and then laugh...a really funny and humorous guy. I liked him right off.

I hopped in the back seat, and down the street we went. As we were driving through the streets of Tay Ninh we saw a jeep approaching us from the opposite direction. We were both traveling at about the same rate of speed, about 25 mph. The other jeep contained Dai Uy Duong. Suddenly John recognized Dai Uy Duong and shouted at him. The driver of the other vehicle and Dai Uy Duong turned their heads around to see who it was. At the same instant a small child ran out in front of their jeep. The Dai Uy's driver spotted the little child out of the corner of his eye, and immediately swerved hard to the right and slammed on his brakes to avoid hitting it but it was too late. While he didn't hit the child "head on," the child's foot had slipped out in front of the jeep and the sliding tire had torn the child's foot wide open from one end to the other.

Tau turned our jeep around and we raced back. I jumped out and ran over to the little kid. It was a small boy. His eyes were wide with fright. People gathered around from all over, talking excitedly. There was lots of jabbering in that Chinese sing-song talk. I looked at the foot and could see the tendons exposed. The skin was laid back, and I could see the muscle structure vividly. We picked up the child and put him in our jeep and raced over to the hospital which was about two blocks away. John had him in his arms as we brought him in to the Filipino surgical team. They had a wonderful doctor there, part of a medical assistance team from the Philippines. He was an extremely skilled surgeon. He had an assistant with him, too, and three nurses. They were permitted to work on the civilian population, but not Army soldiers. They agreed to operate on the little boy because he was a civilian. We left him there in the best hands possible.

It was at this time that I remembered something from my training about the Vietnamese people. They had all sorts of superstitions and traditions. One of them was that if you met somebody for the first time, and something bad happened to you that same day, then that person would bring you bad luck. Outside the hospital I met Dai Uy Duong. He was very friendly to me. I liked him right off and I could tell that he liked me. I could tell even at that first moment that we were going to be very close friends. But, I also noticed something strange in his behavior toward me. I could tell that he thought that I was going to bring him bad luck because that child had been struck at the same instant we met. At that point, Captain Ramsey recommended that we all go to a local restaurant and have a beer. We ended up at one near the battalion headquarters. It turned out to be a room 15' x 15' with card tables and chairs inside and a thatched roof overhead. The supporting poles were made out of bamboo, and the whole building was open on the sides to allow for ventilation. We sat down and ordered Biere Larues. Each one got a bottle. The manager brought over some tall glasses with slivers of ice inside. (There was no such thing as refrigerated bottles in Vietnam, at least not in Tay Ninh.) So we poured the warm beer over the ice and... "voila," cold beer. It was all very tasty. It was also a low powered beer that didn't have a very high alcohol content, probably only about 3% by volume. The Army doctors back at Fort Bragg told us to drink lots of this beer, because it was pure and healthy for us, and good for our 'innards'.

I sat down next to Dai Uy. I discovered that he had been in the Army a long time. He had started off as an enlisted man in the French Army when they were here. Later, when the government of South Vietnam was established he became an officer in the Vietnamese Army. Then he later joined the Rangers. (The Rangers were an all volunteer unit specializing in long range patrols and commando raids.) He had worked his way up to Captain and was now a Battalion Commander having been in continuous combat for over twelve years. Not once in all that time had he been a staff officer (desk job). All 12 years had been out in the field fighting. He was lucky to be alive. He had been wounded many times. I also learned that he had a wife and a little girl. He showed me pictures of his baby. I could tell he adored her.

About this time Captain Ramsey decided to play a trick on me. He ordered something from the waiter that was hanging up on the ceiling, a little cube about two inches square wrapped in banana leaves, and tied with a string. John told me this was a Vietnamese delicacy, and invited me to eat it. He told me it was something every Advisor should try, and that if I didn't eat it I would be offending the Captain and would lose face. Everybody nodded their heads in approval. So rather than make a scene (I suspected something was up), I decided to go ahead and show them how tough I really was. I opened up

13

the small package. Inside was red meat. It was raw pork with caraway seeds mashed on top. The Advisors called it "putrefied pork." After salting, it had been hung up in that hot roof for days, maybe weeks. I bit into it. It tasted absolutely terrible. I didn't particularly like the caraway seeds either. I managed to get the whole thing down, and followed it up with a lot of beer. But it wouldn't stay settled in my stomach. I could taste it for hours. Even the next afternoon when I belched, I could still taste it. It was really rotten. A great trick by John, and I vowed I would never eat one of those things again.

After this little party with the Dai Uy, we went back to the Compound. I signed for the military equipment that I was to receive as an Advisor. It was a jeep, a PRC10 radio, and one pocket-size AM radio. And how did I sign for all of this equipment? On a little piece of pocket notepad paper! Normally, in the Army, you sign for equipment on very official forms typed out in triplicate. But there I was signing for a very expensive jeep on no less than a piece of scratch paper, and hand printed at that. It did list the serial numbers on it. But still, that's all I had to do. I liked that. No fancy paperwork. And that's the way I planned to pass it on to my successor.

CHAPTER 2

The next day was my first combat operation with the battalion. The troops hopped on the trucks and Dai Uy's jeep took the lead. We roared out with all the trucks following. The route took us down black top streets in the city past nice looking homes with banana trees and flowers growing out front in the yard. Then the road turned to dirt, and we saw thatched roof huts, and others with tin roofs. We splashed through puddles of water scattering chickens along side the road. Little kids waved at us as we drove by. When we got to the edge of town we stopped and dismounted and the battalion fanned out. First and Second Companies moved out up front, with Third and Fourth Companies taking up the rear. Dai Uy and I formed the middle with the Command Group. The Command Group, or CP as it was called, consisted of men who carried the radios for the Dai Uy: radios that could contact the subordinate companies, the artillery, the Air Force and the command post back in Tay Ninh City. We moved out. It was a very peaceful scene. I could tell there was no great danger there. Farmers looked up and waved to us as we walked by. Water buffalo were out in the flooded fields, pulling submerged plows through knee deep water, preparing the rice fields for planting. Only the handles of the plow stuck out of the water as the farmer staggered along behind, guiding the hidden blade around the paddy. There were palm trees everywhere. It was so beautiful and green. About 2:00 p.m. the skies darkened. Dark and heavy clouds magically appeared from no-

15

where. The bright and sunny day suddenly became black. Then it started to rain. It literally came down in sheets. We got soaked through in a minute. We continued to slosh along as we headed South.

We passed through some intermittent brush, and then back out again into some rice paddies. About 5:00 p.m. we came to a village. The battalion moved right into the village and set up for the night. I had an idea that this village was one of the contested ones; loyal to the government during the day but harassed by the Viet Cong at night. The Dai Uy called in the company commanders and had a little meeting with them. He pointed around the village and told them how he wanted to defend for the night. It would be a perimeter defense (a complete circle around the village), with the CP in the middle. One company would set up from 12:00 to 3:00 p.m. as on a clock, another from 3:00 to 6:00, and so on all around the clock until they were completely tied in for "all round" protection. There would be no reserve. In a case like this a reserve wouldn't do any good anyway. It was more important to have people shoulder to shoulder all the way around the village to stop anybody from coming in, than to have one or two companies located in the middle to eject anybody who might penetrate the circle. Besides, if the enemy did get past the perimeter and into the middle of the circle how would we know whom to shoot in the dark? It was best to stop them out front.

The battalion began to settle in for the night. Everybody pulled out their black pajamas from their pack. Then they took off their shoulder harnesses, canteens, ammo pouches, uniforms, and boots, and put on their black pajamas and shower clogs. The black pajamas had about four buttons up the front, and were long sleeved with no collar. They were very lightweight and very cool. This was a good procedure, because we could hang our fatigues to dry during the night, and have dry clothes in the morning. By wearing shower clogs, our feet dried out, too. It was all very, very comfortable. The only problem with it was that we now had 350 men dressed in black pajamas, and every one of them was carrying a rifle. There was no way of telling them from the VC who wore the same kind of uniform.

About an hour later when the battalion had completely set up around the village and it was just about dark, I decided to go for a walk to check the perimeter. As an advisor, my job was to take a look at the battalion and make recommendations to the Captain on the tactics they were employing. On this occasion, I wanted to see how tightly the men were employed, and whether any enemy could slip in through them, and to double check that everybody was facing out. So I started around. As I walked the circle, I could see the men in groups of two or three. Nobody was dug in, but they were in combat positions. Machine guns were at the ready, ammunition inserted, bolts cocked back once as they should be. As I passed by, they would smile and say, "Chao Dai Uy" (Hello Dai Uy), and I would say "hello" back to them. It was fun to get to know them. They were all brand new faces to me. I didn't know a man there, but they were all very friendly, and I really enjoyed speaking Vietnamese with them. Sometimes they would stop me and ask me how old I was, and whether or not I was married, and if I had any kids. I, in turn, would ask them the same thing. Then I would move on to the next position. Somehow or another, on my way around the circle, I walked out of the circle and into enemy country. It didn't take me long to realize my mistake. I had "lost the ring." I made a sharp turn left and headed back toward the village. It was now getting dark, although I could see about 100 yards ahead of me. Suddenly a voice rang out to my front. "Ai!" ("Ai" means "who" in Vietnamese). The voice was excited, almost terrified. I saw this Vietnamese in black pajamas to my front, with a carbine pointed right at me, screaming "Ai, Ai." I had my own carbine down along my side in my right hand. I didn't dare move. I stopped and called out, "Ngung lai, ngung lai," (don't shoot, don't shoot), but it didn't calm him down. He didn't know who I was. I knew he was one of the men from the battalion, but since I was brand new, he didn't know who I was and probably thought I was one of the enemy. It made no difference even though I had a white face. He had probably heard those reports of Russians being with the Viet Cong, and so he was taking no chances. He brought the carbine up again. Again I called out, "Ngung lai, ngung lai. Co van my. Co van my," ("Don't shoot, don't shoot, American Advisor"). He started to lower his carbine a little bit, but he still wasn't satisfied. Then, other soldiers ran up and started talking to each other in that rapid fire, Vietnamese, sing-song manner. Then they all started grinning and motioned for me to come in. I walked toward them slowly saying, "Co van my, Co van my," ("American Advisor, American Advisor"). They all laughed hysterically, and I laughed, too. I explained to them that I had only been in Vietnam a couple of days, and that I was a new man, but they already understood. Probably, one of the men who ran up at the last minute had seen me previously, perhaps when we were loading the trucks. I walked back to the command post. I said nothing to Dai Uy, although I was sure he would hear about it later and would get a good laugh out of it, too.

Supper time: it was time to put a little money in the kitty and pay the farmer's wife for a chicken. I had heard talk that when some RVN Battalions moved into an area, they killed all the chickens, and then forced the people to cook the food for them, without paying a dime for it. But Dai Uy Duong was not like that. He took particular pains to make sure that he and all his men paid for what they got.

I watched as the farmer's wife took a big meat cleaver and proceeded to hack a very good drumstick into four different pieces. She did the same with the wing. She hacked the whole chicken into tiny pieces and then put it into a wok and cooked it in some vegetable oil and soy sauce. Then she placed it into a bowl on the table. The table was a heavy, "picnic type," table, something like ours in the States but without benches. So, we all pulled up little wooden chairs and sat down. The meal consisted of rice, chicken and some vegetables that had been stir fried in a pan. It was absolutely delicious. Somehow or other, beer bottles appeared from nowhere and we had warm beer with the meal.

After dinner I sat outside and listened to the sounds. Many of the Vietnamese soldiers had pocket transistor radios with them, and I could hear those mournful,

18

sing-song, Chinese songs everywhere. Those terrible, sad, haunting melodies floated across the night air. I sat there in pitch blackness knowing I was 8,000 miles from home, just me and one other American, with 350 men in some nameless village in Vietnam. One of the hardest things for me to do was to listen to all those voices in the night, all speaking Vietnamese, and all speaking so rapidly. I couldn't follow them, so I just didn't know what was going on. The music was so strange, too. Haunting. Even so, I felt pretty comfortable. I wasn't afraid, at least not yet. Then it was time to go to bed. I had one of those "Ranger" hammocks that Tau, my driver, had procured for me. I think I paid him about five dollars for it. The hammock was made out of nylon with parachute cords tied to each end. The whole thing rolled up into a tiny ball that you could stick in your pocket and yet when strung up it could support the weight of a grown man. It was just the thing to take on long range patrols. After the hammock was strung up, the way you got into it was like this: first, you sat in it sideways and rested your full weight on it. Once you knew it could hold you, then you swung your legs up and around, and at the same time lowered your body into the hammock. I had previously strung my hammock up between what appeared to be two good size tree trunks. Later, after dark, it was time to go to bed. I walked over to my hammock, put my carbine across my lap, sat down on the hammock and tested it. It held my weight. Then I pulled my legs up, swung around and stretched out full length in the hammock. Ka-boom! One of the trees that I had tied it to keeled over and crashed right on top of me. All the leaves and branches fell right on top of me. Suddenly, flashlights came on all over the place and everybody started laughing at me. The "new man" had tied his hammock to a tree that wouldn't hold his weight. What a laugh. Jerry had a big laugh on me, too, as well as the Vietnamese. They all thought it was the funniest thing they had ever seen. I could hear them say "Dai Uy," and then something else in Vietnamese and then they would all crack up. I laughed, too. Then I got up and tied my hammock to two strong trees and went to bed.

When I first started sleeping in a hammock while on patrol, I didn't know what to do with my carbine. I knew that if I laid it "crossways" across my lap, it might fall out in the middle of the night and get sand in the barrel, and then I wouldn't be able to fire it. Another option was just to lay it flat on the ground underneath me but somehow or another I didn't like that either. I finally decided to lean it up against the tree trunk by my head, where I could reach out for it in a big hurry if I needed it.

I was fast asleep. Suddenly, in the middle of the night, bam, bam, bam. There was a Thompson submachine gun firing not more than 10 feet away from me. Was it firing at me? Was it one of our guys? Were the Viet Cong making a rush? I didn't know what was going on, and I didn't take time to think twice about it. I rolled out of my hammock and hit the ground. At the same time, I grabbed my carbine with my right hand, and looked out to my front where I had heard the firing. I couldn't see a thing. It was pitch black. I knew I couldn't open fire because there were people to the front of me and people sleeping all around me. The perimeter to my front was full of our own men. Then I began to hear lots of shouting and lots of talking back and forth in Vietnamese. I could also hear Dai Uy's voice louder and stronger above the rest. After about five minutes of excited sing song talk, things started to settle down and then it got completely quiet. I knew Dai Uy was just a few feet away, so I went over and asked him what had happened. He told me that one of the men had his weapon loaded and cocked for the night and had fallen asleep and somehow or another had accidentally caused the gun to go off. It had fired off three round before its startled owner woke up. Fortunately nobody was hit.

Morning arrived. Chickens were "clucking" all around. They were not penned up. They just walked around the village at will. Little kids laughed and giggled and chased each other in the streets. Women were busy cooking over their fires. The men got the water buffaloes ready for the field. The water buffalo had big rings through their noses with ropes tied to the rings to lead them around. Walking up and down the streets, I listened to the sound of a Vietnamese village coming to life. Our troops cooked tea in little pots. Since we had all brought along loaves of french bread, breakfast that morning consisted of hot tea and delicious fresh bread. After breakfast, it was time to move out.

We were going to cut east and head back towards a dirt road and then take that road back to Tay Ninh City. We initially followed an ox cart trail out of the village. The troops fanned out on both sides. Then we moved across some rice paddies. It was a beautiful scene. The sun came up in magnificent splendor; bright and clear, with the bluest sky you've ever seen. There were palm trees, coconuts, rice fields. It was all so beautiful. And there was no trouble. Not a shot was fired. Eventually we hit the dirt road going back to Tay Ninh and turned left. We continued to put out flankers (soldiers to our far side to protect us from anyone who might try to fire into us). Then it started to rain. We paused for lunch. It came down in sheets. We all got soaked. I could see the buildings of Tay Ninh to our front but we were still a long way from town.

Then we passed through some sugar cane fields. The stalks were about two inches in diameter and grew very tall, about fifteen feet high and had tassels on top. Local farmers were out there hacking away with their machetes. They would sever it at the bottom and then hack off the top and then stack the stalks along the road. One woman, who I imagine was in her forties, had been doing that all day. She had been cutting the sugar cane down and had been stacking it up on the road waiting for an oxcart to take it to market. Unfortunately for her our battalion came down the road at this time with tired and thirsty men who loved to munch on sugar cane. It was a real treat. Each soldier, as he passed by, stole a stalk of cane from her stack. By the time our CP group arrived probably 150 men had filed by and taken 150 precious stalks off her pile. The woman was crying when Dai Uy and I arrived. When he saw what was going on, he became furious. He got on the radio and hollered something into the mike and the whole battalion stopped dead. Then he walked forward to the head of the column, shouting and kicking the men as he strode along. When he got up to the first Company Commander, he chewed him out royally,

21

pointing and gesturing. Then all of the men turned around, took the stalks of sugar cane that they had stolen, and put them back on the woman's pile. After that, we all turned around and then headed back for Tay Ninh City again.

As we hit the outskirts of the city, I noticed that it was surrounded by a huge protective wall, not of mud or stone, but of bamboo. In some places the bamboo was dead and had been driven into the ground like stakes. But in other places it was alive, planted and growing very closely together, so close that a man could never walk through it. The stuff was ten feet thick. It would have taken the Viet Cong three hours to hack their way through all that bamboo with a machete. It made a great protective wall.

Finally I saw the trucks. Tau was waiting for me and grinning as usual. I hopped into the jeep and we raced down the street. Tau drove like a madman. People in Vietnam, particularly soldiers, didn't know what a speed limit was all about. There were no police cars. Sure, you might see a policeman on foot from time to time, but he was not going to argue with an Army jeep bristling with armed soldiers. Tau was doing 40 mph down this dirt road, splashing through mud puddles, scattering chickens right and left and driving within inches of little children playing in the street. I told him to slow down but he just laughed and shouted "bool sheet." But I was concerned. I knew that if one of those little kids made one false move we would wipe him out. So I kept insisting in Vietnamese for Tau to slow down. Finally he did, to what he thought was a reasonable pace, but it was still too fast. At last we drove into the compound. I was safe at home after my first combat operation and there hadn't been much to it.

That night I was the duty officer for the compound. Basically, what I had to do was make sure we were in touch with the Vietnamese, so that if anything did happen they could contact us and alert us. Sometimes they asked for Captain Shook to get airborne and look around. Other times, they might want to get hold of one of the Ranger Advisors to tell him that the battalion was moving out. Or, maybe they needed to tell us that the town itself was under attack as it often was. Whatever might come up, I was the man to be notified and I in turn would notify my fellow Americans. It was a routine job, passed on from night to night amongst us all, on a fair share basis.

It all started off as a routine night. We had supper in the large dining hall. The Vietnamese lady cooked a delicious meal for us. We had mashed potatoes and steak. It was "American" food, not the Chinese style cooking that was served in the battalion. Then after supper we showed the nightly movie. We always received "first run" movies or, at worst movies, a year old.

Around 9:00 p.m. we heard a tremendous amount of firing near the house. It sounded close, less than five blocks away. It was coming from the direction of the wall that ran around the town. The VC were, in fact, attacking the town. Our telephone rang. I got a report that the Viet Cong were at the wall just a few blocks from our house and that we should be prepared for a possible assault. I immediately sounded the alert. (I did that by banging on a 105mm shell casing with a steel bar. It made a terribly loud noise.) Everybody poured out of the house grabbing their ammunition and rifles as they went. We all took up positions on the wall. I peered down the street but could see no one. Then I decided to climb up on the roof for a better view. From up there, I had an excellent view all the way around. From this vantage point I could see over our own wall, and could look down at anybody who might be approaching. I could also see the flashing of guns five blocks away. I didn't know it at the time, but my own Ranger battalion had been alerted to drive the VC from the town. (They grabbed whatever was available at Battalion Headquarters, about forty men, and put an officer in charge. He went to the scene of the fighting, drove them off, and that was the end of that.) We later found out it was only a squad of about 9 to 11 VC who came to the edge of the wall to fire into the town to terrorize people.

CHAPTER 3

The next day, it was my turn to go up with Captain Shook as he made his reconnaissance flight over Tay Ninh Province. Colonel Tansey, the Senior Advisor for the Tay Ninh Province, had a policy that "Howie" never flew alone. The chances of him being hit were pretty good. A bullet could put out the engine, and he might have to crash land somewhere near the Cambodian border. Most pilots were not extremely skilled at making their way "cross country" overland, particularly in enemy territory. They just didn't know how to hide out in the jungle, or how to escape and evade. Infantrymen, on the other hand, knew the jungle. They knew how to move at night, how to use a compass, and how to move "cross country" successfully. It was, after all, how they made their living. Colonel Tansey had a policy that Captain Shook had to take an Infantryman with him on all flights. In case they got shot down, the plan was that they would get as far away from the plane as fast as possible, hide, and then later that night hike back to Tay Ninh City. It would have been pretty easy to do, in fact, very easy for an infantryman. You would simply hide out during the day and move cross country at night. It would have been impossible for the enemy to catch them. Of course, if you moved during the day, or down trails, then you'd end up in a POW camp.

I climbed into the back seat of the L-19, a two seat airplane. The pilot sat up front, the passenger right behind him. It looked like a Piper Cub and cruised at 70 mph. Mounted on each wing was a rocket launcher, with two rockets inserted in each launcher. The rockets were made of white phosphorous. When the pilot spotted the enemy, he would dive down toward them and fire off a rocket. When the rocket hit the ground, it would explode into a huge, white cloud, thus marking the location of the enemy. Then fast moving attack fighters, fully loaded with bombs and napalm, would come in and destroy the target. Captain Shook was "the eyes and ears," so to speak, of the attack fighters.

We taxied to the end of the runway. It was my first flight in an L-19. He "poured the coals" to her and we roared down the runway. It was a hot day and it took a long time to get off. We lifted off slowly and climbed up to about 200 feet, then banked left and headed for the Cambodian border. Once we reached cruise altitude (about 1,000 feet), we leveled off. I could see rice paddies and people working below. Later came intermittent patches of forest and jungle and then finally nothing but jungle. I could see the fortifications of the enemy up ahead. They owned the area over there. There were no towns, not inhabitants, nothing but trackless jungle.

You had to rid yourself of any idea you might have had of a traditional border, such as the one that exists between the United States and Canada. Here in Vietnam, there was no border station, no guards, no roads, no nothing. It was impossible to tell where Vietnam ended and Cambodia began. The enemy took sanctuary in this area, just across the border in Cambodia. They lived in huge open camps over there. And nothing could be done about it. They were, after all, in another country and we weren't allowed to cross into it. However, just in case we did decide to go attack, they had cut the road leading to Cambodia. They did this by digging trenches across the road ten feet deep and ten feet wide. There were hundreds of them. That made it impossible for any invading force to approach from Saigon.

All along the road were fortifications; pill boxes and bunkers. It was a regular "Maginot" line. The Vietnamese Army would never have been able to charge through all of those fortifications. So there the enemy sat, safe and sound on the other side.

We flew around this area checking it out. Occasionally, Captain Shook would cut the engine and glide silently like a giant bird. The L-19 had two small windows in back that popped out sideways, each supported by a metal bar so they wouldn't fall down. It gave me an unobstructed view of the ground below. We glided silently over the fortifications on our side of the border and looked around. It was empty. Nobody was there.

Captain Shook turned on the gas again and the engine roared to life. We flew around at an extremely low altitude, maybe 100 feet, checking things out. Since we didn't see anything, we started climbing. Suddenly, I heard small arms fire all over the place. I heard rifles going off below, and saw the muzzle flashes as they fired at us. Then tracers started coming up (bullets with brightly burning fire in the back of them so the guy firing the bullets can trace where they are going). They passed by us like little orange balls. Whoever it was missed. It was probably just a couple of VC. Not worth calling up the Vietnamese Air Force to bomb the area. We circled back looking for them but could find no one. Then we turned southeast and headed back for Tay Ninh. The scouting mission was over.

Later that night, the enemy hit the outskirts of town again, just opposite our compound and only a few blocks away. What a tremendous volume of fire! Tracers stitched out into the night. Then the artillery opened up. Their shells whined overhead and exploded on the other side of the town wall. Hundreds and hundreds of rounds were fired in the darkness. Of course, we were on the alert and had already grabbed our rifles and ammunition pouches. I climbed up on the roof again as the others took up positions along the wall. It was a very moonlit night. I could see about a block and a half away. Suddenly, it all stopped as quickly as it had begun. The night became quiet again. We later found out that all the commotion had been caused by our own popular force soldiers who had spotted a squad of VC and had opened up on them.

24 September 1964 - 2:00 P.M. in the afternoon.

A day off, or at least it was supposed to be. But we were alerted. "Move out quickly," they told us on the telephone. Cha La, a village directly East of town was under attack and in trouble. So Jerry and I grabbed our rifles and red berets, ran for the jeeps and tore up the road to join the battalion. Everybody was ready to move out. We formed a truck column and headed East. The village we were heading for was not really a part of Tay Ninh but was a couple of miles outside of town. We would be in a secure territory until we got to it. The road along the way was under strong government control, so we didn't have to fear an ambush. As we raced along, local soldiers waved at us. Past the outskirts of Tay Ninh City we roared across two miles of open area and then arrived at Cha La. We quickly dismounted. Up ahead along the road leading out beyond the village, I could see rice paddies, and then a line of jungle past that, about a mile away. I knew the rice paddies were disputed territory. In the day, they belonged to the people, but at night they belonged to the enemy. And that jungle line a mile away...that belonged to the enemy.

First and Second Companies jumped off their trucks and moved out on line. Tactically, they looked very good. They moved as fast as they could across the large rice field. Dai Uy and I took up the middle, and Third and Fourth Companies fanned out behind us. It didn't take us long to find out what was wrong. Seven of their local soldiers had been shot dead in the rice paddy just ahead. They had been on patrol, protecting the rice field, when they had made a big mistake. They had walked single file down a dike. Some enemy in the dark woodline to their front, had opened fire with an automatic rifle killing all seven of them in a single burst. They were now lying face down in the mud and the slop.

Our Rangers picked them up. They weren't wearing regular Army uniforms just mismatched civilian clothes; black pajamas, an Army suspender harness here and there, ammo pouches. Their rifles and carbines lay where they fell. Evidently the VC, and perhaps it was only one man, had fired and run away.

Since we were about a half a mile from the village, it was too far to carry the bodies back. So, the Rangers decided to drag them over to a road which ran through the middle of the field. There a truck could pick them up. Soon, a three quarter ton truck did arrive, and they lowered the back tailgate and commenced throwing the dead bodies onto the back of the vehicle. The truck turned around and we followed it back to the village.

I watched the mud covered bodies bouncing around in the back of the truck. I knew that in a few minutes there was going to be a bad scene ahead because these dead soldiers were local boys who lived in this village. Their families, wives, and children were waiting in the road for them. It was just too horrible to watch. They began recognizing their dead father or husband, or son, and burst into tears. They cried their poor hearts out. Some screamed and beat their chests. Others flailed their arms in the air. Still others bent over, sitting there on the ground, moaning, rocking back and forth in incredible grief. It was all so sad. Nothing could be done. They were all dead. One lone enemy had taken them out. It taught me an important lesson. Never walk single file down a dike.

I looked around at the villagers. A lot of curious bystanders came to look at the bodies. They just stood there staring. Lots of little children came up, too. It didn't take long for the little children to fix their eyes on me because I was a foreigner. Maybe I was the first foreigner they had ever seen. So they stared at me. Normally, I would play little tricks on them, or act like a monster and take off after them or tease them but not this time. Dead men lay at our feet. Everybody was quiet, and of course, I was quiet, too. The little children looked at me and I looked back at them. They were beautiful little kids.

About one out of every twenty had a cleft pallet. This was something unique to Vietnam, perhaps caused by unsanitary conditions or perhaps genetic problems. But whatever the cause, many children were born with cleft pallets. One of the things that the Filipino team back in Tay Ninh had been doing was to repair that big gap in their gum. They would put the children in surgery, cut that portion of the lip that was indented, stretch it back to normal and then suture it up thus covering the gap. Of course it was only cosmetic surgery. If you lifted up the lip you could still see the cleft pallet below. But it did so much good for the kids' morale. At least they "looked" like everybody else. And that was so important. Those Filipino surgeons were doing wonderful work.

It was time to move out, time to go back. There was nothing more we could do. Dai Uy picked one platoon to stay behind on night ambush. They would try to get the guy who did the shooting. I remember it was so dark and gloomy that day. It had been raining. Black clouds gathered as darkness fell. There was an area mid way between the village and the jungle line, that had some tall grass in it. I saw our ambush platoon move out towards that area. Of course they weren't going to be dumb enough to let the enemy see them lay down in that grass before dark. They would move into another ambush site after dark, in order to surprise the enemy. If any enemy did come from that jungle tonight, they were dead men. And I hoped they would. We climbed back into our vehicles and drove back to Tay Ninh.

The next day we launched a sweep operation from Suoi Dai, a Special Forces camp northeast of town. We were to move cross country from Taye toward Cha La (the village where those local soldiers had just been killed the day before). We trucked out to Suoi Dai. It was a very large camp, very well defended. I noticed all kinds of people in this camp; Cambodians, Chinese, as well as Vietnamese. I was told that Special Forces used this camp to monitor the enemy moving down trails from North Vietnam into Cambodia.

Our operation was closely coordinated with Special Forces. We had to make sure that none of their own troops were in the vicinity before we moved out. Then we struck out for Cha La. It was the same routine. Immediately we hit jungle. It was quiet in the jungle. You couldn't hear a thing. We moved slowly. You didn't hack your way through the jungle with machetes, like you see in the movies. You simply held your rifle at the ready (at a 45 degree angle to your front), peered through the bush, and then stepped in between the leaves and bushes or whatever happened to be growing there. Most of our area was composed of thick brush and tall jungle trees. If we hit anything like a real tangle of vines, we simply crawled underneath. But in most cases we moved through the jungle by simply keeping our left hand out, pushing the branches back and looking ahead for any movement.

Suddenly we stumbled across a VC base camp. They had just left, evidently in a big hurry. Fresh cooked pots of rice were tipped over on the ground. I looked around. They had been using little "lean-tos" as shelters. The lean-tos were made out of bamboo poles, thatched with huge leaves to ward off the rain, and were open on the side. This was not a village, but a makeshift camp. They had been burning their fires in small holes in the ground. I suppose the reason they did that was to keep the flames from being seen, but there was no danger of that. You couldn't see more than 25 yards in the jungle, anyway. The fires were still burning.

As I moved around, I spotted a small lamp on the ground. It looked like a typical American hurricane lamp only in miniature. The whole thing wasn't longer than four inches. It was cute. So I picked it up and kept it as a souvenir. From this place we kept moving south until we ran into the rice paddies of Cha La, and from there across to the village. We didn't catch the guys, who did that awful shooting the day before but we wanted them really badly. The trucks came to meet us and took us home.

There were four villages immediately west of Tay Ninh, on the opposite side of the river. Tay Ninh City stopped at the river, but if you crossed over the bridge and then cut left, you came to a village called Tan Dien. Tan Dien was under government control. But beyond Tan Dien there were two more villages: Cu Chi Hai and Cu Chi Ba ("Hai" means two and "Ba" means three). Cu Chi Hai was a contested village; sometimes under government control, sometimes not. Cu Chi Ba was completely under VC control and there was always a lot of fighting over there. (That's where all the noise came from every night.)

It was Sunday morning, 10:00 a.m. We got word that Tan Dien was under attack. That put the VC very, very close to the city. I grabbed my rifle and combat gear and ran up to the old fort. The battalion was already moving out and they were in a hurry. Many only had time enough to put on their pants and nothing more. Most were wearing shower clogs. They just grabbed their rifles and ran. Some ran directly over to the area. Others tried to hop on trucks heading over there, or jumped in jeeps.

Tan Dien was about 1500 yards from town. We crossed the bridge, turned left and got ready to move south. I could see the Vietnamese Air Force overhead. They were flying A1E propeller-driven fighters. The plane had a large radial engine, weighed 12,000 pounds and could carry 12,000 pounds in bomb weight. That was amazing. And it could loiter overhead for five hours. (Most fighters carry a very light load and stay over the target only a few minutes.) The A1E's were over Tan Dien and were bombing and strafing. That meant local forces (the village guards) were pinpointing the targets. It looked like a big fight. There would be big trouble today.

There was a long straight road, with rice paddies on both sides, leading to the village. Someone said that the enemy was on the other side of the rice paddy, in a tree line to our front, and on the right side of the road. The Rangers moved rapidly down this road. Most were running. The situation was very tenuous. We didn't know if there were "friendlies" up front for sure or not.

One of the Rangers had brought along a .30 caliber light machine gun. He had placed it on the edge of the road, and was firing it down the edge of the road and into the tree line to our right front. But he was so spasmodic. Bullets were flying everywhere. Some splashed into the rice paddy, and others hit dangerously close to the road. The machine gun was jumping up and down all over the place. He just didn't know how to handle the weapon. (He should have put some weight on the tripod to keep it steady.) I was in mortal fear that one of those bursts would leap from the rice paddy onto the road and kill half our men, so I moved up next to him and helped him adjust his fire more to the right and into the tree line. Once I got him squared away I moved down the road myself. (But I was still afraid he would shoot me in the back.)

Then we started hearing firing to our front. We didn't know what it was. Was it the enemy? Or was it the local guys? Finally we made it across the paddy. I moved up the left side of the road. There were some local forces there.

31

Luckily, we hadn't fired into this area. We moved past the local forces and headed for the VC.

At this time Dai Uy Duong turned to me and told me that there were enemy to our front, and that I should call in a UTT. (A UTT was an attack helicopter that had four machine guns and two rocket pods attached to it. It could come in really close and strafe the enemy position.) Since there was already such a helicopter in our area I shouted back "Yeah," and that I would mark our position. Marking our position was important, because from the air, all villages looked alike (at least these three did). So, it was necessary to mark our own position with smoke. I then threw out a green smoke grenade, told the helicopter pilot that I was standing on the green smoke and that the enemy was south of the green smoke, and that he should shoot anything that moved south of that smoke. He "rogered" my transmission.

I heard his blades, whomp, whomp, whomp, banging in the air as he approached from my left. (I had previously told him to attack across my front from left to right. That was the best way. It was very dangerous to have them come in from behind, because if the pilot sneezes, or dipped his aircraft, you got it in the back. It was much safer to have them make their pass from left to right across your front. So, that's the way I oriented him, and that's the way he was going to do it.) He was now "in bound" off to my left.

I had in my possession a PRC-25. It was a brand new radio put out by the Air Force. The Army had not yet adopted it. The Army still used the old PRC-10. The PRC-10 had a movable dial and didn't work very well. The movable dial always seemed to get knocked off channel and the radio, itself, was not very powerful. But this new PRC-25 locked the channels in place and was extremely powerful. When you spoke into it, people heard you.

The helicopter began firing and I heard the rockets launch out of the tubes. Suddenly, boom! There was a big explosion, right in front of me. Then four more huge explosions, one right after the other and lots of white smoke. Then thousands of bullets began impacting into our position. It sounded like someone snapping a whip over our heads a thousand times a minute. I knew immediately what was going on. The helicopter was coming in on us and not the enemy. I grabbed the "hand mike" of the powerful PRC-25 and yelled, "Cease fire, cease fire."

The guns stopped immediately. They had hit us by mistake. One soldier, right in front of me, had been wounded. A thin piece of aluminum from one of the rockets had hit him in the leg. A piece of shrapnel, about three inches long and an inch wide was sticking out of his leg. We were all excited and breathing hard but after a minute we started settling down. The wounded man laughed, and pointed to the piece of aluminum sticking out of his leg. Then the medics came over. They pulled it out, cleansed the gash and put a bandage on his leg.

I then asked myself "What in the world went wrong? Why did he fire on us?"

Then I started thinking to myself, "One more year to go! Would I make it? This time our own bullets almost cut me in half. A year is an awful long time."

Well, what should we do now? We had to move south and drive the enemy out of the village. But we didn't want another accident, either. So Jerry and I decided that we would move well forward of the battalion and mark our position again, so that if there were a mistake, our men wouldn't get hit. It had to be us because, we were the only ones who could speak English to the pilots.

Jerry and I struck off down the road. We didn't walk on the road, but off to the side. I moved on the left, Jerry on the right. We moved slowly, sneaking through the tall grass. We didn't know where the enemy was, or who was going to catch the first round so we moved very cautiously. We moved, stopped, listened, and then moved again. When we got about 300 yards in front of the battalion, I figured we were far enough out, so I picked up a red smoke grenade and threw it in the direction of the enemy. Then I oriented Captain Shook on the target. He was up now in his L-19. The UTT helicopter had, meanwhile, run out of fuel and had gone home.

Captain Shook spotted my red smoke, dove down and marked the area to our front with white phosphorous.

Then he brought in the VNAF fighters. They strafed the area with machine gun fire. When they had finished he called in artillery fire. About this time I heard Captain Shook on the radio. "My toy is broke," he radioed. While flying over the enemy they had fired at him and put some bullets into his plane. One had penetrated the engine and he was having trouble staying up. He radioed that he was going to try to make it back to Binh Hoa Air Force Base, and have it repaired.

After this we moved south again. Nobody was there. The enemy had run away. We swept all the way down through Cu Chi Ba, just to make sure it was clean. Then we turned around and walked home. The "Battle of Tan Dien" was over.

CHAPTER 4

One of my duties as an Advisor was to notice training deficiencies in the battalion, and to make recommendations to the Dai Uy on how to correct them. One of the things I noticed right away was that they were very, very bad on marksmanship. They couldn't hit the broadside of a red barn. In fact, it was extremely dangerous to be in front of them, not because they were aiming at you, but because they hit everywhere else but where they aimed. They were so spasmodic. Bullets would impact everywhere, from just a few feet in front of them, all the way to going straight up in the air. And they weren't doing this on purpose. They just fired like crazy and simply weren't aiming. An infantry battalion should practice fire discipline, that is, fire only when required, and then very accurately, to save ammo. But that wasn't the way it was with this Battalion. So I drove over to the Army Training Center, in a suburb of the southern part of the city, and found a man who worked with targets and marksmanship training. I studied up for a while, picked out the necessary manuals and training aids that I needed, and then drove back. It was my intent to make the battalion "better shots."

Later that day, the Caribou (our cargo plane) came in. It had on board a movie destined for the Special Forces troops out at Sui Da. A chopper was then requested to fly the film out to them, and it was my job to deliver it, because my battalion had the day off. I sat in the back of the helicopter. I watched the pilot increase the engine

35

speed of the helicopter before we lifted off. The blades kept turning faster and faster. Then he gently pulled up on a long metal stick located next to his left leg (the collective). This caused the blades to bite into the air and the helicopter hovered. Then he took another stick (located between his legs), and pushed it forward. The aircraft then nosed forward, and we started down the runway. At the same time, he pulled up harder on that stick to his left and we climbed out.

We flew across some jungle, then across some open rice paddies, across jungle again, and suddenly, there was Sui Da. Sui Da was, of course, out in "bear country." The whole area belonged to the VC. There was a road out there, but it had to be cleared every time you used it. You more or less had to fight your way from Tay Ninh City to the camp. Even after you cleared the road, your hair would turn white, wondering if someone hadn't sneaked in behind, who might put a bullet through your windshield. It was a long way out there, and there was an awful lot of jungle in between. It would only take one man with a rifle to do you in — or a few hiding along the road to capture you.

But today we were flying over the problem. We landed at the compound, and a Special Forces Sergeant came out. I handed him the film out the door and we took off again. On the way home, about a mile out of Sui Da, a VC squad of about eight or nine people opened up on us. I could hear the rifle fire down below, but we were up too high to worry about it. I could hear the pop of their rifles, and see a little bit of smoke and a muzzle flash here and there. Being up so high, I personally couldn't hear very distinctly, but the pilots were very aware of what was going on. They seemed to have a sixth sense about this and could pick it up better than we Infantrymen. The ship was not hit, and we returned safely to Tay Ninh.

John Ramsey, the man that I had replaced with the Ranger Battalion, was still in Tay Ninh City. He hadn't flown home yet. He didn't like his new job working at the District (county) Headquarters. He worked as an Advisor to the District Chief (a sort of county commissioner) helping with training, working with the local forces and the government in general. His big problem was that he did not like the man he had to advise — the District Chief. The guy was a mousy type, and an outright coward. Wherever he went, he always carried a small army with him, usually five or six men armed with Thompson submachine guns and rifles. They were his personal bodyguard. And this guy looked scared all the time. He never ventured any place where he might encounter the slightest danger. Naturally, John couldn't stand him and neither could I.

I do not want to detract from the fact that the life of a District Chief is a dangerous one. All village chiefs and district chiefs were targets for assassination by the Viet Cong. But this man lived in Tay Ninh City. It was pretty safe there. Nevertheless, even in this safe area, he persisted in moving around with his private army at all times. He leaned on that security too much. He "never ever" took a chance. He never drove anywhere by himself like going over to a restaurant. He could have if he had picked an odd hour and never set a pattern. Then he would have been all right. You met all kinds of Vietnamese in Vietnam, some very brave, professional soldiers, outstanding in every respect. And then you had this ten percent dud factor, like the District Chief. A complete "scaredy cat." It really showed on his face. He was in constant terror. He exhibited no leadership whatsoever.

It was difficult for a country like Vietnam to survive and grow, when so many of its leaders were like that. Most of the good officers were out with the battalions, fighting in the jungle. The people that were always trying to get out of something had all the safe jobs. They served at the District level, or at the Province level (state headquarters) in staff jobs and in nice offices. We complained about this through the American Advisory chain of command. We told them that the real soldiers ought to be running the country, not these cowards and politicians.

The leadership of the country, at the county and state level, was corrupt, too. We knew they took bribes. Only in the fighting forces did you find real solid leadership. Regrettably, however, it was at the district and province level where we were supposed to be building up the country, to make the people proud to be Vietnamese, to want to serve, to fight, and to stand up against communism. But we had a serious flaw in the plan. They had the wrong guys in the wrong jobs. Anyway, John despised the man and consequently didn't like his job as district advisor either.

I could also tell that John did not like me too and that there was bad blood between us. Partly, it was my fault. I was too cocky. Here I had this elite battalion, and I was still young enough and dumb enough to think I could survive anything. I exhibited too much pride. And now that John had lost his job with the battalion I sort of needled him about that, too. John did not like the stigma of being at district, and I made matters worse by making fun of him for it. I made up a song that went, "Hi diddle dee dee, the district life for me, where every day is a holiday, and you always get your combat pay, Hi diddle dee dee, the district life for me." We used to sing it around the table and it made John furious. I could tell he really hated me.

One night we were watching a movie in the compound and it came time to change the reels. Of course at that time everybody got up and headed for the latrine. Somehow or another John and I ended up as the last two guys in there. We finished our business and were washing our hands, when John said something smart to me, and I said something smart back to him. We squared off facing each other. Then something inside me told me to apologize to John for my cockiness. I knew that I had been out of line. So I told him that I knew he had been with a Ranger battalion longer than any one else, and I respected him for that. John then admitted that he had been angry at me because I had taken his battalion away from him. He said it wouldn't have made any difference who had replaced him. He wouldn't have liked him anyway. We both smiled at each other, I stuck out my hand, John stuck out his, and we shook. We became best friends from that moment on.

The next day John invited me to go with him to a Special Forces camp. He had some business out there on behalf of the district, and wanted me to come along so he could introduce me to the Special Forces guys and show me their camp. He said he could also get me a "free" rifle. I was interested in that, because I had been issued one by the Army in Saigon, and if I ever lost it, I would get in a lot of trouble, and probably get some sort of letter in my file. And it was highly possible in the year to come that I might lose that carbine somehow, through theft or whatever, so I decided to get a free one.

We took off in his jeep. It was a very dangerous drive. We left town and started across the rice paddies. Initially, we could see people working out there. They looked up at us for a little bit, and then looked back down. We knew that they were from Tay Ninh City and friendly to us.

As we approached the jungle up ahead, I saw a tree line across the rice paddies to our front. The road ran right through the middle of it. As we got closer, I wondered if anyone was up there waiting to shoot us. The road was allegedly cleared by the local forces, but they were incredibly inefficient. Sometimes they just didn't do it at all. But I felt sorry for them, too. They had no leadership, no training. They didn't know what to do and were so poorly equipped. Most wore tennis shoes without shoe strings, and their uniform was a "mix match" of whatever they could get their hands on. Some had army trousers, others not. A few had Army shirts. They carried old, single shot rifles. When given a mission like clearing a road, they usually ventured out as far as they thought it was safe to go. Whether the rest of the road got cleared was not their concern.

John and I had no choice. We had to drive down the road. Occasionally, we did see a couple of local forces grinning at us along the road but they were spaced a good three miles apart. What was in between? No one knew. Around every curve in the jungle I just wondered when we were going to get it. Were there 50 men waiting to kill us? Would they put 500 rounds of ammunition through our jeep and "take us out?" But eventually we arrived safely. We drove through the main gate and right into the camp.

The camp was circular in shape. A defensive wall ran all the way around the camp bristling with barbed wire, fighting positions, fox holes, and bunkers. John waved at someone he knew. It turned out to be a lieutenant. He came over, shook hands, and introduced himself to me. John then told him that I had come along to get a free carbine. The Lieutenant then took me to his warehouse. It was a modern type warehouse made of metal, the kind you see back in the United States.

We went inside, and I was amazed. There, stacked from top to bottom, was row after row of carbines, rifles, automatic rifles, machine guns and pistols. The place contained thousands and thousands of weapons. The lieutenant told me to pick out any one I wanted. I wouldn't have to sign for it. It would be a gift. So, I went down the line of racks and found a beautiful, brand new, mint shape, fully automatic, M-2 carbine, with a selector switch. The selector switch allowed me to shoot it single shot if I wanted to and I liked that feature. It had a beautiful blond stock without a scratch on it. They just gave it to me.

After this, we walked over to the little house where they lived to meet some of the other personnel. There were some Sergeants there and a Captain. My initial impression was that their camp was a little slovenly bordering on "pig pen." Nothing was picked up. They hadn't done any house cleaning in long time. Things lay all around. Beer cans were on the floor, out on the porch, everywhere.

This base had a secret mission, a mission that I still don't know to this day. I do know if it involved reconnaissance. (Reconnaissance is the art of spying on the enemy through patrols or from secret hiding places in the jungle, without letting him know you are watching him.) I do know that they flew out in helicopters and landed along the Cambodian border. I suppose they even went into Cambodia. I heard tell they lay along the Ho Chi Minh Trail, counting the enemy as they came down from North Vietnam.

Our Ranger battalion had been designated a reaction force for these Special Forces people at Sui Dai, in the event they got into trouble. John literally saved their lives one night. They were attacked by a large Viet Cong force who, I guess, simply got tired of having them in the area and had decided to kick them out. John ran out there one night with all the Rangers and drove the enemy off. They thought the world of him. Of course, John was an ex-Green Beret himself.

I was also told that they had a foot locker full of money

40

out there and that any time they needed anything, whether for labor, or to recruit volunteers, or to pay the soldiers, they simply opened up the foot locker and dished it out. No receipts of any kind were given, and nobody asked any questions. They ran their own show.

I did see a lot of Cambodians in the camp. Cambodians differed physically from the Vietnamese. The Vietnamese look like Chinese people. The Cambodians have a thicker face and are very, very dark. They are not totally black, but you can spot the difference, between a lighter skinned Vietnamese and a darker skinned Cambodian a mile away. These Cambodians wore large black and white checkered scarves. I was told that the reason they wore these, was that if they got into a fire fight in the jungle and got all mixed up with the enemy, they simply shot anybody who didn't have on a checkered scarf.

My own battalion had some problems with these Cambodians. The Cambodians and Vietnamese were historically enemies. When the Cambodian troops came into Tay Ninh City and started drinking beer, the fact that these two groups had been enemies for centuries was not easily forgotten, and a fight usually broke out between the two. I remember one night, guns were drawn and shots were fired in the air but it turned out to be a "Mexican stand off." By the time the police arrived, Dai Uy had calmed the situation down. To keep the bad blood down between Special Forces and the Rangers, a decision was later made not to allow both of them in town at the same time. When the Rangers were in town, the Cambodians couldn't come in and when the Cambodians came to town our troops were restricted to barracks. But usually this wasn't much of a problem as both of us were out in the field most of the time anyway.

41

CHAPTER 5

Saturday Morning: we were not going out on an operation. It was a day off. We heard that the Filipino nurses were coming down to our compound to play volleyball. What a weird war. One day you are out in the jungle fighting for your life, and the next you're out playing volleyball with beautiful women. Unbelievable. Just like the movies. So, the girls came down and we chose sides and played volleyball. We had lots of fun.

About an hour later, I was standing over by the edge of the volleyball court near the road, when I looked out the gate and saw a three quarter ton truck go by loaded with dead bodies. Arms and legs were sticking out everywhere. Bodies were stacked from top to bottom. I couldn't believe it. I jumped in my jeep and followed the truck. It pulled into the hospital complex and drove over to the morgue. Evidently, this hadn't been the first load delivered because, as I walked into the morgue I found the floor literally covered with bodies. There were maybe fifty dead Vietnamese in there, all laid out stiffly. One man had been propped up on a large board. The board was leaning up against the wall at a 45 degree angle. I walked over to look at him. He was definitely dead. His normal color had changed to a very pale, drained yellow. He had been shot right through the face. Dried blood covered his face and flies crawled all over him. The horrible part was that his eyes were open and he was looking right at me. I turned and gazed at all those poor dead men. It was an incredible sight.

I got back in my jeep and quickly drove back to tell LTC Tansey. I told him there were at least 50 to 70 dead men in the morgue with more arriving all the time. He knew nothing about it. As it turned out, there had been a big fight in a town south of us, about 40 miles away. They had been fighting all night, along with their American Advisors. The Advisors worked for LTC Tansey and hadn't called in, or told him anything, so the Colonel was furious. I don't know why the advisors had failed to inform higher headquarters of their situation. Perhaps they just weren't there, gone to Saigon for the day or maybe their radio got shot up and they couldn't call out. Or maybe they got pinned down in an isolated part of the camp, where they had no communications. All I know is that LTC Tansey was raving mad. Here it was, 10:00 a.m. the morning following a gigantic battle and he had still not been informed.

We later learned that the famous Dong Nai Regiment had attacked the town and the Vietnamese fought back bravely all night until the enemy broke contact at 5:00 a.m. The VC weren't able to penetrate their positions and lost a lot of troops trying. The RVN soldiers did a very good job. One small base, a little outpost, was overrun, but the rest held on and fought like tigers all night. I remember this town, Go Dau Ha, very specifically because of a terrorist incident that had occurred there a month before. It was a murder.

Terrorist attacks were, of course not, unusual in Vietnam. School teachers, officials, post office workers, district chiefs, etc., were murdered every night in Vietnam. Sometimes the VC disemboweled them, plunging a knife into their stomachs while they were still alive pulling out all their intestines. Later, they would tie a rope around their neck and run them up the flag pole for all to see. Other times they would cut off people's hands. They did all sorts of terrible things to terrorize the people.

I remember one particular incident in Go Dau Ha, because it pained me very much. There was a man down there who had a wife and five children. He was running for an elective office in the village. One night the VC knocked on his door. When he came to the door the VC shot him right in the face with a pistol. They murdered him right there in front of his five kids. It was a despicable act. But then, it was just another one of ten thousand murders that occurred that year anyway. But back to the battle. It ended up in ARVN's favor, and I was happy about that.

Later that night, after supper, about 9:00 p.m., fighting broke out on our town wall again. There was heavy fighting, lots of firing. The telephone rang. It was the Filipino medical team. They had received word from the Vietnamese that they were targets for assassination, and they wanted to know if they could come down and stay with us for awhile, or at least until the firing was over. They were closer to the fighting than we were, being only about a block away. Naturally, we said yes. We were very happy about it because the Filipino nurses were beautiful. There were three of them, and we liked to talk to them and see them.

Usually, they didn't have much to do with us. Oh, they would occasionally come down and play a volleyball game, but they never came down to watch a movie, or to have a beer with us, or dance. But that night, with all that heavy firing, right outside their house, they hopped in their truck and barreled on down to our place and we were happy to see them. Upon their arrival we manned the walls and were on the lookout for an attack.

After a while it looked like the same old story. Knowing the girls were inside, we all went back in and opened up a beer or two and had a big party, leaving the Vietnamese to "fight for democracy." Gradually the firing died down and the girls went home. The next night we were hoping that the enemy would attack again so that the nurses would run down to our place once more and we could have another party, but it didn't happen.

The Headquarters had planned an operation for us down to the two villages of Cu Chi Hai and Cu Chi Ba. I had heard bad things about the Cu Chi area. It was across the river. The first village belonged to the Vietnamese government, but everything south of that was under enemy control. It was full of fierce, fanatical, suicidal type, local Viet Cong. They would allow themselves to be overrun by the battalion and then stand right up in the middle of everyone and start shooting back. They were fanatically brave. It wasn't going to be easy.

The time came to move out. We crossed the bridge and turned south through the secure village of Tan Dien. Moving through the village and out the other side, we entered "bear country." To our front was an abandoned rubber plantation. We walked through it without a problem. Then we came to a rice paddy. It was about half a mile wide. Beyond that there was a wood line. We crossed this area and again we didn't receive any fire. That was quite surprising to me. When we moved into Cu Chi Hai we could tell that the VC had been there, because of all the little Viet Cong flags that were pasted all over the place.

We continued to move south. The enemy could not be found anywhere. Beyond Cu Chi Hai lay another rubber plantation, and just beyond that was an old abandoned school house. We almost got all the way through this second rubber plantation when a sniper opened fire. The bullet passed just over me and sounded like the crack of a whip over my head. It was close, very close. Jerry and I were standing right next to each other and we both dove to the ground instantly. The sniper had us in his sights. He knew exactly where we were. He fired again, just inches above our heads. Jerry and I lay down in a ditch. It really wasn't a ditch so much as a shallow, sandy depression. We were definitely pinned down. The sniper had zeroed in on us and we couldn't move. If we got up, we would be killed.

We just lay there, deathly still in the sandy depression. It was sheer terror. If we popped up, he would put a bullet through us. Lying on our backs, we got out our cigarettes. We each put one in our mouths, flicked the lighter, and lay there on our backs smoking. I reached out, got hold of the radio mike cord and drug it to my ear and called the district. In my very calmest voice, I informed them that we were pinned down and could not move. The radio operator on the other end responded with a disinterested "Roger." (Evidently they had heard it before.)

They were not going to run out and get LTC Tansey. I guess something like this happened all the time. It was

45

just routine for them. Well, it wasn't routine for me. It was the first time I had been pinned down by a sniper who had my name on his sights and I lay there hugging the sand.

Some Rangers, hidden from view of the sniper and off to our flank, moved out after him. We heard firing and shouting. Then silence. Dai Uy called me on the radio and told me that everything was now okay. They had run him off. I quickly jumped to my feet and ran to the flank, to get behind some trees. Everything seemed to be all right. The Rangers were now advancing and requesting .60 millimeter mortar fire.

A mortar squad of about four men, located next to me, responded. They set the mortar up in the middle of some trees. (A mortar is a tube in which you drop a bomb, with a shotgun shell in the base of it. When the bomb hits the bottom of the tube the shotgun shell goes off, propelling the bomb out of the tube and into the air toward the target.) These little Vietnamese troops were sitting there dropping the shells down the tube as fast as they could. Pop, pop, pop, off they went, straight up through the trees. Of course, if any one of those shells had struck a branch overhead, it would have exploded, killing everyone below including me. But there they are, grinning away and having a good old time firing as fast as they could, oblivious of the danger above them and obviously not caring too much where the shells were landing, either. I just hoped they weren't landing on any of our own Rangers.

I looked at Jerry, he looked at me and we both rolled our eyes skyward. What a war. The mortar squad was completely ignorant to the fact that they were just inches away from their own self-destruction. Finally, they stopped.

We moved out and up to the school house and paused. It was deathly quiet. We listened intently. All you could hear was the chirp of a bird. I saw the Rangers standing silently, looking around. No one was here. We moved back to Tay Ninh City.

CHAPTER 6

Scenes from Tay Ninh City

Our compound was a pretty place. It was located on the corner of an intersection, and had a high white wall all the way around it. The only opening in the wall was at the front and led to the street. There was a very large iron gate there which could be locked. The wall itself was very high. You couldn't jump over it. Even someone standing on top of someone else's shoulders couldn't make it over, without having to reach up and pull themselves over by their finger tips. It didn't do much for us from a defensive point of view, because it had no firing ports (holes) through which we could fire but it did eliminate the possibility of the VC making a sudden and direct charge into the building. And if we were alerted, we could pick off anybody coming over the wall. The top of that flat roof gave me an even better view, and offered a spectacular sight all around the fields of fire.

Inside the villa were some Vietnamese people who worked for us. Actually, it was a family: a man, his wife, and their little boy and girl. The man was a gardener and took care of the yard, the wall repairs around the house, or whatever. His wife served as our cook and made some really delicious meals. And the kids had the job of going around and sweeping out all the rooms every day. The broom they used was very different from ours. It was nothing more than a bunch of straws tied together at the top to form a handle, and that fanned out around the bottom to form a broom. It was about two foot long. You

47

had to bend over to use it. Of course, the little boy could use it standing up. So the family made a living by taking care of our personal items and the house. It was a nice arrangement all the way around. There was also an unusual animal that graced the walls of our compound. It was called the "fook you" lizard. I don't know the biological name for it, but that's what all the advisors called it. As you lay on your bunk and looked at the ceiling, you could see those green lizards slither across upside down. Then you would hear them call out, "Fook you, fook you." Their voices were almost human. It was as if they were mocking us.

We also had a gazebo out in front of the house. The floor was concrete, with bamboo shafts running up the sides supporting a circular thatched roof. It was really nice to sit out there in the evening. Sometimes it would rain. The rain would come down in sheets, but we would be nice and dry inside the gazebo. It could hold about 10 or 15 people, with chairs all around. I used to go out there at night and listen to the sounds. I could hear a 105 artillery battery fire off east of town. Then the shell would whistle overhead; then, a few seconds later it would impact on the west side of town, over by Cu Chi Ba where the VC were always fooling around. The sequence was this: a loud cannon would fire off behind me, then it would make a whistling sound as it passed overhead. Then it would explode off to my front.

One night, we had a new officer report in who was on his way to an assignment out in the bush. He was an "old guy," and had been in World War II, Korea and now Vietnam. He had a good sense of humor and was really funny. On his first night in Tay Ninh, we sat out there together in the gazebo drinking a beer. Suddenly, I heard the cannon go off. I casually told him that in a few seconds he was going to hear a round whistle overhead. Sure enough, after a few seconds, it whistled right past us. A few more seconds later I told him, "Now you are going to hear it explode to our front."

Sure enough the moment I said that, the shell exploded west of town. I had it all down to the last second. He was pretty impressed by all that. We had a big laugh.

The old guy was later assigned to a village near the Cambodian border. It lay along the blacktop road that led to Cambodia. There was a river between Tay Ninh City and his new home. It was a very wide river. Unfortunately for him, his village was located on the other side of the river and not on our side. And, of course, the bridge had been blown between. He would be completely isolated over there. The only way he could get over there was by air. So, he had to fly to his new assignment by helicopter. I always thought about what a terrible job he had. There he was, in an area completely surrounded by the enemy, on the wrong side of the river, with the bridge blown behind him. Tay Ninh was surrounded, but at least in Tay Ninh we had an infantry battalion and all kinds of local forces. This guy had nothing between him and thousands of the enemy. He was really in a very precarious position.

Another man, who lived in a scary place, was an Advisor, a Major, assigned to the Boi Loi Woods, another real hotbed of enemy activity. The Boi Loi Woods was where the Dong Nai regiment had its training camp, and a base camp with many supplies. His village was located about 1,000 yards out from the edge of this forest, in the middle of a rice paddy. The enemy used to attack it regularly, most times just to train their new recruits. It was probably the "hairiest" place in all Vietnam. There he sat, all night long looking at that black, ugly tree line to his front, knowing it was completely filled with enemy soldiers, and wondering what night all 5,000 of them would come screaming out to kill him. The Major assigned down there couldn't take the stress. He started drinking too heavily. In fact, he drank so much that Colonel Tansey had to pull him out and send him back to Saigon to a different job. He just went to pieces staring at that black jungle every night. I, for one, never blamed him.

Our airstrip was located off the Northeast edge of town. It wasn't very long, but it was big enough to bring in an Army Caribou (a twin engine supply plane). Every Tuesday at 10:00 a.m. we would drive over to the airstrip, park, and wait for that plane because it brought in something rather special...our mail from home. It was so quiet waiting for that plane that you could hear a pin

49

drop. It might have rained the night before but in the morning the sky would be brilliantly clear. The air was clean and crisp with a sense of quiet that only comes after a heavy rain. We looked south and listened. No one would speak. The silence would only be broken by the occasional sound of a match being struck as someone lit up a cigarette or a man moving in his jeep seat.

After a while, someone would pick up the sound of the engine. Then a shout, "I hear it, I hear it. It's coming."

Long before we could see it we could hear it coming, its engines steadily droning. Then all eyes would rivet south. Finally, a voice would holler, "I see it, I see it."

A finger would stab skyward, and we would all shoot our faces in that direction. Finally we could see it, a small speck moving against a sea of blue. Gradually, it got bigger and bigger. Then the plane would circle the city. It would approach from the east at 1,000 feet and then dive straight down. It looked like it was on a dive bombing mission to the end of the runway. But at the last moment it would flare out and land, tires squealing. After a short roll, it would taxi over to our location and stop. We would unload the food boxes, a mail bag and a 55 gallon barrel of kerosene while the engines continued to turn.

As soon as the last item was off the plane, the pilot would rev his engines and taxi back to the end of the runway. There he would turn, point the plane back to the east, and pour the coals to her. Halfway down he could have lifted her off, but he never did. He kept roaring down the runway at a terrific speed. Then suddenly, at the end of the runway, the nose would poke skyward and the plane would climb almost straight up. It was impossible to believe it, unless you saw it. The plane looked as if it would fall backwards out of the sky but it never did. It just kept going straight up. At 1,000 feet (and safe from sniper fire), the pilot would level her off and head for the next outpost. Meanwhile, on the ground, we greedily searched through the mail bag, throwing letters at each other as we found them.

Right behind the airfield, at the end of the runway, was a vestige of the old French Empire: a large building, a fort about the size of a football field with very high walls.

The walls were 12 feet thick with firing ports. Back in the 1800s and early 1900s, the French would fire through these narrow holes at the enemy. Inside of the fort were rooms where the officers and men of our battalion lived. The rooms were build right into the wall. This was our barracks. The soldiers hung their hammocks on hooks embedded in concrete. The commander, Dai Uy, also had his office there. We parked our jeeps there at night too in the middle of the parade field. It was probably the safest place in town, because that's where the entire Ranger battalion slept.

We had movies every night at the Advisor's house. They were brought in weekly on the airplane. Of course, while the rest watched the movie or drank beer, one man was appointed the night duty officer. In addition to his job of maintaining contact with the local Vietnamese by telephone, he had another job. He was to stay in touch with a Special Forces team of nine men, who lived on top of a very high mountain in our province. It was the only mountain around. The Vietnamese called it Nui Ba Dinh (Black Lady Mountain). It was very black and rose straight up out of nowhere. It was very ominous, very mysterious. Just to look at it gave you a feeling of foreboding. The mission of this team was to maintain contact with Special Forces Patrols operating in the area below. From on top of that mountain, they could broadcast their radio beams to the teams operating in the flat jungle country for miles around, or even over into Cambodia. That little outpost in the sky could be easily attacked and overrun, because they were so completely isolated up there, not to mention the fact that they were totally surrounded by VC. So our job was to stay in constant contact with them, in case they got into trouble.

To do this, they gave us one of their own radios called the HT-1. (I understand it was developed by the CIA.) It was the size of a Velveeta cheese box and was painted black, and had a long telescoping antenna on the end. It was very easy to use, because you didn't have to dial in a frequency. It only had one frequency and that was pre-set. All you had to do was turn the radio on. The frequency was a very high one, similar to the type used by the Air

51

Force, and could even broadcast through cement walls. So, we could watch a movie and monitor those poor devils at the same time by just laying it down on a chair next to us. It would transmit right through our building. None of our Army radios could do that.

A funny thing happened one night while we were watching one of the movies. It was a war movie, the kind that didn't have any real plot, just lots of combat. From the time the first reel started until the time the last reel ended, there was nothing but firing; firing of machine guns, bombs, explosions, hand grenades, and mortars. There was an immense amount of noise in this film, just continual combat sounds from start to finish. Finally, the movie ended. The projection screen turned bright white from the lamp as the film started whipping around on the reel as it usually did. We were preparing to return to our rooms for the night when we continued to hear firing and explosions. And they weren't coming from the movie! They were coming from outside the house. It was the real war. We all jumped up, grabbed our carbines, and ran for the wall. The VC were only two blocks away, attacking the town as usual. We hadn't realized it because we thought all the explosions were coming from the movie. The Vietnamese had been too busy to call us at the time, so we hadn't been informed that the town was under attack again. What a laugh!

CHAPTER 7

It was morning, about 8:00 a.m. Another operation was planned for the day. Some of the troops had already trucked over to Tan Dien. Tan Dien was the village across the bridge from Tay Ninh, and south along the river, the same place where we ran out to, on such short notice that Sunday morning. I had a funny feeling in my stomach. I was a little afraid of Tan Dien. I knew that south of that first friendly village there were snipers. They owned that country, and they knew it. They had spider holes to hide in that were very cleverly camouflaged. They were fanatical too, and not afraid of us. Now it was time to move out and get them. I hopped in my jeep with Tau. We drove through downtown Tay Ninh, across the bridge, and then turned left down the old dusty road. As we drove along I recalled how, just a few Sundays before, a machine gun had been firing across that rice paddy. Now it was so peaceful. The first village was still under government control. We pulled into town. The battalion was there and ready to move out. Our job was to move south and secure the road down to an old school house, so that some trucks and bulldozers could come in and work on the road. We headed out.

The first patch of ground was through a rubber plantation owned by the Michelin Company. It was easy walking. As we walked through the rubber, I noticed something. If I looked in one direction, it seemed that there were trees all around me. I couldn't see very far at all. But soon I began to realize that the trees were in rows, and if I looked between the rows I could see a great distance; in fact, all

53

the way down to the end of the plantation about a half a mile away. Walking a few steps further, and looking in another direction, it was all one big forest again.

We had moved about 500 yards south through the rubber when the battalion stopped. Dai Uy wanted to make a map check. He got out his map and held it with both hands. I moved over and stood beside him. We were both standing there looking at his map, when suddenly, "crack," a bullet passed right between us. It smacked a rubber tree two feet behind us splitting the bark. In a thousandth of a second, I looked to the right from where the shot had come. There, I saw a black pajama figure running down an open row of trees, about 200 yards away. I grabbed my carbine, raised it, and in a split second brought the sight to my eye. At the same instant the enemy darted left and was lost in the trees before I could pull the trigger. After a moment, we both breathed a huge sigh of relief. That was a very close call. The bullet had missed us by only a few inches.

It was time to move south again. The rubber ended and we entered some jungle. The jungle cleared after a couple hundred yards and then I saw a rice paddy to our front. At this point, there was a road on our left, jungle to our rear, an open rice paddy to our front, and more jungle off to our far right about a quarter mile away. That piece of jungle off to our far right extended in the same direction we were moving, and eventually curved back to our front again. We had come to an open rice paddy and had to cross it. There was no other way around it.

When I got to the clearing my suspicions were confirmed. It was a bad spot. There was a sniper off to our right, and he had the area covered. We now had two choices. We could either run across the rice paddy, one by one, as fast as possible and let the sniper fire at us intermittently, hoping he would hit no one or we could turn to the right, attack through the jungle a quarter mile away, and try to find him. The latter action would of course take time and would mean casualties, too, because if we maneuvered toward him, he would open fire and get a couple of us before he took off running. It would be an exercise in futility. Besides, our mission was to go down to the schoolhouse, not to clear the jungle.

Dai Uy decided correctly to ignore the sniper, and to have everyone run across the rice paddy. I arrived at the edge of the jungle and looked across the rice paddy to my front. Some men had already made it across and were standing in the tree line on the other side. As each man got ready to run, he hunched his pack tight on his shoulders, hefted his rifle up into his right hand, got on the dike and then took off running as fast as he could. Meanwhile, the sniper would take a bead on him and decide whether or not he would kill him. Several men, directly to my front, took off in a dead run. They made it across. Now another man. He made it, too.

Now it was the turn of the man directly in front of me. Off he went. He got about half way across when the sniper fired. I heard the bullet crack. It sounded like the loud pop of a whip. The man fell face down in the water. I knew he had been hit and was probably drowning. Since I was brought up by our Army to go after the wounded, I instinctively crouched and started to run out to get him. But a Vietnamese soldier behind me put his hand on my shoulder and held me back. He pointed at the man lying face down in the water and gestured that I should wait. Suddenly, the "dead" man, who was lying face down in the water, leaped up and ran for cover. He made it. He had been "playing possum."

Now it was my turn. Heart pounding, I grabbed my carbine and took off for the fastest run of my life. I flew down the dike but it seemed like an eternity. I was held back by the weight of the harness, grenades, canteen, carbine, and 200 rounds of ammo. One thought raced through my mind. Was I in his sights now? Only a few yards to go. I flung myself into the safety of the jungle. I made it. And the game went on. Others followed. My heart kept pounding. I was still out of breath. What excitement! Alive one minute — dead the next.

Everybody got across so we moved South again. This time it was through mixed terrain; some bush here and there, a rice paddy, but always keeping the road to our left. Finally we reached the schoolhouse. Upon arrival we set up a perimeter, fanning out around it for several hundred yards. We didn't have to worry about the back side of the schoolhouse, the part that faced the road, because there was a river over there, and it was almost impossible for the enemy to come from that direction. We didn't have to worry about them coming from the north, because that was the direction we had just come from. But we did have to worry about them coming from the south, and particularly from the west, because that's where the thick jungle was located. Some of the troops hid behind bushes, some lay out in the open, still others huddled behind a clump of ground or a ditch; any place where they could find cover or concealment.

It was then I heard the crack of a bullet. I was standing on the enemy side of the schoolhouse, about five yards out from the schoolhouse, in a small patch of meadow. It was a sniper. He was firing into our group. The bullet passed over my head with a sharp crack. I crouched down, ran back around the schoolhouse, and took cover behind it. Shots were now being fired about every five minutes. There were three snipers out there: one to our left, one to our front, and one off to our right front. You always heard the crack of the bullet first, and the noise of the rifle second, because the bullet travels faster than the speed of sound. Sometimes we heard the thud of a bullet first as it smacked into the ground or into a tree or into a soldier.

We all crouched down behind the schoolhouse. Two medics ran back toward us from the jungle, bent over. They were dragging a man who had been hit. They laid him down on his stomach inside the schoolhouse and proceeded to cut away his fatigue jacket. I took a look. He had a big gaping hole in his back. Not a neat, small, bullet hole like you see in the movies, but a large ragged hole with lots of blood pulsating out of the wound. They placed a large bandage over the wound to stop the bleeding.

The firing went on. About every five minutes a wounded man would be dragged in. The sniper was hitting someone every five minutes. Now more wounded. The medics placed them on a low table, worked on them and then laid them off to the side.

I watched this macabre scene for about an hour. We were taking hits like clockwork, and I realized we were at an impasse. We couldn't stay there. The enemy would just pick us off one by one. It was just stupid to lie there and take it, and Dai Uy appeared to be visibly upset. In fact, he was in shock. He couldn't react. He had gone to pieces. He wasn't blubbering or anything like that, but he was shaking. I went over to talk to him. He told me that he had once had a nervous breakdown and that he had that same feeling now and that he just didn't know what to do.

I urged him to make a decision, to attack the enemy or withdraw, one or the other, but we couldn't stay there and take it on the chin. He said he couldn't. He had to obey his orders. His colonel had ordered him to secure this area, and that was what he would have to do until the trucks and bulldozers arrived to do their job. We had to stay until 5:00 p.m. to give them protection. I looked at my watch. It was 1:00 p.m., and not a work crew was in sight. There were no trucks, no bulldozers, no nothing. We were just sitting there like ducks in a pond for no reason at all. This didn't make sense.

I told the Dai Uy to try and contact the district and ask them what was going on. He said he had tried but they were shut down for siesta. This simply meant that while we were out there dying, the people back at the Vietnamese headquarters were having a nice long lunch, and were now probably lying down taking a nap. He couldn't raise a soul on his radio.

Then I thought about Colonel Tansey. Why not contact him? I got him on the radio and told him my problem. He then informed me that the work crew had never shown up in Tay Ninh City. (They were evidently coming in from out of town and no one ever arrived.) I then got back to Dai Uy and told him that nobody was coming and that we had no reason to stay out there anymore so "let's move." But he said he still couldn't leave, not until he had cleared it with his colonel, or he would be in big trouble. (Orders can never be disobeyed, reinterpreted, or modified in the field by the Vietnamese Army.) So he tried to contact his superiors once again but they were still taking a nap. It was all so useless. Headquarters was all shut down. But there we stayed, the whole battalion being chewed to pieces bit by bit in one afternoon and all for nothing.

Then I got an idea. I asked the Dai Uy, "Dai Uy, if I told you that your colonel was trying to reach you but couldn't and that he was sending a message through my colonel to me over my radio would you obey it? Would you move out? Would that cover you?"

He said, "Yes."

If he received orders through me then he could head back home. I got on my radio and pretended to talk to my headquarters. After a moment or so, I went back to Dai Uy Duong, and told him the following: "Dai Uy, your colonel has been trying to contact you, and he can't. He told my colonel to tell you that you no longer have to stay here and that you can do anything you want."

Suddenly Dai Uy sprang to life. He started barking orders to the Rangers all around him and to his staff. We began to pull out. We fell back across the road to our rear, towards the river, and then headed back north toward Tay Ninh City. But, we had only moved a couple of hundred yards when Dai Uy Duong decided to attack the enemy again. I don't know why. Maybe he just wanted to get one last lick in, to outflank them and to come in from behind. But it was a good move.

However, at this particular time, as the battalion cut left toward the enemy, I found myself all alone in the jungle. I had been the last man in the file when suddenly the battalion just disappeared. I guess they had cut left on me when I wasn't watching, and had disappeared in all that brush. I stopped for a minute, just to get the feeling of being out there all alone. It was eerie, almost enjoyable. But then I got scared. I realized that at any moment enemy soldiers could step out of that jungle, and I would be a prisoner of war. There was no one around to help me. So I put my carbine in my right hand, hung my arms down along my side, and took off in a dog trot.

Eventually I caught up with the battalion and began to work my way forward toward Dai Uy, when shots rang out. It was those snipers again. But this time the Rangers were mad as hell. This time there would be no lying down and taking it. We were coming in on their flank and we were going to "clean their clock." Everybody got up on line and opened fire. The Rangers started screaming and hollering and ran toward the snipers. They wanted to kill and kill bad. I did, too. I hoisted my rifle to my shoulder and ran firing at the enemy. I screamed, "Ranger, Ranger," at the top of my lungs. We drove them off. It was all quiet. We poked around a little bit and then headed back north, back to Tay Ninh City. The operation was over.

It was 9:00 p.m. the same day. The telephone rang. It was a call from District. The village east of town where those seven poor men had been shot dead, was now under attack by the VC. We were told to get ready. The battalion was to move out and save Cha La from being over run. A few minutes later, my jeep pulled up with Tau at the wheel and we raced down the street in the darkness toward battalion headquarters. Everybody was already loaded up on 2 1/2 ton trucks and were ready to roll out. Truck engines were running and the headlights were on.

Dai Uy was standing by his jeep briefing his officers. When he was finished I warned him of a possible ambush enroute. It wouldn't have been the first time. It was an old VC trick; send a small force over to a village, fire at them and get them scared, so that they will call up the reinforcements, and then lie in wait somewhere between the village and town and shoot up the reinforcements as they came hightailing it to the rescue. But Dai Uy Duong told me he'd already figured that one out. He said he knew that was probably exactly what the VC had in mind.

We took off in a roar towards the village. As we entered "bear country," the trucks stopped. We dismounted and plunged into the jungle. Then we moved cross country in the darkness toward the village. Eventually, I saw lights up ahead, flares hanging in the air. I peered through the jungle. It was the village.

We burst out of the jungle. To our front was a large rice paddy, and beyond that the village. Dai Uy got on the radio and told the villagers we were coming, and that help was on the way. We staggered across the rice paddy and into the village. Were they happy to see us!

In the meantime, of course, the VC had bugged out. We hung around for a while but there was nothing more we could do. It was time to go home.

Dai Uy radioed for the trucks and they came barreling

down the road. They pulled into the village and turned around. Everybody jumped on and we headed home. But now we were doing something dreadfully wrong. Yes, we had used our brains coming out. We had moved cross country to avoid a possible ambush. But now, we were heading right back down the same highway we had come out on. No precautions had been made whatsoever. Now was the perfect time for an ambush. The VC knew we had to take this road back to Tay Ninh. So there we were, "moving ducks." I was right behind Dai Uy. He was in the lead jeep, lights on. It was terrifying to drive through the jungle at night, headlights on, knowing there was no protection on either side of you and that anything could happen at any time. But it didn't. Once again, God in his mercy had let us make it safely back to the city. I let out a big sigh of relief. This was sheer madness!

A few days later, it looked like we would launch another operation down to Cu Chi (the schoolhouse area where Dai Uy went into shock). As the men gathered at the battalion, I could tell that they were not extremely happy about it. It meant heading back to those snipers again. I could just tell by the look on everybody's face. It wasn't fear or terror that showed, but everybody did have a sour expression.

We moved over to Tan Dien, the last friendly village before Cu Chi Hai and Cu Chi Ba. Then we began to move south. At this point the artillery observer, a Lieutenant who was not a member of the battalion, but who was attached to us to call in artillery fire, stopped and claimed that he was not going to go any further. He had turned coward. He was refusing to leave Tan Dien Village. Dai Uy was furious. He shouted at him and kicked him. After being kicked and beaten for a full minute the man agreed to come along. But I could tell from the look on his face that he was in terror (and so was I). We moved out and headed for the schoolhouse again. Two hundred yards short of the schoolhouse we heard the sharp crack of bullets overhead. It was those snipers again. Perhaps only two this time. Dai Uy halted the battalion and hollered over to the observer to call in artillery fire. It was a good move. Soon artillery shells started falling in front of us, hitting the ground by the VC, throwing shrapnel everywhere. They were using "variable time fuses" (a fuse that causes the shell to explode 50 feet above the ground and showers hot steel down on the enemy). They were calling in 155mms.

Normally, infantry uses 105mm shells in close support, because the shell is smaller and can be called in much closer. But Tay Ninh did not have any 105mm guns. All we had was 155mm guns located at Ben Kieu. This 155mm shell was enormously heavy and was chock full of explosives. When it went off it literally shook the earth. What a terrible blast. It blackened the trees and threw out pieces of hot shrapnel everywhere for hundreds of yards. It was extremely dangerous to use that close but it was all that we had available.

I was scared. It was frightening to know that the shrapnel called in that close might sail through the air and hit me, too. I was also frightened by the fact that somewhere, miles away, there was a little Vietnamese fellow looking through a gun sight and if he made just the slightest error, even a fraction of an inch in his aim, the shell would land on top of me and blow me to kingdom come. However I did have a lot of confidence in the crew. They were all very well trained. All of their officers had been trained in the United States at the best artillery school in the world (Fort Sill) and were extremely proficient. Still, when those shells screamed through the air and landed right out in front of me with such horrible violence, it did worry me.

At this time, Jerry and I were a little bit behind and to the left of the battalion. We were lying down in a graveyard. The Vietnamese (including the VC) were terribly afraid of graveyards. They will always walk around one, or lay down on the other side, but they will never lie down inside one. However, Jerry and I found it very useful to protect us from the snipers. Each grave had a ring around it, about four inches high marking the spot where the deceased lay. Sometimes it was made of poured concrete, other times of stone. Either way, it offered excellent protection.

Today, it was the same old story. There was a sniper

hidden out there, somewhere in a spider hole. He would slide that rifle of his out of his little hole, fire, wound someone and then pull his rifle back inside and hide. You could never spot him to shoot him and it was just too thick and dangerous to maneuver against him. About all you could do is call in artillery fire and pound the area senseless and hope to kill him that way. Later, you could shift the artillery fire and try to outflank him. That's what Dai Uy was trying to do in this case. He was moving the third company off to the flank while the artillery kept the sniper pinned down.

While all this was going on, Jerry suddenly had to "take a crap" in the worst way. As you know you can't do that lying down. You have to squat. He just couldn't stand it anymore. The whole thing had come on him real quick. I don't know what he ate but he told me he had to go and he had to go now. We glanced around quickly for a safe spot to do the job. The best place seemed to be across the road. The enemy was not normally in this area and we would be further away from the sniper as he was off in the other direction. So we grabbed our carbines and ran for it. I pointed my rifle back in the direction of the sniper while Jerry took care of his business. What a predicament he was in, answering a call of nature while under sniper fire. But the sniper did not fire at us. Jerry finished his job and we ran back and jumped once again into the protection of the graveyard. Then we laughed ourselves silly about what had just happened.

Soon the artillery lifted, and we heard the Rangers shouting and firing as they attacked the sniper. I don't know what happened to the sniper. I suppose he ran away. Maybe this one just dropped down inside his camouflaged tunnel and waited until we all had passed over him. At any rate, he and his friends were not a threat to us anymore. We continued south and arrived at the schoolhouse. Again, the battalion fanned out into a circle. I didn't know the purpose of our stopping there at that particular time. It was Dai Uy's decision. He was coordinating with the company Commanders inside the safety of the schoolhouse. But it was not safe outside. The snipers in this area started opening up again.

Cowboy, my Vietnamese bodyguard (who also carried my pack and food and cooked for me) had wandered away. He had been right next to me all day but now, somehow or another, he had slipped away. I suppose he went over to talk to a friend in one of the companies up front, closer to the snipers. Anyway, at this time, one of the snipers saw him and shot him through the arm. He fell down. A buddy picked him up and slung him across his shoulder, and trotted back with him toward the schoolhouse and the medics. Then the sniper fired again. This time he hit him in the other arm. It was so odd that both bullets would catch him in the elbows.

Dai Uy didn't want to stay around today, with all this going on, so we pulled out. Meanwhile, Cowboy was being taken care of by the medics. They put some bandages on him, laid him in a hammock, slung it on a bamboo pole, and started dog trotting back toward the safety of Tan Dien village. We followed. An ambulance was waiting there. They threw Cowboy inside, and the vehicle roared off for the hospital. Tau was waiting for me at the village, too. I got into the jeep and we sped off for the hospital.

When I got to the Army section of the hospital, no one was there to help. No one knew where the Army doctor was either. So they sent someone to try to find him. He should have been on duty, but he wasn't. While at the hospital I ran into the Filipino surgeon and the two nurses. Since my friend was badly wounded and bleeding, I asked the surgeon if he could help. (In reality I preferred him over the Vietnamese Army doctor anyway, because Filipino surgeons were outstanding.) I pleaded with him to help Cowboy but he said he couldn't. He told me sadly that it was against the rules. He was in Vietnam as a guest of the government, and could only help civilians. He could not participate in any war related activities at all. He just couldn't help. Finally, the Vietnamese Army doctor did arrive. I didn't like him from the start. He looked snobby and lazy. But Cowboy was in his hands now. I had to leave. All I could do was to go back to the compound and wait.

The next morning, bright and early, I got up and went to the hospital. I arrived at the ward. It was not air conditioned. It was nothing more than four big concrete walls with a tin roof overhead. There were big open windows on the side, so that air could pass back and forth through the rooms. Sometimes when it rained real hard it the rain blew right into the room. But the wards stayed cool that way; lots of shade with big open spaces.

I found Cowboy's bed. His wife and kids were there, too. I noticed that he had casts on both arms. He was conscious and gave me a big smile. I looked at his casts. The casts were soaked with blood at the elbows. He looked down at his elbows and told me in Vietnamese, "xau lam, xau lam" (very bad.) I knew to what he was referring. The bleeding was supposed to have been stopped before the casts were put on. This only meant that a sloppy job had been done and he was now bleeding from the inside. They were supposed to do all the surgical work first, and then put on the cast.

I left the room and went looking for the Vietnamese doctor. I found him in his office. I told him that something was drastically wrong with Cowboy's arms. The Doctor immediately turned unfriendly. I could tell he didn't like me telling him what to do. As he didn't want to talk to me anymore, I had to leave. The next day I went to see Cowboy again. It was the same story. They hadn't changed the casts and they were still bloody. So I went to see the Vietnamese doctor again. This time I was very nice to him. I tried to bribe him. I gave him a carton of cigarettes. I begged and pleaded with him. But in the end I could tell he was not going to do anything. I was so frustrated because I knew that, day after day, irreparable damage was being done to Cowboy's arms.

About a week later, in desperation, I asked the doctor if I could move Cowboy to Saigon. I asked him, "If I can get him a ride to the National Hospital at Cong Hoa will you agree to release him?"

The doctor said, "Okay," but that he wouldn't order a Vietnamese chopper for him. On the other hand he wouldn't stop him from being transferred either. So I contacted Major Stewart who ran our U.S. helicopter company and asked him if he would pick up Cowboy. He agreed.

The next day the chopper arrived. All arrangements

had been made. I got Cowboy over to the airfield. I couldn't go along but everything had been set up down south to receive him. Major Stewart said he would fly him to the National Hospital in Saigon where they had better facilities. I felt good as I watched the helicopter climb into the sky taking my friend to better care. At least he was getting away from this "quack" in Tay Ninh.

CHAPTER 8

It was in the afternoon after the usual siesta, about 3:00 p.m. A special meeting had been called by the Province Chief. All of the District officials were there. The meeting was held in a large room at the old fort. I walked into the room and looked around. There were various members of the Vietnamese Army there, as well as the local District Chief, the Province Chief, some American Advisors, and the Artillery Liaison Officer. The room was dark. I peered around at all those shadowy figures in dark fatigues. The only light in the room was a small lamp clamped to a large map on an easel in the front of the room. We took our seats and listened. I didn't understand Vietnamese fluently but I knew an operation when I saw one. I could tell by the symbols and drawings on the map. It looked like we were going up to Nui Ba Dinh the large mountain north of Tay Ninh City.

It appeared that, on this operation we would move north, sweep along the base of the mountain and then head back south again. Needless to say, I was scared. I knew once we left the northern edge of Tay Ninh City and headed for that mountain we would be in enemy country, really bad enemy country. They owned every inch of real estate from there to Hanoi. There were in fact, roads that ran from Hanoi, right down into our sector. We might run into anything out there including Ho Chi Minh himself, with the entire North Vietnamese Department of Defense.

After the briefing, I walked forward with Dai Uy to look at the map. Our biggest concern was to make sure that we would not walk out of artillery range. A Howitzer had an effective range of 12 kilometers (or 6 miles.) I drew a line on the map using the artillery battery as the base and ran the line out for 12 kilometers. As it turned out the operation would take us to the outer edge of that 12 kilometer line. Technically, we would be within range but it would be at the very maximum range the artillery could fire. We took the rest of the afternoon off as we would be moving out the next day.

Morning came. We trucked north to the edge of the city and disembarked. The edge of Tay Ninh City was not so well defined in the north. It was hard to say where Tay Ninh ended and "bear country" began. There was a gate guard out there, so we disembarked and began to move out. I knew that the people we would meet from here on out, lived and worked outside the city limits so that meant that they were probably VC. They might smile at us and pretend to be on our side but once we crossed that gate we were for all intents and purposes in enemy country. Perhaps some of them supported the VC out of genuine sympathy for their cause, but others did so out of fear. Who knew who was on who's side, and for what reason? We would have to be suspicious of them all.

At first, we sloshed through some rice paddies. Later there was lots of tall swamp grass with water at the bottom. The swamp water came up to the top of my boots, but it was not too bad to move through. Somehow or another, I got behind in the formation. Normally I walked right behind Dai Uy's radio operator, but today I was behind a little Vietnamese soldier. He was carrying a loaded M-1 rifle, round in the chamber, with the barrel sticking right in my face. I kept thinking about how much I trusted that little guy. If the safety went off and he accidentally slipped, it was "good-bye" world. It was just one of those things I had to put up with. If I ran around all day long correcting every little thing I didn't like, the troops would lose face and subsequently their confidence in me. So I accepted a lot of things the way they were and walked behind that little guy all day long with his rifle pointing right in my eyeball.

We left the swamp grass and began to move into

jungle country. There was brush here and there. We moved right up along side the bottom of Nui Ba Dinh mountain and then swung left. I was thankful Dai Uy hadn't received orders to go up the mountain. If we went up the mountain, they could shoot down at us, and that would put us at a big disadvantage.

I had an odd feeling about this operation from the very beginning, as if we were playing a little game with the VC, and both sides were aware of it before we started. Captain Ramsey told me once that he was sure that there were spies in the Tay Ninh District Headquarters because one day, when he was out on patrol, he captured an enemy soldier with a copy of their own operations order on him. Perhaps today, too, someone told them where we intended to go, and they were just playing cat and mouse with us. They might decide to leave us alone. There were plenty of reason for them to do that. After all, there were 350 of us, all heavily armed and mean as sin. On the other hand, with advance knowledge of where we were going, and with the larger forces that they had at their disposal, they could ambush us and wipe us out entirely. So, the question was, "what was going to happen today?" Would they attack, or leave us alone?

We swung a little more north. At this point we reached the maximum range of our artillery. Then we took a hard left. We walked for a couple kilometers along the extreme edge of our artillery support and then began to bend back toward Tay Ninh City.

About this time, the battalion halted to my front. I walked forward to see what was up. They had captured a suspect. He was wearing black pajamas, but didn't have a weapon. He looked extremely scared. His hands were tied behind him with commo wire (telephone wire.) They were tied very tightly. Too tightly. The blood was not going into his hands. He looked terribly afraid. He had this look on his face, that indicated to me that he had been beaten just before I got there.

That would have been typical of the Vietnamese. If they caught someone it was standard policy for many units to tie their hands behind them and kick the living tar out of them until they talked. You had to understand all this in the light of the frightening situation in which they lived. Everyday, these soldiers saw kids blown up on school buses, teachers shot in the face, people hung from flagpoles, hands cut off and thousands of other acts of terror. So, when they caught somebody from the other side, they naturally had a tendency to punch him in the face and kick him in the stomach, to pay him back. It was just pent up emotion. However, I made a note to talk to Dai Uy about this. I knew this man had been kicked many times before I got there and I couldn't go along with that, from a personal point of view.

We tramped on back into the swamp grass area. It was not a very good place to stop, but since it was fairly dry in the area in which we were standing, we decided to take our noon chow break there. As Cowboy was no longer with me, I had to carry my own pack and food. Tau had made a rice ball for me before we moved out that morning. They made them like this: when the rice was hot, you scooped it up in your hands, formed it into a ball about the size of a softball and then let it cool. Once it cooled, you wrapped it in wax paper. Oddly enough, it tasted great cold. All you had to do was sprinkle a little salt and pepper on it and it turned out to be really delicious. We also opened up a can of Spam. I shared that with my radio operator, Chan, and his buddies. We also had brought along a loaf of French bread so we sliced that down the middle and made sandwiches.

About this time Dai Uy's bodyguard, a kind of thin, old man, took out a pipe. The pipe had been made out of a discarded aluminum tube which, at one time had been a parachute flare canister. This tube had a hole poked in the bottom, through which he had stuck a hollow stick thus converting it into a pipe. Then he took a substance out his pack, stuck it into the pipe, lit it, and puffed on it until it was glowing red hot. He then sucked the entire load of smoke inside of him without breathing, and without letting any escape. I never saw anything like it. Finally, he laid the pipe aside and began to let the smoke flow slowly out of his nose and mouth. (I found out later that he was smoking opium.) He was the only man in the battalion who had this bad habit. It didn't take long for the smoke to take effect. He was sitting opposite me when suddenly he was "gone." He had this very glassy stare. He was off in a dream world. And he would be there for another half an hour or so.

After lunch we moved south. Eventually, we hit black-top. It was an old macadam road put in by the French. It was still in good repair, and ran all the way over to Cambodia. However, you could no longer drive to Cambodia because all the bridges had been knocked out between here and there and the road had been cut up. But from this particular spot, from here to the city, the road was in good shape and was used daily by the farmers.

As we left "bear country" and walked along side the road, I could see more and more signs of life in front of me. Little kids came out to watch us go by. Many were only five or six years old. They looked so small. Some were tending huge water buffalo. The water buffalo were the size of large oxen and had long curved horns, and were extremely vicious. Yet, these little children kept these water buffalo under control with only a piece of string tied through their nose. When they pulled the string, the buffalo meekly followed. Farmers, too, worked in the field. Some were hoeing. There was an ox cart right in front of me. It was a very simple affair: two large wooden wheels, connected by an axle, with a flat wooden bed on top. Two long poles stuck out in front, to which the ox was harnessed. The ox moved at an extremely slow pace, probably at only one mile an hour. Since we walked at a pace of three miles an hour, we quickly passed him by. Unlike the water buffalo, the ox did not become frightened by me. He did not snort or bolt, like his brother bovine. He was a very calm and contented animal. I looked up ahead and saw the city. We were home.

The next day, I agreed to meet Dai Uy for a little talk during lunch, before he went to take his afternoon nap. We met at a roadside restaurant. It was nothing more than a couple of card tables set up under a thatched roof hut. We ordered a couple beers. The waiter, if you want to call him that, came to our table, and gave us two large plastic glasses with some chipped ice inside. We then opened up our warm beer and poured it over the ice. It was extremely delicious and refreshing. We also ate a couple of pickled pigs feet, which we fetched out of a jar sitting on the table.

I told Dai Uy what I wanted to talk to him about. It was the subject of the treatment of POWs. I began by telling him that, as an advisor, I wasn't going to interfere with his command, or pretend to have the solution to all the world's problems. Nor was I going to point out all the minor deficiencies of the battalion. American Infantry battalions have their share of problems, too. But I did want to address one major issue. I told him that when I arrived on the scene yesterday, I had a feeling that the prisoner we had picked up that day had been kicked around quite a few times. I then told him that if I was going to be an advisor to his battalion, I would have to insist that they treat all prisoners kindly.

I told him that I knew that there was a lot of hatred between both sides, and that I understood that. But I also told him that I knew the VC were fighting for a cause, and that they believed in what they were doing just as much as we did and if they could believe in their cause enough to go out and fight for it, and maybe be wounded or crippled for life, then when we captured them, we ought not to mistreat or beat them. After all, we were both infantrymen. Dai Uy agreed with me.

We continued to talk about it for a while. Although he did not stand up and play the "Star Spangled Banner," I could tell by his nod and assent that what I had said had sunk in, and that he would do this for me. (During my tour of duty with the battalion I never once again witnessed any incident of mistreatment. Later on when we captured prisoners, we didn't even tie them up. We just put them in the middle of the 350 Rangers. If they wanted to make a "run for it," that was their business. Of course they weren't about to do that. They stayed right with us on the patrol until we finished and then we took them back to Tay Ninh City, where we turned them over to the police.)

I had a feeling that when I finished talking to Dai Uy, he really wanted to do this for me. I could feel there was a special bond between us now. And something more than just a bond, something unique, a friendship forged by the war and sealed by having gone through so much together, having shared so many hardships in the jungle, and having been shot at side by side. You can't fool people and you can't fool the Vietnamese. They know if you are a sincere person and if you genuinely like them. I had always liked Dai Uy, from the day we had met. Now there was this great friendship between us. I could just tell that this was one of the things that he would do for me, out of mutual respect for one another.

The next day, another operation, this time east of Cha La. We would to be a "blocking force." (This meant that we would set up on a line, stand shoulder to shoulder and face the enemy. Then the friendly forces...in this case an infantry battalion of the Fifth Division...would act as beaters, and drive the enemy into us.) The plan was simple. We were to slip in behind the enemy. Then the RVN Fifth Division would attack from the front and drive them into our waiting arms. So we trucked out of Tay Ninh City to start the operation.

I was not too happy with the way things were going. We were driving far too far down the road without security. Finally, we stopped at a clearing. The tailgates came down, and everybody jumped off. But we took too long to get moving. I didn't like it at all. There was a rice paddy off to our flank, and beyond that, the jungle. If there had been Viet Cong over there, one machine gun could have taken us all out. Eventually, we got organized. A couple of men started wading across the swamp, acting as point. Then a few more men moved off to the left, and a few more to the right (flankers). Then some more started across. When the security element got about halfway across, more Rangers jumped into the water and begin sloshing their way forward. Eventually, the lead man reached the edge of the jungle to our front.

At this time, Dai Uy halted the entire battalion in the middle of the paddy. It was an extremely calm, quiet morning. I could hear birds chirping all they way across the paddy. Dai Uy was receiving a call on his radio. He put the handset to his ear, listened for a moment and then dropped the mike. He told me he had just been notified that the Fifth Division was going to be two hours late.

72

How utterly ridiculous! If an American Battalion Commander showed up two hours late to a LD (line of departure), he would be fired on the spot. There was absolutely no excuse for this. It had to be due to gross inefficiency, and the Fifth Division had a great reputation for that. But there was nothing we could do about it. We would just have to live with it.

We continued moving toward the jungle. We were going to go ahead and occupy the blocking position anyway, not that it would do any good, of course. Why set up a blocking position two hours before the force that is going to beat them into your arms even starts out? How utterly futile. We continued to slosh through the rice paddy. The water was pretty deep, halfway up to my knees. When you walk through water like this, your socks loosened up and fall down inside your boot and then ball up under your foot. It can be the most aggravating thing in the world. But I found a solution for the problem. I always pulled my socks up as high as they would go, and then folded them down over the top of my boots, and then wrapped a rubber band around them. That way they never slipped down inside my boots. I should have patented the idea.

Eventually we worked our way over to the blocking site. It was located in a rubber plantation. We got on line from left to right and faced the enemy. Of course, we all knew they wouldn't be coming for another two hours. So people laid down. Some sat with their backs against the rubber trees, rifle across their legs. Others smoked cigarettes and talked. We all knew this was just going to be another exercise in futility.

The whole thing slowly turned into a picnic. As I looked left and right, I could see the Rangers laid out along the row of trees. When I looked to the front, I could see for a long distance through the rubber. At any rate, it was a good place to be. We would really catch them in the open, if they did come this way. But all day long there was no contact. Finally about 3 p.m. Dai Uy got a message that the operation was over, and that it was time to return home.

We took a different route back toward the City. I was

happy for that. At least we wouldn't get ambushed taking the same route back. We moved out in the direction the enemy was suppose to be coming from, but found none. We left the rubber, walked through some jungle, and then came to a deep stream, which was about chest deep. It wasn't flowing very fast, so we didn't need a rope or anything like that to cross it. We could just wade across. It was an extremely hot, muggy day. As I stepped down into the water it was like stepping into an ice cold mountain stream. It was very, very refreshing. Then up and out; we helped one another climb up the slippery bank and headed back to Cha La. The trucks were waiting for us in the village. We were home again.

Vignettes

I learned that Dai Uy had been in the Military for 12 years when we met. He had started off as an enlisted man in the French Army, and rose to the rank of Sergeant. Later he received a commission as a Lieutenant. He had fought mainly in North Vietnam. After years and years of fighting in the jungle, he finally had a nervous breakdown but was able to overcome it and return to duty. At the time that I joined him as an "Advisor," he'd already been in combat for twelve years.

One day my jeep driver, Tau, came to me with a big sheepish grin on his face. He had VD. He asked me to give him some of my tetracycline. He knew it would cure VD. But this could create a problem for me, because if the word got out to the rest of the Rangers, they would never stop pestering me for tetracycline, and I wasn't suppose to give them any. But in the case of my jeep driver, a personal friend, I gave him the medicine and told him keep his mouth shut.

One of the more humorous things in Vietnam is that they have an equivalent for the American phrase "seven year itch." They say when a man is about 35 years old, he starts fooling around. After being married for a while he gets bored and, according to the Vietnamese, becomes a "woman chaser" at that age. Although I was thirty, I always told them that I was thirty-five or "ba muoi lam" as it was spoken in Vietnamese. Wherever I went, the first

74

question people would ask me was, "How are you?" and I would always reply, "Fine." The second question they would always ask me was, "How old are you?" and I would reply "ba muoi lam." Then they would burst into laughter. Of course, I knew the meaning behind the words, and I knew what was going on. But it was all so funny to watch. They thought they were pulling something off on me. They would point their finger at me and shout to the others, "ba muoi lam, ba muoi lam," and everyone would start laughing hilariously. Of course, I didn't mind. It was a good way to "break the ice" and to make friends.

On one of the operations, I decided to play John Wayne. I had always wanted to carry a Thompson submachine gun, just like the gangsters in Chicago. So one day I left my carbine at home and got Tau to get me a "Tommy gun" out of the battalion's weapons stock. It had a straight clip running out of the bottom and held 20 rounds (bullets). Each round was heavy and, of course, with 20 of those rounds in the clip, the whole thing turned out to be extremely clumsy to carry. The additional ammo was also heavy. I could only carry about four extra clips. So, with one clip stuck in the weapon, that only gave me a total of five clips or 100 rounds of ammunition. (With my carbine I could carry three times as much.) But I wanted to play John Wayne, so I opted to carry the Thompson.

On the plus side, the Thompson was short and easy to carry through the brush. On the minus side, it had a very short barrel and consequently was not very accurate and I didn't like the way it fired. It fired from what is called an "open bolt" position. That meant that you carried it with the bolt cocked back, held back by a portion of the trigger which protruded up. To fire it, you simply pulled the trigger down, and the bolt slid forward, propelled by a coiled spring. But it took so long for that bolt to slam all the way home and fire the bullet, that it seemed like an eternity before the round went off. In fact, if you fired the gun at a running target, you had to follow the target with the barrel until the gun went off. Conversely, with a normal weapon (like the carbine), the instant you pulled the trigger it fired. You could drop a target in its tracks.

Another problem associated with the Thompson was that it had an extremely slow rate of fire. It was horribly slow. "Clack, clack, clack." I just didn't like it. It wasn't fast enough. So it didn't take me long to figure out that the carbine was a much better weapon. You could carry a lot more ammunition, and when you pulled the trigger, it fired instantaneously. Plus, it was fast. Out where we operated, there was only the "quick and the dead." So the carbine was the weapon for me. I gave the Thompson back to Tau and stopped playing John Wayne.

The advisors were funny guys. Every time I left to go on patrol someone would shout out "dibs on your boots." What they meant was that if I got killed, the person who yelled out "dibs" got first choice on my boots when they brought my body back. Actually, it was a gesture of good luck, shouted in the same vein as actors who tell each other "break a leg" before each performance.

I learned that Lt. White would be leaving the battalion. His time with the Rangers was up. Jerry was a good man and very brave. I predicted he would go far in the Army. But, in the future, it meant that I would be all alone with the battalion...just me and 350 Rangers.

One night, we got word that a village south of us was under heavy attack. A small outpost of 10 to 11 Vietnamese soldiers was being hit by a battalion of VC (about 500 men). Our job was to move out and drive the VC away. I rushed up to the battalion, met Dai Uy and we talked briefly. We took a look at the map. Meanwhile, the troops were shouting and loading, and getting onto the trucks. Headlights were on.

I warned Dai Uy of the potential for ambush. It could be a typical VC trick again: hit an isolated fort somewhere in the middle of nowhere and then ambush the reinforcements coming to the rescue. But Dai Uy was already on top of the situation. He had decided to come in through the back door, cross country through the jungle. We moved out on the trucks. We didn't take the main road down to the village that the VC expected us to take, but we took a different route. About half way to the village, the trucks stopped. We all dismounted and moved out into the pitch black jungle. About 40 minutes later, the area started to open up with a little bit of spotted brush here and there; then later, a road, some drainage ditches, rice fields and vegetable gardens. We were getting close to the village.

Earlier, I had heard our artillery coming in, but now I didn't hear it impacting anymore. In fact, I couldn't pick up a thing. It was deathly quiet. As we got closer to the outpost, tension mounted and we sensed that we were going to run smack dab into an enemy trying to retreat back to his lair. They always did this when dawn came. They always operated in darkness and then ran for cover when the sun came up. Only this time, we would be between them and their hideaway. My heart began pumping hard. I knew in a few minutes that there would be heavy fighting ahead for us.

It was getting much lighter, almost daylight. I looked off to my left. I could see the Reconnaissance Sergeant off about 200 yards to our left, and all on his own. That was his job, to be scouting around on his own looking for signs. Sometimes he was off to the flank, and other times he was out front. He would talk to people, or check the trail. In general, he acted as the eyes and ears of the battalion. For some unknown reason I decided to walk over and join him. Once there, we moved together slowly. As I looked back at the battalion, I could see that they were moving slowly too, like cats stalking their prey. Everyone knew the enemy was very close. Every eye searched nervously ahead. Our carbines were at the ready. The Reconnaissance Sergeant and I were taking half steps, moving ahead very cautiously. We stopped, we listened, we looked, then moved out again.

About this time we glanced at the ground. We both saw it at the same time. It was a cigarette butt still smoldering. We exchanged glances knowingly, and then looked all around. Our eyes swept toward the jungle, then off to the flank, then over to the bushes, then across the field. Where was the enemy? He had to be close. They had to be very close because that cigarette butt was still smoking. Suddenly, BANG, a bullet popped right over my head. I dropped to the ground, heart pounding. I fell flat, carbine up. I waited breathlessly, head low, looking around. Where did that shot come from? Where was he? How many? I waited and listened. The whole jungle was deathly quiet. The birds stopped chirping.

Suddenly, I heard laughter rolling in across the fields coming from the direction of the battalion. It got louder and louder. Then the Reconnaissance Sergeant got up on his knees and hollered over. A loud exchange took place. Quickly we learned what had happened. It seemed that one of the men from the battalion had seen some kind of game bird, that was very good to eat, sitting on a tree directly over our heads. He had just decided to fire at it without warning. But it took two years off my life. It was really a stupid thing to do but there was nothing I could do about it.

I stayed with the Reconnaissance Sergeant as we continued to inch our way forward. Gradually, the battalion's path and our's merged. I was up front now, "point man." We came to a ditch about ten feet long and three feet wide. There were pools of blood in the bottom. Scattered around the ditch were lots of bamboo poles. We knew what this was all right. It was the enemy's "first aid" station, where they had brought the wounded back for care. They had put them in this ditch to shelter them from gun fire. After they were bandaged, the wounded had been placed in hammocks, the hammocks were then strung on bamboo poles and the wounded were then carried back to their base camp. Somebody had been hurt really badly here today. We could see that.

As we approached the outpost, I could see that a fierce battle had taken place. Artillery had exploded all over the place. We later learned what had happened. The village defense force had been driven back from their positions around the outskirts of the village, to a concrete bunker located smack dab in the middle of the camp. This bunker had firing ports on the side so they could fire out, and it had a very thick roof on top. It became their "last ditch" stand. They abandoned everything else and then called in artillery on top of themselves. The artillery impacted on top of their roof killing the enemy all around them. The local forces had requested "variable time fuses," too.

These shells came hurtling out of the sky, exploding

50 feet above the ground, showering hundreds of pieces of shrapnel down on the enemy. Each piece was about six inches long and one inch wide. Those terrible, razor-sharp pieces of shrapnel had smacked into the bodies of the VC below. The local force, of course, had been protected by the thick concrete roof, but the exposed VC were not, and they had taken a horrible punishment that night. That was evident from the blood all over the place and from what the soldiers told us about the fighting.

While walking around, I noticed something hanging from the barbed wire fence, located just outside their bunker. It was two human fingers and a part of the back of a hand. That was all that was left of some VC's hand; two fingers and a long trailing piece of flesh dangling from the wire. The razor-sharp pieces of shrapnel had done their job well. The VC (who never leave their dead behind) had, evidently, not noticed this little bit of flesh hanging in the wire.

I moved over to the bunker where the defenders were. They were just local boys, recruited from their own village, and not professional soldiers. They looked so poor in their floppy hats, makeshift uniforms, and cheap tennis shoes. They jabbered away about the fight. They had been fighting all night since midnight, when the attack began. They told us of how they had abandoned their outer positions, and then had fallen back on the bunker, calling in the artillery fire right on top of themselves. It had been brave thing to do. And it had gone on all night.

We later found out that the famous Dong Nai Regiment had attacked them. Imagine that, the Dong Nai Regiment being held off and defeated by a little band of rag-tag soldiers. About this time the Commanding General from Tay Ninh flew in by helicopter. He lined up those brave little troops in front of our battalion so we could all watch. We stood proudly at attention as he decorated each of them on the spot. He pinned a medal on every single one of them and they richly deserved it.

The area was now secure, so we moved over to the black top highway. It was the main highway between Tay Ninh and Go Da Hau. We got on the trucks and went home.

That same night, LTC Tansey came downstairs to see

me. He informed me that he had just found out, from the American Advisor in Go Da Hau, that they were out of ammunition. He was absolutely furious. Somebody down there had not done their job. Since the Dong Nai Regiment had been very active on a line between Tay Ninh and Go Da Hau he could not take a chance that they would not attack that night. So, in conjunction with his Vietnamese counterpart, they had decided to run a convoy of artillery shells from our location to Go Da Hau. We would leave immediately. The 33rd Ranger Battalion was to go along as security. It would be a night run. This was all so unbelievable. It was too scary to think about. There we were, ordered get on some trucks, turn on the headlights, and drive smack dab down a highway that ran through the heart of Viet Cong territory in the middle of the night. We would be "moving ducks."

But I couldn't argue; I had to go. I kept thinking about some remote outpost that might need those shells that night. Tau showed up with the jeep and we drove up to the battalion. Dai Uy looked at me and I looked at him, and we both knew what each other was thinking. This insane decision had been made by both our bosses and we had to obey it. It must have been extremely urgent. LTC Tansey didn't make stupid decisions. Dai Uy's jeep lurched forward, and we headed south out of town. I followed right behind him. Behind me I could hear the 2 1/2 ton trucks gunning their motors as they roared out. It was a long line of headlights as we "snaked" out of town. In the middle of the convoy were the trucks loaded with the artillery shells. In front and behind them were the Rangers. But what good could we do? What kind of security was that, driving down a jungle road in the middle of the night, in the heart of enemy country?

We sped through the jungle. We were really moving out, 30 to 40 miles per hour, fast for a truck convoy...then 45 mph. I laughingly told myself that we might accidentally run over some VC, who might be casually strolling down the road in the middle of the night. What a laugh! One thing I didn't fear was an ambush. The trip down had been decided too quickly for word to have leaked out. Ambushes occur on pre-planned operations when the VC get the word in advance. However, I was afraid that we might run into some VC camped alongside the road, and they might open fire on us as we drove by. We would just have to take our chances.

Mile after mile we race down the blacktop road, jungle on both sides, down straight stretches, around curves, headlights probing ahead. Was there anyone down there? So far so good. We drove like this for an hour. Finally, I saw the lights of Go Da Hau ahead. We had arrived safely. What a comforting feeling it was to drive through the gates of the town and into the security of the Army camp. The trucks lined up and we all dismounted. The artillery shells were quickly unloaded and stacked on the ground.

Our job was finished, and we could all get a good night's rest before we headed back tomorrow. I knew we wouldn't be going back that night because only a fool would drive back up a road he had just come down. He might be lucky enough to make it through once, but not twice. But, to my surprise and horror, Dai Uy told me we had to head back that very minute. He didn't ask for my advice, and he didn't need it. He was not that dumb. Obviously, he had been ordered back by his boss in Tay Ninh, and he had to obey even though there was no logic to it. He couldn't even discuss the matter because that wasn't the way things were done in the Vietnamese Army. Besides, Tay Ninh was pretty defenseless now without us. So, he hopped in his jeep and I hopped in mine, and we took off with the trucks following.

I was speechless. I couldn't believe it. As we headed out of town I just knew we were going to get it on the way back. Every Viet Cong in Tay Ninh Province knew we had driven down that road a few hours previously, and now here we were coming right back up it again. There would be no survivors. We would just drive up the road, and they would be waiting for us; the world's largest ambush. My heart pounded, and my eyes stuck open wide with fear as I stared down the lonely dangerous road ahead. We drove mile after mile through the jungle. My carbine was fully loaded, the safety was off, and my finger was on the trigger. I was ready to fire, waiting for the opening shot. I could either try to run through the ambush, or jump out and fight back. It would all depend on the situation.

Our jeep sped around a curve. The headlights probed ahead. I couldn't see anybody, but then, you never did. Where were they? I asked myself. Curve after curve, stretch after stretch I peered into the night. Maybe it would be here, right now at this point. It was a ride of sheer terror. Then, suddenly, BOOM...a horrible explosion off my right side. My heart literally jumped out of its cavity and hit my throat. I whirled, pointing my carbine in the direction of the sound, terrified. Tau floored the jeep. But there was no accompanying gunfire, no further explosions. What was it? A mine? Did we catch the tail end of an ambush?

We drove on further. Now we were safely past it. I leaned back a little and relaxed. Then Tau told me that the explosion had come from a friendly artillery battery, located right along side the road at Ben Kieu. They were the ones who had made all that noise. They had fired a cannon at the exact moment my jeep had passed by and I got the full blast of the muzzle. If only I had known that it was there, it wouldn't have been so bad. If ever I had a chance to "do it in my pants," it was then. Suddenly, we began to see little hootches along the side of the road, then more signs of life. It was the outskirts of Tay Ninh City. Thank God we were safe. But I never wanted to see another night like that as long as I lived.

The next day we were alerted to look for a VC company that was supposed to be down by the Cao Dai Airfield. There were two airfields in town, one in the heart of town (where our helicopters and supply plane landed), and the other a private airfield down by the temple, called the Cau Dai Airfield. There was supposed to be about 200 VC down there. You never knew how much truth there was to any of those rumors. Maybe there was a VC company down there, and maybe there wasn't. But you couldn't take a chance and not check it out. You also couldn't help but get a little scared, because there might actually be a company down there waiting for you. So off we went.

We rode down in trucks. When we got near the airfield, we dismounted and swept the area. There was no contact. When we swept over to the airfield we found

Major Nha and LTC Tansey sitting in their jeep waiting for us. They had heard the report, too, and had driven down in a jeep to take a look for themselves. They hadn't taken any security along. They had just driven down by themselves. That took guts.

Two nights later, the Viet Cong attacked Go Da Hau, the place where we made that night run to deliver all those artillery shells. They had employed the entire Dong Nai Regiment in the assault; three infantry battalions and one heavy weapons company. Only one battalion of the Fifth Division was stationed there, and it was split up into two different locations at that. The Viet Cong attacked both positions simultaneously. However, on this particular occasion, the Fifth Division had its act together, and killed over 55 of the enemy while suffering only 28 casualties themselves. One position was partially overran, but they managed to drive the enemy back. The following day, the newspapers came out with a story on the battle, with lots of pictures of dead enemy bodies and captured weapons. The papers declared it was a great victory. And it was. Any time one battalion (500 men) can hold off an entire regiment (5,000 men) they are really doing something.

CHAPTER 9

Advisors

A Vietnamese Infantry Battalion consisted of 250 to 350 men, and would normally have two American Advisors assigned to it. The Senior Advisor would hold the rank of Captain, and the Assistant a Lieutenant. I found out that the Assistant Advisor to our battalion (who had been there before Jerry) had been shipped home before he had completed his tour. I never knew his name, but I do know that the Vietnamese hated him. I never did find out what his problem was. Perhaps he just didn't like Vietnamese.

I personally never found that a problem. I got along with all of them. All you had to do was respect them, and they would respect you back. Of course, if you were prejudice or had some other hang up, it wouldn't take long for that to show up under the circumstances in which we lived.

All I know is that one day, when they were in a fire fight, somebody tried to shoot him in the back. He had taken fire from his own Rangers. When the Senior Advisor found out about that, he had him transferred immediately. I heard he was shipped home early.

I had heard of another case like this, too. There was a Captain down in the Delta who was not too well liked. The Vietnamese had their own way of letting you know how they felt about you. In this particular case, the battalion had been moving through a thick mangrove swamp when they camped for the night. While everyone was "asleep," including the Advisor, the battalion quietly got up, moved out and left him there all alone in the jungle. They did leave him his radio so he could call in a helicopter and get evacuated. But he got the message real fast.

Two days after the attack on Go Da Hau, a mine blew up just a few blocks from our house. We never did find out who it was meant for. The same day we had also received a message that fourteen enemy tanks had crossed the Cambodian border, and were headed our way. The message also stated that this would be the start of a great offensive. The time of the report was 2400 hours (midnight). There was no further information available. I immediately discounted it, because the Viet Cong didn't use tanks and, also, tanks generally didn't move at night. This was just another one of those garbage rumors that got passed from person to person, and later on ended up being an Intelligence report. We rated reports like this F-6 (A-1 means the "very best." F-6 means "utterly ridiculous.")

Tay Ninh City was a pretty Vietnamese city, and bustled with traffic and life. A jeep here, a black Peugeot there, and smoke pouring out of all those three wheeled motor scooters. The three wheeled motor scooters were made by Vespa of Italy, and were the taxis of the Orient. The driver sat up front by the handle bars, and a small cab was mounted in the back over the two wheels. Back there was where the passengers rode. Sometimes, you might even see a pig in there, all tied up, or a large bag of rice.

Tay Ninh was a fairly quiet city and had some really nice homes in it. They were made of concrete, plastered white on the outside with beautiful red tile roofs. The downtown area exuded French architecture; large cement buildings, high portals, high ceilings. The marketplace was right next to the river, with many tables set up there. Some had umbrellas over them, or a large section of cloth strung above to provide shade. Everything and anything was sold at the market; pigs, tomatoes, cucumbers, lettuce, cabbage, beer, trinkets, etc. Tay Ninh was a very productive area. You saw lots of rice, tons of rice, in fact. There was an oversupply of rice. It was everywhere and it was cheap. They sold it in huge barrels, with little signs stuck in the rice denoting the price per kilo (2.2 lbs).

85

There was also a barber shop downtown, where all the guys got their hair cut. We didn't know if the barber was VC or not. If you did go down there alone to get a haircut, you might be giving him the opportunity to take a straight edge razor to your throat. He could then quietly leave for the jungle and collect a sizable reward. (There had been a large reward on John Ramsey's head.) So, we never went for a haircut alone. In fact, wherever I went, to the market place or wherever, I was always followed by a Vietnamese bodyguard. It might be Tau, (my driver) or Chan, (my radio operator) or somebody else.

That was, in fact, Cowboy's job before he got hit. He had been my bodyguard. Dai Uy would never let me go anywhere in the city unless I was protected. A bodyguard would follow me everywhere, mysteriously, quietly, about 25 yards behind with a Thompson, cocked and ready to go. I always knew he was back there, watching over me. Whenever I went in to get a haircut, they purposely went inside with me. They wanted the barber to know they were ready to shoot him if he cut my throat. There was simply no question about that. The barber knew it, and the bodyguard knew it. The barber shop didn't have a fancy chair with armrests, like you see back in the States. All he had was a regular straight back chair. And the barber only used a scissor and a comb to cut your hair, too, no electric trimmers. You got a pretty nice haircut out of it anyway. The only thing unusual about a Vietnamese haircut was that, at the end of it, the barber would take out a straight edge razor and not only scrape around the bottom of your neck, but down your back as well. After that, he would stick his thumb in your ear, turn your ear inside out and scrape the interior. I didn't like that, because I knew it would make hair grow out of my ears later in life, but there was simply nothing I could do to get him to stop. So I just let him do it. However, all the while he was scraping away on my neck, it was comforting to see that bodyguard sitting over there with a Thompson submachine gun in his lap.

Down the street from the barber shop was a restaurant with an open air front porch, where you could sit down and have a beer. One day on my walk around town,

86

I noticed Dai Uy sitting there, and decided to join him. I ordered a large bottle of Biere Larue. As we sipped the golden brew, Dai Uy proceeded to tell me that the city had run out of beer. He informed me that we were, in fact, drinking the last two beers in town. Then he began to joke about the situation and said, "It must be time to open up the road to Saigon again. The town is out of beer."

You see, the city of Tay Ninh was surrounded by the Viet Cong, and the road to Saigon had been cut in a hundred different places. The VC would go out at night with pickaxes and shovels, and dig trenches across the road. Each trench was four feet wide and six feet deep. They would pile the dirt up on the road, so you had a big mound of dirt on one side, and a big gaping hole on the other. It was impossible to drive over it, and also impossible to drive around it, because they always picked a spot in the road where there was a river or swamp or some other obstacle off to the side. Of course, a motorcycle or small motor scooter could squeeze by, so some goods did pass back and forth between the cities. The VC would stop these people at a road block, and make them pay tax on whatever they were carrying.

The VC not only dug one trench across the road, but sometimes as many as 20, 30, or 50 trenches in a row. So that was now the situation in Tay Ninh. They had cut the road in about 30 places, and the beer trucks couldn't come in, and the Army trucks couldn't get out. So, Dai Uy jokingly said that, since those were the last two beers in town, it was time to fight our way south to Saigon. Only he wasn't joking. Sure enough, the next day, we received an order to move south and open the road. Away, we went.

The road was safe all the way down to the trenches, secured by the local forces. As we drove along, we saw them standing along side the road in their floppy hats. Some were wearing white tennis shoes, others black. Most were wearing civilian shirts. A few had on Army pants. What a hodge podge! Some carried single shot rifles, others carbines. It was really hard to tell them from the VC. They stood along the road, grinning and waving. Eventually, I spotted a mound of dirt to our front. The trucks stopped and we jumped out. Dai Uy and I walked

87

up to the first big mound of dirt. Behind it was a trench cut clear across the road. I could see many more mounds further south.

About this time some folks from the Department of Public Works arrived. They had followed us out. They were civilians, and had brought tools with them to clear the road. Their tools looked like potato diggers. Meanwhile, our rangers hadn't done a thing. They had simply gotten off the trucks, had taken no security measures, and were now standing around like dumb oxen.

It was an ideal time for an ambush. However, somehow or other I sensed that nothing like that was going to happen on such a bright, beautiful day. Everyone was laughing. It was so calm and peaceful. I just knew there wasn't going to be any trouble from the VC. So I decided to watch the Vietnamese workmen fill in the ditch. I walked over and stood by them. They held those potato diggers high above their heads, brought them straight down into the dirt, and then pulled the dirt back into the ditch.

Suddenly, one man, who had just brought his hoe down, jumped back and took off running. Everyone else started running too and I didn't know why. I just stood there staring at the whole scene. Then, suddenly, BOOM, a big explosion right in front of me. I stood there stunned. I looked down at my arms and legs to see if I was bleeding. (Sometimes, when you're stunned like that, you don't even realize you've been hit.) But I was ok. Nothing had hit me.

It turned out to be just another VC trick. They had taken a grenade, pulled the pin out, placed it in the mound of earth, and piled dirt on top of it to keep the handle from flying off. When the workmen came along and pulled the dirt off the grenade, it exploded. Since it took four seconds for the grenade to explode, the workman had time to run. In many cases, the helpless victim never spots the grenade, and is still hoeing away when the explosion takes place. But this was our lucky day. About this time, Dai Uy shouted some orders at the men to "spread out" and "put out some flank security," like they were supposed to. We spent the rest of the day filling in the trenches so the beer trucks could roll again.

Advisor Training Note

I observed from the numerous operations that I had been on, that when the Rangers went on patrol, those who carried Thompson submachine guns carried them without the wooden stock attached. All they had in their hands was the metal portion of the weapon. I also noticed that when they got into a fire fight, the weapon jumped all over the place. They couldn't hit the broad side of a barn with those Thompsons. They needed the wooden stock attached, to steady it. So, I decided to conduct a training exercise during which, in a very low key way, I would point out to them the error of their ways. By seeing their error, perhaps they might go ahead and make the necessary corrections. In this manner, no one would be giving them an order, and they wouldn't lose face.

So one day I asked the Dai Uy if I could take all those who carried a Thompson to an "Advisors Training Class." He agreed. We moved out to the firing range. I put up "E type" silhouette targets (targets made out of cardboard, that look like human beings). Then I lined up all the rangers and issued them one clip of ammunition each. We stood back about 25 feet. I told them to open fire without using their stocks. As I expected, nobody hit the target. They simply could not control their weapons. Bullets impacted all over the place, but not on the target. Then I had them put on their stocks. As they tightened them down, I issued them another clip of ammo. Then we opened fire again. This time, even I was shocked by the results. They were able to hit the target almost ever time, probably nine times out of ten. I knew I had made my point, so I didn't drive it home, out of courtesy to their pride. We did a little more firing, just for practice, and then I dismissed them. I couldn't wait until the next time we went out on patrol to see what they would do. Hopefully, they would be using the stocks.

A few days later, the opportunity came. We were going into combat. We moved out. I glanced around at the men. Nobody, I mean nobody, had wooden stocks attached to their Thompsons. They were still carrying just the metal portion of the weapon. Reason? The stock made the gun too heavy. It was simply easier to move through the jungle without the stock. Results: Rangers 1, Advisor 0.

I was beginning to learn that being an advisor was not an easy job. However, I was not frustrated by it. You had to be very patient and understanding, because their culture was completely different from our own. For example, I thought I had a very logical point about the Thompsons. But they simply did not want to accept it. My job was to continue to observe, to do the best that I could, and to point out areas for improvement. And that was exactly what I intended to do.

The day I used the rifle range to test fire the Thompsons, I had to send out troops in advance to clear it, because it was just beyond the edge of town, out in VC country. You couldn't just drive out there and test fire your rifles at targets, because the targets might shoot back at you. That day I gave that job to the local forces. They moved out and checked around the range and beyond to make sure it was safe for us to enter the area. I noticed that some of the Advisors from town had climbed into a jeep and followed us out, in order to fire their carbines, too. But they had another reason for going. Oddly enough, even though they lived in Tay Ninh City, they were not eligible to draw combat pay. If they left the city and went out into "VC country," they would be eligible to draw an extra $55 a month. So, whenever we opened up the range, the Advisors who worked in town would tag along. It was an easy way for them to get in their "combat pay." Personally, I think they deserved it for just living in Tay Ninh City.

A big operation was planned, west of Tay Ninh City, to Cu Chi Hai and Cu Chi Ba (the rubber plantation where we always got into trouble). Normally, we would move directly from Tay Ninh into these areas and take on the snipers. But this time we didn't plan to head directly toward them. We planned to sneak out at night and come in on their rear. It was a good plan, and I liked it.

It was around midnight when we moved out. No trucks, no jeeps, just infantry on foot. We formed the battalion into a single file, and snaked our way out of town. As we approached the wall of the city, I could see a small gate in the middle of some bamboo poles. The popular forces were standing there in their black pajamas, carbines and floppy hats. We walked silently by them and slipped into the jungle. I was excited. This was my first night patrol. It was an extremely moonlit night. Off to my right, above the brush, I could see a Catholic Church with its high steeple, and the cross outlined against the sky. I took it for a good sign, knowing the Lord was with me. We moved on silently. I was amazed how quietly the Rangers could move. No machetes, no chopping. Just a gentle bending of their bodies left and right as they moved through the brush, always moving straight ahead.

About a half an hour down the trail, I had to go to the bathroom in a really bad way, I mean, a real big bowel movement. I just couldn't hold it anymore. It was terrible. I had to go, but I couldn't stop the battalion and have it wait just for me. Besides, I couldn't tell the Dai Uy. I wasn't with him. He was somewhere up front, and I was way in the back among a bunch of Rangers I didn't even know. And I couldn't explain my problem to them, as my Vietnamese wasn't that good. Besides, they weren't going to stop an entire battalion just so one American Advisor could drop his trousers and do a "duke job." But I was afraid to get out of line, because I didn't know any of the men around me. If I did get out of line and squatted along the side of the trail, perhaps somebody coming along later might see me out there in the dark and shoot me. I was also afraid that if I stayed out there too long, the battalion would pass me by in the darkness and leave me behind and I would never find them again. But the call of nature was too strong.

I moved off the trail to my right about 10 feet and "dropped trousers." As I was squatting there doing my business, I could see the shadowy figure of the Rangers pass by. Now, the men in the column didn't know I was out there. But none of them looked my way. They were too busy looking straight ahead. I finished my job, pulled up my trousers, and stepped back in line. No problem. I just kept following the man in front of me.

About dawn the battalion started moving very, very slowly. We were now in an area of panji stakes. When the VC built their base camps, they usually put out panji

91

stakes all around, to give them protection and early warning. (A panji pit is a hole dug into the ground about the size of a shoe box and six inches deep. In the middle of the hole, they insert a sharpened bamboo stick, point up. The point is extremely sharp. Usually it is dipped in dung or urine, to contaminate it, so it will cause an infection to anyone who steps on it. The whole thing is then carefully covered with leaves or branches. When someone comes walking along, they innocently step on the camouflaged trap and impale their foot on the stake.)

It was getting light. I had on a pair of boots with a metal foot pad in the bottom, so I didn't have to worry about the stakes coming up through the bottom of my boot. In fact, in general we didn't have to worry about booby traps or mines, because the VC just didn't use them in our area. As I walked along, I noticed that many of the panji pits were so old that they were no longer operable. They had rotted out or fallen over. In many cases, the heavy rain had exposed them. But some did work. Some of the Rangers who were wearing tennis shoes had stepped on the stakes, and were now injured. I felt sorry for them as they hobbled around. It was painful to watch them pull the bamboo stick out of their foot, and then limp forward with the rest of us.

Later, we stopped along a trail and fanned out, ambush style. I could see a trail through the brush to my front. We were hoping the enemy would come down this trail. The trail led from Tay Ninh City to their base camp, and we were hoping to get the jump on them. I got very excited lying there. It was a broad trail, obviously used very often. Suddenly, I heard a noise. It was a creaking sound. An oxcart was coming down the trail. It moved very, very slowly, and was coming from the direction of the enemy base camp. There was a man sitting on top of the cart. Nobody opened fire, because nobody knew who he was. Perhaps he was a VC sympathizer coming back from delivering a load of food. Or maybe he was just an innocent farmer out collecting wood. In all probability, he was VC, or at least a good friend of theirs. But no one opened fire because we didn't want to give away our position for just one man.

We waited there until about 8:00 a.m. No one came down the trail. It was getting too late for an ambush now, so we began to sweep through the area. It was thick, hot and steamy. Time passed, but there was no contact with the enemy. We saw no signs of the VC anywhere. We patrolled through this extremely hot, humid jungle, always heading east, back toward Tay Ninh City and the two Viet Cong villages of Cu Chi Hai and Cu Chi Ba. Our plan was to come in on the rear of these two villages and surprise them.

At 12:00 p.m. we stopped for lunch. (Once again, it was cold rice balls and cucumber slices.) It was the traditional time for all Vietnamese to take a break. It was true not only of the soldiers, but the farmers, too. Everybody. Due to the extreme heat in the afternoon, most people ate their lunch from 12 to 1 o'clock, then slept from 1:00 p.m. to 3:00 p.m. The Viet Cong did this, too. There was no formal agreement on it. Nobody ever talked about it officially. But there was, in fact, an undeclared truce between both sides every day, from noon to 3:00 p.m. I noticed the Rangers were not particularly alert then. They did fan out and form a security circle, but mostly they slept.

After our "siesta," we got up and moved out again. No contact. Many times after lunch we did take rifle fire. But today we were coming in on their rear. They didn't know we were there. It was extremely hot, like being in a steam bath with no breeze. We moved further east toward Cu Chi Ba. As we approached the village, I remembered my words to Dai Uy Duong the night before. (I was beginning to get a sixth sense about combat, I could almost feel danger coming up. The hair on my head would bristle when I pointed myself in a certain direction.) Even though we had been behind enemy lines all night long (on the way to their base camp), I had sensed that there would be no danger on the way. I just knew nothing would happen. I just knew in advance that we would make it all the way there without contact.

Now, as we headed back toward Cu Chi Ba Village, I had that strange feeling. I knew we would soon be in a fire fight. I had told Dai Uy all this the night before. I had told

93

him, "Dai Uy, we are going to move all night, and nothing is going to happen. We are going to move all day and nothing is going to happen. But when we come back to Cu Chi Ba, we'll make contact."

Dai Uy was beginning to believe me, because I had been right before. Sure enough, nothing happened all day. But as soon we began to move across some open farm fields near Cu Chi Ba, the enemy opened fire on us. I could hear the rounds snap overhead.

It was a long way across all that open farm land to the village, and it was extremely dangerous to cross all that open terrain without some kind of support, so the Rangers decided to shell the area with artillery. The artillery was to be fired from in front of us, from Tay Ninh City. Hopefully, it would fall short of where we were and on the village, and not on us. I heard the cannon go off in the distance, and then later saw the rounds impact. Dust hurtled skyward with each explosion. It was impacting right in the village, right from where we drew that fire. I wondered if there were any people in there. Of course, that didn't make any difference to the Rangers. They had drawn fire, and they were going to fire back. After pounding the village with artillery for about 10 minutes, the Rangers fanned out and moved across. No one fired back. Evidently, the Viet Cong had slipped out of the back of the village and fled.

When we got to the village, there were people there; old women, old men, young women, and children, all scared to death. They looked at me. Terror was in their eyes. They were frightened because the artillery had fallen on them. But they were also frightened, because they believed that the Rangers were going to kill them because they were Viet Cong sympathizers. (It could have easily been done. All that was necessary was to have taken them off to the side and shot them, and then later to have claimed that they were victims of "artillery fire.") But that was not going to happen, because that was not the way this battalion operated. Of course, the poor villagers didn't know this. They had been told by the VC that the Rangers would kill them all and torture them.

I wondered how they survived all that artillery fire,

until Dai Uy showed me. Under each house was a bunker six foot by six foot square. Heavy logs served as the roof, and dirt was piled on top of that. It could have easily withstood a direct hit. We of course, for our part, could have claimed that these were "Viet Cong fighting positions." But they were not, and we knew it. They were just holes the villagers had dug to protect themselves from the constantly raging war.

The enemy was gone and it was quiet. We fanned out on both sides of the road that ran through the village. One element cut through thick jungle on the right, and the other through the rubber on the left. We headed north and returned to Tay Ninh City on foot.

When I got home, I looked at the map. We had walked from 11 o'clock the night before to 6:00 p.m. the following day and traveled a distance of 21 kilometers. That's 13 miles! Thirteen miles through some of the worst jungle in the world. I believe we set a record for total distance traveled in Vietnam in one day. The Rangers were great.

CHAPTER 10

Occasionally, I would play badminton with those beautiful Filipino nurses who lived up the street. They would drive down in their little green ambulance. I really enjoyed the safety of Tay Ninh City. Here there was laughter and life. When the badminton net went up, and we were batting the shuttlecock back and forth, I always felt like I was in a dream world, a fantasy land. I had always despised war movies with beautiful women in them, because they were so unrealistic. War was a dirty, slimy job performed by men who smelled bad and crawled through the mud. Women were just not a part of that scene. Yet, here in my own situation I found these pretty girls living right next door. I was safe here, too, in town. It was if there was no war at all. But all I had to do was pause between badminton serves and look out over the horizon, to the jungle beyond, and know that death was out there waiting for me, calling me. And that was no game.

All along the road between the major cities were guard towers, monuments of stupidity left behind by the French. Many were still occupied by the Vietnamese. On top of each tower was a platform. Two men would sit up there all night. In former times, French soldiers would sit up there, far away from their homes, watching the sun go down. Night would fall, and then the enemy would move in all around them. It was weird to see these towers sticking up in the darkening sky, with black jungle behind them. One evening, I stood by a tower that had two Vietnamese soldiers in it. We were getting ready to move

96

out and go back to town. I wondered as I left, what purpose did that tower serve? Would the VC come and kill those two after we left? Would another tower fall to the enemy? And for what purpose?

I discovered that the Vietnamese were a very polite people, and would always say "yes" to anything you asked them. They always smiled approvingly when asked to do something, but this didn't mean they would do it. It was just their way of being polite. If they didn't want to embarrass you by telling you "no" (or tell you that you had a bad idea, or that it was something they just didn't want to do), they just smiled and said "yes." "Yes" meant that they had received your message, nothing more. There's an analogy to this in Army radio talk. "Roger" means "yes" I have received the message. "Wilko" means "yes, I have received it, and will go ahead and do it." When the Vietnamese say "yes" they are simply saying "Roger," I understand what you are saying. It has nothing to do with "wilko" (I am going to do it).

We went on patrol just about every day. Usually we saw nothing. It was the same old routine. We would leave early in the morning, just after dawn. Initially, we would be in friendly territory. People in this area worked the fields for miles around, and lived in the city at night. They were pro-government, and their farm fields were pro-government. It was safe.

You would see all kinds of peaceful life for miles around; for example, farmers plowing their flooded rice paddies with water buffalo. The plow was hooked up to the animal's large horns, and then pulled through the water. The water was higher than a man's calf, and very gooey at the bottom. Yet that water buffalo could pull that plow right through all that slop. Modern machinery couldn't handle that. Yet here they were, farmers, even little kids working those fields, bossing those huge, vicious water buffalo around, getting the job done. When you were close to the city, they waved. They looked up and smiled. They were friendly.

When you got further out, people stopped waving. They never looked up. They kept their heads down, doing whatever they were doing, and you knew what that meant. It meant they were VC, or friends of the VC. Finally, you got out to a point where there were no people at all, just jungle. Yet, even out there, you could see an occasional rice paddy. Somebody was working those fields. But who? The enemy, of course.

The area around Tay Ninh was all rice paddies or jungle, with some rubber trees and rubber plantations. But, for the most part, it was just thick jungle. The jungle was not as thick as you might think from watching the movies. Sure, there were occasions when you ran into some really impassable areas, like bamboo. Bamboo grew in thick, huge clumps, sometimes three to six feet deep. And it was wide, too, maybe 200 to 300 yards wide across. When you hit that there was just no way through. You had to walk around it.

From the air the jungle looked impenetrable, thick and full of tall trees and vines. But, when you got down at ground level, you would find that there was always room for a man to walk around. No one used a machete to chop their way through. You just slithered your way through, bending your body here and there, like a snake. Occasionally, you were forced to crawl on your knees for a yard or so, but never more than that. Usually, we just walked upright, brushing the vegetation aside. There were paths all over the jungle, too. But we never followed a path. The enemy might be waiting for us on it. We always moved "cross country." It was amazing how fast we could move through the jungle. An animal the size of a large dog could literally race through the jungle, without ever stopping.

The interior of the jungle was dark and very shadowy. But when you started to reach the end of the jungle, you could see light up ahead. You could always tell when there was a clearing up ahead by the light. The jungle stopped at the clearing as clean as if a knife had cut along its edge. Then suddenly, there it was, an open field. When you came to one of these clearings, the bright light of the day almost blinded you. Peering out from the edge of the jungle, you most often saw a rice paddy to your front. Across the rice paddy, for a half a mile or so, you could see the bright green rice shoots growing. It was beautiful and unbelievably green in that bright sun. Beyond the rice, on the other side of the paddy, would be the dark, shadowy jungle again. Every time I crossed one of those open areas I asked myself, was anybody over there? Did they know we were there? Were they going to wait until we got in the middle of the field, and then hose us down? We never knew. Every time you crossed one of those fields, you took a chance. My heart and head would pound. You might make it across a hundred times, but there was always the chance that "this time" would be your last.

You couldn't walk around it. It was just too far. Those clearings extended for miles. It would take too long. Besides in most cases, the operations order required us to patrol straight ahead. So, the first company would get on line, fan out left and right, and then start across. The rest would wait on the edge of the jungle to see what would happen. When the first company was about half way across, the remainder of the battalion would then move out. It was slow going. The water was knee deep.

We would plod our way across the freshly planted rice. You could hear a sucking sound as your boots slipped in and out of the mud. Eventually, people got tired of walking through the slop and headed for the dike. Then, once again, the battalion would end up in one long line, walking toward the enemy.

Sometimes, a Ranger would fall off the dike. He would lose his balance and fall off into the slop and just lie there. At that time, everybody would laugh and giggle at him, as if it were the funniest thing they had ever seen. I think part of their laughing was to alleviate the tension. We all knew we were just one step away from death, "hanging out there" in the middle of nowhere. If the jungle to our front erupted in gunfire, we were all dead men. Yet, in the midst of all this terror and anticipation, the men would just laugh hysterically and point at the poor victim lying in the slop. He, in turn, would flash back a buck tooth grin.

Most times, as I passed by a Ranger stopped on the dike, he would ask me, "Dai Uy met qua?" (Is the Captain tired?). That question was asked of me a hundred times a day, and constituted ninety percent of my conversation with the troops. And my reply was always the same: "Dai

Uy khong met qua." (The Captain is not tired.) They loved it!

Finally, to our front, we would see the elements of the first company plunge into the jungle. We were safe. Now the rest of us would make it safely across.

One day we were on an operation south of Cha La. The plan called for us to move through rice paddies and jungle, and then into a rubber plantation. All morning long the battalion had been just horrible. They couldn't do a thing right. It had been bad from the very beginning. First of all, they had debarked from the trucks right out in the middle of a rice paddy, with jungle all around. That wasn't too smart. And then what did they do? They just stood around in a gaggle, waiting to get organized. There was absolutely no security. I didn't know what their problem was. Maybe the Dai Uy hadn't issued his plan yet. But, meantime, the battalion just stood there in one big heap, waiting to get massacred. After about a half hour of this madness, we moved out. But we did not move like we were supposed to. Instead of fanning out left and right, and sending scouts ahead to see if there was anyone waiting for us in that jungle, the whole battalion simply moved out in single file. Three hundred and fifty men, one behind the other, walking toward the jungle, after the enemy had been given a chance to observe us for the last 30 minutes. I couldn't believe it. I was expecting the enemy to open up and kill us at any time. We were just making it too easy for them. Finally, the lead Ranger made it to the jungle line and plunged in. No gun fire erupted. We had beaten the odds again. But it could have been disastrous. Battalion after battalion in Vietnam had been lost like that, exhibiting the same kind of stupidity, but today we had lucked out. We moved ahead into the jungle.

After a while, I saw light up ahead. We were coming to another clearing. Surely they would do things right this time. But no, the battalion moved out again, one behind the other across the rice paddy. There was no security, no scouts, no nothing. It was almost as if they wanted to die that day. All morning long it was the same story: walk through the jungle in single file (which was right), and then walk across the rice paddy in single file (which was wrong). We were going to get it, and we were going to get it badly.

Finally, we came to another clearing. The men started to move across again in a single file. This time I had "had it." I was not going to get killed on account of their stupidity. So I called Dai Uy off to the side, and I told him that this was the last rice paddy that I was going to cross like that. I told him the battalion was no longer trying, but had given up. Walking in a single file was like asking to be hacked to death. I told him quite forcefully, "If they walk across this rice paddy in single file, I am going to quit. I am going to walk back to Tay Ninh by myself."

I meant it, and he knew it. Dai Uy looked at me, acknowledged my message, but didn't say a word. Then he walked off to the side. I did not follow. Fortunately, none of the men around us spoke English, so they didn't know what had transpired. The Dai Uy waited about ten minutes, looked at his map and pretended he had things to do. He casually talked to some of the men around him, and then later looked around in his pack for something. I could tell he was stalling for time to save face. He did not want to let the men see me talking to him like that, and then immediately respond to my ultimatum. If he took a direct order from a foreigner, it would make him look bad. But the men around us did not understand what had happened, and now, with the passage of time, they were unable to put "two plus two" together.

The time was now ripe for Dai Uy to act on my request. He picked up the radio and barked into it. I could tell he was angry. He really chewed them out in that sing-song language. Suddenly the men sprang to life. They started to do things right. They fanned out all over the place. Dai Uy didn't look at me and I didn't look at him. He didn't want to give any sign of recognition that he was doing it my way, and I, for my part, was not interested in gloating over the incident. Neither one of us wanted it that way. We just wanted it to be right. Again the unwritten rule was working. Both of us understood each other. The operation continued without incident, and we returned home.

At seven o'clock the next morning, Tau showed up

with the jeep. We were going on patrol. It was the first I'd heard of it. Usually, I got advance word. I hopped in the front seat, and we tore out through the gates of the compound, turned right and headed up the street at a high speed. We were already late. A few chickens in the road squawked and ran off to the side. As we turned into the battalion compound, I could see the trucks were already loaded with men. Some of them were starting to move out. Dai Uy's jeep was moving too. We fell in line behind it.

As I looked around, to my horror and amazement, I notice that the entire battalion was wearing helmet liners. What a switch. Normally, they wore red berets. That's what I was wearing. But it was too late to turn back and get my helmet now. I'd just have to be the only one out there wearing a red beret that day. The trucks moved out, and after about a half hour drive we arrived at the line of departure. The Rangers disembarked. The jungle was quite close to where we were. I didn't see any security out. I supposed it was safe. The Rangers fanned out and we moved toward the jungle. We slipped into the jungle single file. Three hundred men couldn't walk abreast through the thick jungle. It just wouldn't work. Eventually, one group might get separated from the other and would open fire on each other. So, we walked along silently, one behind the other.

Eventually, we stopped. I moved forward. I could see daylight up ahead. There was a rice paddy up there. I moved up, past the line of Rangers in front of me, to the edge of the jungle, and peered through the leaves and branches. I got an eerie feeling looking across that rice paddy. It was a cloudy, dark, morose day. A feeling of foreboding came over me. I didn't like it. Who was on the other side? Were they waiting for us? Was there a sniper out there?

The time came to move out. The Rangers got on line. First and Second Companies moved across first. Now it was my turn. I stepped out into the swamp and mud. The water in the paddy was about half way up to my knees. The mud sucked at my boots. Each step was labor. Every time I pulled my foot out of the mud it made a sucking sound. It was torturous. It was agonizingly slow. We took heavy, deliberate steps. All the while we were hanging out there... in the middle...vulnerable. I looked out across the wide expanse of rice paddy, to the dark and ominous tree line to my front. I wondered if a bullet was going to come flying my way, but we made it across.

Back into the jungle and single file again. After a while, we saw light up ahead again. It was another clearing. We fanned out and slopped through the mud. We reached the jungle on the other side and moved out again. Days like this were just hot, monotonous and boring. A walk in the sun. But, all the while, it was in the back of your mind that you were just a fraction of a second away from death. We came to another rice paddy. We fanned out. First and Second Company crossed first. We let them get about half way across. Then we (the command group) started off.

The long radio antennas of the command group stuck into the air. I looked around. I was the only man wearing a red beret. And I was also taller than the rest of the people. With all of those antennas sticking up into the air, it was a clear signal to anybody that we were the command group. We made it to the center of the rice field when BANG, there was a sharp, whiplike crack. A bullet snapped right past my ear. It felt as if someone had just slapped two boards together right next to my head. What a loud explosion! I could feel it. I could actually feel the air, pushed by the bullet, rush into my ear. I dropped flat on my face in the mud. It was a sniper. He must have missed my head by a thousandth of an inch. I laid there frozen. The noise actually hurt my head. What a shock. What a terrible surprise. Slowly, I raised my head, I looked around. Other Rangers were lying face down in the slop, too. Some had taken cover behind a dike.

I heard Dai Uy talking excitedly on the radio. Then artillery shells started impacting to our left front, where the sniper fire had come from. Dai Uy was going to use artillery fire to cover our walk across the paddy. I saw the shells impact along the edge of the jungle. Black smoke poured up from the tree line. "I hope they get the bastard," I muttered.

Now it was time for me to finish crossing the paddy.

103

We all wanted to get out of there as fast as possible, because we weren't sure the artillery could keep the sniper down. I picked up my carbine in my right hand, dropped it to my side, crouched down low, and began to run. But I couldn't run. It was the mud. Each step was torturous, each step slow. The mud sucked at my boots. I tried to run, but it was impossible. I felt like a figure in slow motion, agonizingly hanging out there in the middle of nowhere.

After about 100 yards I stopped, exhausted, out of breath. We all came to the same conclusion at the same time. The only way we would cross this paddy was laboriously, one step at a time, sniper or no sniper. What a horrible feeling it was, to be out there in the open, knowing that the sniper was still over there. I put my head down and pushed, slowly, onward, each agonizing step by step.

Finally, I got to the other side. We moved into the jungle. Then I discovered I had a terrible headache. It lasted the rest of the day. It had come from the loud pop of that bullet passing by my ear. Eventually, we hit rubber, moved through that, and then crossed a stream. The water was about waist deep and 10 feet wide. Up the stream bank and through the rubber and onto the other side. Finally, we arrived at a black top highway and the road back home. I looked back at the jungle and told myself, "I almost got killed today. What will tomorrow bring?"

Tomorrow came. A long operation was planned, to a distant village far out in the jungle that belonged to the VC. Our mission was to "propagandize" the village; that is, to try and convince the people that they should be loyal to the government. It was a Viet Cong village. The VC owned it "lock, stock, and barrel." These people lived too far out to be under government control. In the vacuum left by the government, the Viet Cong had moved in. The people belonged to them.

We moved out. It was a long hike, mostly through jungle. We approached the village from the back side. We could have taken an old ox cart trail that led directly to the village, but that would have been too dangerous. The road would have been watched. Better to come in from behind. So we did.

After a long march we arrived. As we spotted the

village up ahead, the Rangers fanned out. They formed a circle around the village and surrounded it. This circle was not for the people, to hold them in, but for our own protection. If we just walked into the village and stood around, it was quite possible that we could be attacked by the enemy. The enemy was everywhere out there. This action gave us the "all round" protection we needed.

As I walked into the village, I noticed that there are no men, only women. The women wore black pajamas. They had no shoes, but walked around in bare feet. And they ignored us. It was amazing. Here a whole battalion had arrived at their village, men they had never seen before, strangers from the outside world, and they couldn't see us. It was as if we didn't exist at all. We all knew what that meant. It meant we were the enemy, and the Viet Cong were their friends. Little kids were absent, too, but later I began to see them. They were hiding behind buildings, their cute little faces peering out from behind every corner. I could see terror and fear in their eyes. They were afraid of the Rangers, and they were afraid of me. They had been told that we would kill them. Also, since they have never seen a "white man" before, I was a bit of an oddity to them.

The VC had posted propaganda all over the village, too. Most of it was in the form of paper flags. These paper flags were about the size of a 5x7 card, and were painted with the colors of the Viet Cong flag (red on top, blue on the bottom with a yellow star in the middle.) Propaganda posters were pasted everywhere. We could tell this village belonged to the enemy one hundred percent.

Later, an ARVN G-5, a Lieutenant who had accompanied us on the patrol, started to work. His job was to present the government side of the story. (He worked for the Ministry for Propaganda and Public Information.) Unfortunately, he didn't do his job like the Viet Cong. The Viet Cong used personal lectures, one-on-one conversations, and highly entertaining plays and skits. But not this ARVN officer. (I could tell he was lazy.) He had brought along a battery powered loud speaker, with a tape recorder attached to it. All he did was turn it on, and then sit under a tree and smoke a cigarette. The machine

105

belched out Vietnamese sounds in a high squealed pitch. Nobody listened.

I walked around the village. Little children started to follow me. They had never seen an American before. This village was too far out. It had no TV, no newspaper, no magazines, nothing. Absolutely no contact with the outside world. Some of the people in the village thought I was a Frenchman, even though the French had left the country ten years ago. The little kids started to get closer. They wanted to get a good look at me. Some of them, the more daring, came a little closer and walked behind me. Soon all the children in the entire village were following me. I felt like the Pied Piper. So, I decided to have a little fun with them. I decided to play "monster." I turned around toward them, shaped my hand like a claw, bared my teeth and, dragging one foot behind me, started off toward them. They were terrified. They screamed and ran. Immediately I stopped, resumed a natural position and smiled at them. They knew right away that I was only joking. So they started to come a little closer. Again, I assumed the monster crouch, hand outstretched, foot dragging behind me, lower teeth bared, grunting. They screamed and laughed and ran to hide. But each time I played the game they came a little closer. They now knew that I was not going to hurt them.

One of them came up close to me, too close. Quickly I reached out with my monster claw and grabbed him. Everyone screamed. The little boy was terrified, too. Immediately, I released him. Then I smiled to let him know that I did not intend to hurt him. All the rest started to giggle. More and more of them dared to come closer now. They all wanted me to catch them. So I did. I would grab one just for a second, let him scream and than turn him loose. After a while they were all around me. They were no longer afraid. We were all laughing and having such a good time. I wish I had something to give them, like chewing gum, but I didn't. When you travel in the jungle, all you have room for is ammunition and cigars. I began to talk to them. I asked them how old they were. They giggled. They were surprised I could speak their language. Then they asked me how old I was. I told them, "Ba muoi lam." Immediately, they all laughed and giggled. They asked other questions, too, like whether I was married, whether I had any children, if I had a little girl or boy. I was having a wonderful time. Some of the women hung around about 20 or 30 yards away, watching discreetly.

After a few hours, it was time to leave. The ARVN G-5 Lieutenant has done his job. He had played his tape recorder to the villagers. The world was now safe for democracy. The Rangers got organized for deployment, and we moved out. As I left the town, the little kids followed me. I waved good-bye. They all smiled and waved good-bye back. It had been a wonderful experience. But that night, the VC would move back into the village and tell them how evil I was.

CHAPTER 11

One night we were invited to a party in Tay Ninh City. It was hosted by the Commanding General of the province, a Brigadier General. He was also the leader of the local Cao Dai religion. He was appointed to his position by the government in Saigon and it was a very good move politically because it allowed the people to have one of their own and not someone sent from the capital. He lived in a large, white, French home. It could almost be called a mansion. It would have looked like a mansion if it were located outside of town up on a hillside with a long road running to it. But it was not. It was located in Tay Ninh City, tucked behind a wall, along a busy street. It looked quite ordinary in this setting. As I approached the house I could see how easily someone could have driven by and tossed a grenade right through the front window. Maybe someday they would.

I walked into the yard of the house. There was a large outdoor garden area with lanterns hung everywhere. The lanterns were Chinese style in festive colors of green and red. Electric light bulbs burned inside making them brilliant. They were just beautiful.

The General himself was there. He was a very large man, big for a Vietnamese, at least six feet tall and huge (but not fat). He projected a very happy, effusive, "hand shaking" type personality and yet at the same time, I could tell that he could drop that facade and be all business-like if he wanted to. He looked like an ideal military man and politician combined. He was throwing the party to honor our Ranger Battalion.

Our Ranger Battalion was the only Regular Army troop unit furnished by the Saigon government for the defense of his city. There were other forces, of course, small village forces (or "local" forces as they were called) and also regional forces (county forces) but they were not very well trained. The local forces might consist of 10 or 15 men in each village. Above that, at the district level or regional force level, you might find a few professional soldiers under the command of a District Chief with a small army of his own, perhaps two hundred men. But the Rangers were the only real, well organized, regular army fighting force in Tay Ninh City and the General was grateful to have them.

Later on we went inside. The whole downstairs of the house seemed to be one large room. On the left side of the room a nine piece band played American style music. Everything was free including the drinks. I could see a lot of red faces among the officers. The Vietnamese were particularly enamored by scotch. For some reason or another they thought that "scotch and water" was the American drink. I guess they got that from the movies. Anyway, after one scotch, their faces turned bright red. I don't know why. I don't know what it was about the Vietnamese. Perhaps it was their physical make up or the chemistry in their bodies but after one scotch, they got extremely red in the face. They all looked like they were drunk but they were not.

Later on, to my amazement, I saw two Ranger Officers dancing together. It was a slow romantic tune. Also, I saw other Rangers holding hands like they were boyfriend and girlfriend. I soon learned (to my relief) that this did not mean that they were "gay." The Vietnamese were a very affectionate people and thought nothing of two close friends, including males, dancing with each other or walking hand in hand down the street. (I noticed that when these two officers had finished dancing with each other that they then went over and asked two girls to dance.)

There were many pretty Vietnamese girls there, each wearing the traditional Ao Dai Vietnamese clothing. The

Ao Dai consisted of white silk slacks and a white blouse. Over the long sleeved white blouse they wore a large colored piece of cloth that slipped down over their head and hung front and back over their upper torso. Most of these girls worked for the government as secretaries or school teachers or were daughters of some of the people in town.

L-19

It was my turn to go flying with Captain Shook. He was a real wild man, a typical Air Force pilot. Sometimes on our short air strip he took off "down wind" which was a big "no no." But today he was going to do it right. We taxied down to the end of the runway. He spun the aircraft around, poured the coals to the engine and we moved down the strip. l was in the back seat looking out through the plexiglass window. Suddenly the tail came up a little bit. We continued to gain speed. Then the nose came up and we are off the end of the runway climbing into the sky.

We made a slow turn out of Tay Ninh City, trying to get up to about 1000 feet, (our patrolling altitude) to look for the VC. Then we headed northwest for the Cambodian border. After a while we stopped seeing gardens and rice fields and the ground below turned to dark, trackless jungle. It was beautiful yet eerie and mysterious. We flew further on over deep jungle country. If the engine quit now we would have to glide down and "hoof it" home. Occasionally, I could see the landscape pock marked by a bomb crater, the scene of a previous air strike and I wondered what the pilot had seen down there that day.

Eventually we arrived over the "free fire" area. This was an area totally under enemy control. If you saw anybody down there at all, you were authorized to shoot at them, "no questions asked." Just ahead was the Cambodian border. We followed the old French black top road. It used to have a lot of traffic on it in the old days but now it looked like a washboard, all cut up with trenches across it. There must have been a hundred of them, one after another, in even rows, all the way up to the Cambodian border. The VC dug them to stop the Vietnamese Army from ever coming up the road in tanks and trucks to invade Cambodia. The South Vietnamese certainly had good cause to invade. Across the border in Cambodia was the headquarters of the entire Viet Cong Army; base camps, supply dumps, training sites, even a radio station. Of course, the VC operated on our side of the border too, in miles and miles of trackless jungle but they kept their headquarters on the other side, inside Cambodia, safely out of range of any possible South Vietnamese attack. If the South Vietnamese crossed that border then it would be an international incident. But when the VC operated over there, the United Nations just looked the other way. You couldn't think of this border as some well defined area with a fence and houses on both sides. There was no such thing out there. It was just trackless jungle for miles. A person could walk back and forth between Cambodia and Vietnam a hundred times and never know he crossed a border.

There was no action around the trenches. Usually Captain Shook could pick up somebody moving around and would call up the fighters but today it was all quiet. We patrolled south in a general direction back towards Tay Ninh City. I had my windows open on both sides in the back seat. All you had to do was just push the flat window up and out and lock them into place with a metal bar. I got lots of fresh air that way. The window was about 1 feet high and 2 feet long. My job was to fire my rifle out of that window if we came into contact with the enemy.

It was World War I all over again. I knew what to do from talking to the other advisors. If I spotted the enemy Captain Shook would dive down, hit the VC with a white phosphorous rocket and then pull up to about 100 feet. As he pulled up he would bank left and my job would be to fire my rifle out the window at the enemy below. We were cruising along over a river very slowly and at a high altitude when we spotted a boat below. There was a man in the boat poling his way up the river. We were too high up to see what he had in the boat but we knew he was not supposed to be there. After all, this was a free fire zone. He had to be VC. Probably a messenger. Or perhaps he was bringing supplies from Cambodia.

Captain Shook shut off the engine so the man would

not hear us attack. It became strangely silent. I could hear the wind moving past the windows. It made an eerie sound. The we started down, slowly, gracefully, like an eagle. Captain Shook pointed the nose of the plane at the man in the boat. The plane kept diving, slowly, slowly, closer and closer. The man didn't see us. We fell lower. He still hadn't seen us and he wouldn't. Like a bird of prey we would approach quietly from behind and then BANG! the rocket fired out of its pod. It spiraled downward, smoke trailing from its tail.

We follow it. It took a slow deadly track toward the boat. Before I could see where it hit, we pulled up. It was a hard, violent move. Blood rushed out of my head and down into my feet. Gravity, like an unseen hand mashed me down and pinned me against my seat. My vision blurred. I lost track of the boat. Then we banked left. The blood returned to my head. Now it was my turn, I stuck my carbine out the window and looked back at the river. I saw the man poling the boat madly, heading for the bank. We had missed him. I aimed the barrel of my rifle at him and start pumping off rounds. I followed the tracers down. I was way off target, I started another stitch of tracers, this time moving them towards the boat. About the time I got the tracers onto the boat, the man disappeared into some foliage growing along the bank. I continued to pump the foliage full of bullets. We leveled out and I stopped firing. We circled low, almost at tree top level in a tight arch above him, looking for him. There was no sign. Maybe he was dead. Or maybe he got away. I would never know.

I didn't mention it to Captain Shook but I felt bad about firing at the man. I personally hoped I didn't hit him. It was just not my kind of war, this air war. It was too impersonal. Maybe he had been just an innocent farmer out collecting wood. Who knew? Sure I had the right to kill him. He had been in a free fire zone and he didn't belong there. But I just didn't feel good about it. I hoped I missed him. It's different when they try to kill you on the ground. You fight back with everything you've got. But in the air...well, what can I say. As we headed home I told myself I hoped I never had to do that again.

One day we had a "Saigon Commando" fly in from the capital. Saigon Commando was the nickname we gave staff officers from the Saigon Headquarters. They were Army officers like ourselves but they never got out into the field. Naturally there was a little bit of animosity between us. Many times the animosity was real and was caused by the fact that they just didn't understand the problem. They were called Saigon Commando because they had never been shot at. They sat in air conditioned offices back in Saigon wearing jungle fatigues trying to look like "Jungle Jim" which they were not.

This Captain came out to get a briefing on what was going on in Tay Ninh City. He wanted to know how many villages were under enemy control, how many were under our control and if we were making any headway in getting more villages under government supervision and what were the problems concerning the pacification program. He was District's problem, not mine. They had to take care of him. He would be attending briefings on personnel, intelligence, operations, supply, and government. When he arrived I got my first look at him. I didn't particularly care for him. He appeared to be very, very naive. He was wearing a beautiful pair of boots and freshly starched jungle fatigues. Everybody knew he was just out there to get his combat pay. All Saigon Commandos did this once a month. They had to go out somewhere, to a village or fly over enemy country or something. He was just another bureaucrat out gathering statistics and nailing down his combat pay at the same time. But I did get involved in his visit after all.

Lieutenant Colonel Tansy wanted me to take him out to the Special Forces Camp located to the northeast of Black Lady Mountain. It was a huge base. So we took off. As we approached from the air I could see that it was shaped like a star and was completely surrounded by jungle. I saw bunkers, barbed wire and fighting positions all around the perimeter. I could tell this star was an excellent design for defensive fighting. I had never seen a defensive position like this before but I liked the concept. No matter how the enemy attacked, he would always have his back to one side of the points of that star. I didn't

113

know what these Special Forces guys did for a living out there. I assumed they went on patrol into Cambodia to see what was happening on the other side. I was told that this camp was built by a Special Forces Captain who simply flew in with some civilian engineers and construction people. He just hired a commercial company to put it up. I also heard that this camp hired mercenaries and that they hired Chinese. These mercenaries were supposed to be very, very tough soldiers. (But I wondered if there wasn't some element of cruelty among their ranks.)

We landed. Our guest took off for the Special Forces building to get a briefing and I remained with the pilot shooting the bull. I opened up my ammo packet and pulled out a packet of Dutchmaster Panatella cigars. They fit just perfectly in my ammo pouch and were the same size as an M-14 ammo magazine. I lit one up and sat around talking until the staff officer came back.

It was time to fly home. As we climbed out of the camp and headed back towards Tay Ninh City he looked at me very naively, pointed down at the jungle and asked, "Is that where the bad guys are?"

Inwardly I just shook my head in disgust. He had no concept of the problem. Here was someone who worked at the National level, who was in the same army that I was in and he just didn't understand what was going on. He didn't understand that the VC owned everything outside of town. They controlled all of these villages through terror and assassination. They isolated these villages by putting mines in the road and by tearing up the road and killing anybody who was dumb enough to drive up the road. Their whole concept was based on terrorism. They sent saboteurs into government controlled towns and threw grenades right in the middle of the market place, right into the middle of women and children and the vegetable sellers. It was horrible. Or they kept the farmers from bringing food to market. When the vegetables weren't brought into town the people had nothing to eat.

You would think that the people would hate the VC for this because it was the VC who stopped these very farmers from bringing their food into town. But actually it had a reverse effect. Instead of blaming the VC, the people blamed the government. The VC spread the word that the government was weak and helpless and that it couldn't protect them. However, they said when they took over, the fighting would stop and there would be peace and the people could have all the vegetables they wanted. Oddly enough this worked. The people believed it. This grotesque form of backward psychology actually worked. Instead of blaming the VC, the people blamed the government. They blamed the government for not being strong enough to keep their roads open and for not keeping the vegetable trucks rolling.

Another thing the VC did was to assassinate anyone who ran for public office, like a councilman or a village chief. Others who disagreed with the VC were disemboweled. The VC would take a knife, cut open the helpless victims stomach, pull out his guts and let them dangle around his feet. All this occurred while the poor victim was still alive, screaming in horror. Then they would tie a rope around his neck and run him up the flagpole for all to see. It made a big impression on anybody standing by. You soon got the idea. You should not run for public office, support the government in any way, or allow your son to serve in the Army. You could see how difficult it was to find men to run for office under those circumstances. If they were not killed during the campaign they would be killed later. Perhaps it would come when walking down a street or while sitting in a restaurant or at home with their families. It made no difference. Eventually somebody would come and kill them. It was hard to build up a country when it was torn down like this. There was simply no continuity of leadership because the leaders were constantly being replaced every three months. It was hard to bring stability to the government under those conditions.

I read in the *Stars and Stripes* of an unusually horrible act of atrocity committed on the part of the VC. A man had quit the VC and had gone over to the government. To make matters worse he had enlisted in the Vietnamese Army. But he made a big mistake. He left his wife behind in the village. (You don't quit the communist. That's the worse sin, to quit.) So, they went to the village,

115

found his wife and cut off her hands. What an absolutely despicable act. And it was happening all the time. Over ten thousand people a year were being assassinated and murdered; and that's not counting people accidentally caught up in the war; mistakenly shot or bombed, or the helpless victims of the fighting. No, it was people who, in a premeditated and preplanned way, were shot dead, disemboweled or purposely maimed. Ten thousand a year. It had a stupefying affect upon the population. And now, here was this young Captain sitting across from me who was supposed to know all these things and he simply didn't know what was going on.

I couldn't help but think what a gap there was between me and him. And I had to ask myself another question, if there was a gap between us, (and we both lived in the same country and served in the same army) what kind of gap existed between Saigon and Washington?

My thoughts were interrupted by tracers coming up from the ground. We were too high up for them to do any good. Never the less the bullets kept coming. Probably it was some lone VC firing his AK-47 at our passing helicopter. He couldn't bring us down but there was an odd chance that one of the bullets might hit the plane. Many times the bullets came right up through the skin of the airplane and hit a man in the buttocks or foot. When I travelled in a helicopter I always sat on a flak jacket (bullet proof vest) or something that would stop a bullet because the one place I didn't want to get shot was in the "behind." It was too embarrassing. (Not to mention the chance of hitting my private parts).

Eventually the pilot turned around and told us that we were being fired on. I looked over at the Saigon staff officer. He was just amazed by it all. His eyes grew as large as silver dollars as he peered out over the side of the helicopter. It must have been his first trip out of Saigon.

Captain Ramsey was now working as an advisor to the District Chief (County Commissioner). I didn't know the District Chief's name but his home was in Tay Ninh City. He was a real mousey kind of guy. I could see right through him. He was always afraid. In fact, he was an

116

absolute coward. You could see it in his face. Wherever he travelled in Tay Ninh City he used a pick up truck instead of a jeep so he could put his own private army in the back. There were always five or six men back there armed with Thompson submachine guns, carbines and automatic rifles to protect him. True, he was a target for assassination, but no more so than anybody else.

One of his problems was that he only drove around to safe areas. He never took any risks and never ventured out any further than where it was one hundred percent safe. How could a man like this ever get his job done or get out to meet his people? His fear of assassination kept him a prisoner in his own headquarters. Many District Chiefs were like that. They were appointed by the Province Chief and not elected by the people. So the people had no loyalty to them at all. In this case, the man was despised by the villagers. He just didn't know how to do his job. (Of course, many times these appointments came about because they couldn't get other people to run.) This District Chief's incompetence was clearly shown by what happened one Sunday.

The week before, the Tay Ninh City government had put out a call for all the men from the local villages to volunteer to serve in the Local Force Army. (We called them "Ruff Puff." These men would not serve in the Regular Vietnamese Army or be required to leave their own county but could serve at home in something like the local National Guard. They would be stationed in their own village. It was a good idea. Volunteers were told to show up at a training camp the following Sunday. So John and I went over there to watch the reception. Hundreds of volunteers showed up, people faithful to the Cau Dai religion, also many Catholics, people willing to fight the VC, who wanted to get into uniform. Unfortunately for them, not one person from the Vietnamese government showed up to welcome them or even to tell them what to do. They just stood around for hours. No arrangements had been made to welcome them. The District Chief had taken the day off. (After all it was Sunday.) What a horrendous foul-up. Why did they purposely pick a Sunday and then do nothing about it? We'll never know. But after waiting all day for the government to show up they finally got discouraged and went home.

The Cao Dai religion was unique to the Vietnamese scene. It was practiced only in Tay Ninh Province. It started in the 1800s and the people were very faithful to it. They had a very large temple. There were many other religions in Vietnam too. The largest of course was Buddhism. You couldn't think of Buddhism as a religion centered around the local congregation or church like in the States. It just didn't work that way. It was a religion that was passed on more by tradition and by word of mouth than by any congregational structure. The next largest religion in Vietnam was the Catholic faith. After that you had many smaller sects such as our own local Cao Dai Religion. Painted on the side of this huge Cao Dai Temple in Tay Ninh City was a very large eye. The Advisors referred to it as "the big eye in the sky." The people of Tay Ninh City were a very happy people. Kids on the street laughed and giggled and waved at us as we drove by in our jeeps. Adults waved and smiled too. The whole town was filled with happy, friendly, prosperous people.

It was time to go on an operation again. This time it would be southeast of Tay Ninh City, mostly through rubber. We trucked out to Cha La and moved out. Not too much later we passed by an airstrip carved right out of the rubber. It was an active airstrip. It belonged to a Frenchman who lived on a large plantation near here. Rumor had it that the VC operate in and out of this area all the time with the collaboration of the French. I, for one, believed it. It would have been easy for the Ho Chi Minh Government to have flown planes from North Vietnam into these strips at night. They could have come in at low level, landed, met with the local communist forces and then taken off again. Other flights might have brought in messages or maps or orders from the high command in Hanoi. It would have been easy because we couldn't be everywhere at once. I knew deep down in my heart that this was going on. No one trusted these Frenchmen.

We moved out of the rubber and into the jungle again. It was time for lunch. Once again the battalion formed the usual circle and sat down to rest. Rangers leaned back against tree trunks or whatever they could find, rifles across their laps. After lunch we all went to sleep except for the scouts. About 3:00 p.m. we got up and moved out again. As soon as we left the jungle we hit rubber again. We were about 100 yards into the rubber when suddenly there was an immense amount of firing to our front. The entire battalion was firing. Hundreds and thousands of rounds were being poured into the rubber in front of us. I was really scared. I didn't know what we had run into. It sounded like we had stumbled across an entire enemy regiment. The Dai Uy was talking very excitedly on the radio. There was much shouting and much excitement and much firing going on. Then all of a sudden, it stopped. "At the drop of a hat" it became deathly quiet. I wondered to myself what in the world was going on but I couldn't ask Dai Uy yet. He was too busy talking on the radio and I didn't want to interrupt him. He was very excited and was jabbering away at a hundred miles an hour. I couldn't understand a thing at that speed. Finally he calmed down a bit. The radio operator said something to him, he nodded his head but he didn't pick up the hand mike. I knew it was time to approach him. I walked up to him and said, "What's going on Dai Uy?"

He replied, "Rangers see one man. He run away."

One man? (For a while there I thought we were in a fight with the entire North Vietnamese Army.) But it was only one man? We moved forward. First Company reported they had captured a man. The whole battalion now stopped. As I walked forward I spotted a man dressed in black pajamas. (That's not unusual of course. It was the customary dress of the entire country.) He was shaking violently. I had never seen anyone so afraid in my life. His knees were actually knocking and his arms were shaking uncontrollably. His whole body was trembling violently. And why not. He was the luckiest man in the world. Hundreds of thousands of bullets had just been fired at him and not one had hit him. He had taken off running when he spotted the Rangers but later stopped dead when they opened fire. Then they ran up to him and caught him. As it turned out he was nothing more than an

119

innocent rubber worker working on the trees. He ran away because he thought we were VC.

The Rangers were all laughing. They were not laughing at him but at the situation. It was a unique trait of the Vietnamese, to start laughing when they were scared or when something embarrassing had happened. They didn't laugh out loud but had this silly, toothy grin. It was difficult to explain. When a man got shot or stepped on a panji stake they all got this goofy grin and would start laughing. So here we had this rubber worker with that same kind of embarrassing smile on his face and all the Rangers standing around laughing at him.

I was grateful he wasn't hurt. I walked up to him and gave him a cigarette. He put it between his trembling lips and I lit it. His hands were shaking so badly that he couldn't hold it. I steadied his arm with my hand. I talked to him for a while. We laughed and had a good time. Eventually he calmed down. What a lucky guy. He dodged a lot of bullets and got away with it.

It was time for us to move out again. We headed back north. Leaving the rubber we crossed a stream about 12 feet wide. It was hot and muggy and the water was cold. We moved back towards Cha La when it started getting overcast. Black rain clouds darkened the sky in a foreboding and ominous manner. Then the rain came, seeping down through the jungle getting our fatigues and rifles soaking wet. Eventually we reached the village and returned home.

The next day we went on another operation south of Cha La. This time, we were to be a blocking force for the 9th Regiment of the Vietnamese 5th Division. The battalion moved slowly, very slowly. They looked bad, especially in the open areas. There was no discipline, just one big gaggle of troops walking one behind the other on the dike. I shook my head. One of these days we were going to get it really bad.

CHAPTER 12

Big news. Binh Hoa Air Base, south of us, had been mortared by the VC. It was on the front page of the *Stars and Stripes*. Much damage has been done. Many bombers, particularly the B-57 twin engine bombers, had been destroyed in the attack. The Saigon High Command decided to move reinforcements around the Air Base to protect it and our battalion has been picked to do the job. We will be leaving Tay Ninh City and moving to Binh Hoa immediately. Not much time had been allotted for the move. Of course, it is a lot easier to move a Vietnamese Ranger Battalion than an American Battalion, because an American battalion has all that heavy equipment. A Ranger Battalion travels light. We only have our rifles and machine guns to carry. But they are only giving us one day to get ready and leave. No arrangements have been made for the families. They will have to fend for themselves.

We do know that the road to Binh Hoa had been opened (secured by the 5th Division), so we could now safely convoy down. That also meant that bus service had been resumed, so now the families could follow. They stuffed everything they owned in large plastic bags, or cheap cardboard suitcases, hoped on a bus and followed their men. That's the way things were done. No big logistical problem.

The following day came quickly. All the trucks and jeeps were lined up. The road had been cleared all the way to Binh Hoa, so we headed south. I wondered if I would

121

ever see Tay Ninh City again. It was a wonderful trip down. During the first part of it, we saw soldiers of the 5th Division along the road protecting us. We passed through lush jungle, then a rubber plantation and then jungle again. For a long time we passed through VC country. The roads had been repaired and the trenches were filled in, but they serve as poignant reminders that the enemy was still out there somewhere.

Eventually, we began to see villages and kids waving at us. We were coming into Go Da Hau. At Go Da Hau we turned left and headed southeast. Now I really felt safe, because I knew that the road between Go Da Hua and Saigon was very well traveled. It was very secure. The population from there to Saigon was very friendly to the government. I saw busses loaded with people, three wheeled motor scooters, a motorcycle with a pig tied to the back, people walking along the road and farmers working in the field. The kids ran out from the villages to smile and wave at us.

We picked up more and more traffic as we got closer to Saigon. There was so much noise from all those vehicles. Chickens, too, squawked along side the road. As we passed through the villages, we could see women in the small outdoor markets, squatting down, selling their vegetables. There was a strange smell that I began to pick up, too, a unique smell of the Orient, a sweet smell.

However, the nicest thing about this area was that there was no danger there. Absolutely none. We were genuinely safe, protected by the best police force in the world...a happy and contented people. It made me appreciate what a wonderful thing good government can be.

We arrived at Binh Hoa Air Base. I was informed that I would be living in Train Compound, a few miles from the Air Base. Train Compound was a small Army Camp named after a Lieutenant Train, an advisor who was killed about a year ago. Our battalion's new mission was to protect one half of the air base. Naturally, we got the half that faced the enemy and War Zone D. Dai Uy set up his CP in an old, abandoned French house in the rubber. It looked like something right off a postcard. It had a very high, wide facade, with huge rooms to the left and right of the main door, almost antebellum in character. We got to work immediately. There would be no time off. We occupied the CP, and draped blankets over the windows, in order to have lights on inside the building at night. Dai Uy hovered over a map with the company commanders and gave them their orders. They would move out just before dark, to take up protective positions around the base. The Command Post was very relaxed. We all knew it was perfectly safe here. After all, we are surrounded by our own Rangers. The officers broke out a bottle of scotch and played cards, while the radio in the back room crackled endlessly, with conversation of the companies coordinating with each other.

There was a very comfortable mood in the air. I could sense the men were happy. I was happy, too. Very relaxed. No longer were we surrounded by hundreds and thousands of the enemy. If we did get into a fire fight, it would be "even Steven." We might even outnumber them. It just made things more relaxing. I could see it in the faces of the battalion, staff as they sipped scotch and laughed and talked with one another. Our battalion was now set up in a half circle around the base. Darkness fell.

We had ambushes set up along all the trails, to kill any VC who might try to sneak in and fire a mortar at the airplanes or sabotage them. The back half of this circle was being protected by the local forces. Suddenly, we heard firing. One of our ambush patrols had been attacked while moving into position. I heard lots of talk on the radio. Then silence. We would just have to wait until morning to find out what had happened.

At dawn we learned the truth. One of our patrols had been moving in the dark to set up its own ambush when, they were ambushed themselves. The sad part is that they were ambushed by our own local forces. Evidently, the local forces couldn't read a map well enough to stay on their own half of the circle. I guess they got completely turned around in the dark and ended up in our half, rather than their own. It can happen. You simply get turned around at night and go the wrong way. But it turned out to be a bad night for the local forces, not us. When they opened fire on the Rangers, they missed completely. Our men in turn thought they were VC and fired back, and killing one of them. Then somehow, in the darkness, they were able to determine that they were in a mistaken fire fight with each other and stopped shooting. But it was a bad sign, as to the combat effectiveness of the local forces. They couldn't even read a map. And then, when they sprang a trap on somebody else, they were the ones who got killed. The local forces had a long way to go before they would be up to snuff.

The next day I moved into Train Compound. I dropped by the Headquarters Executive Officer's Office and he assigned me a room. I met my new room mate, a great guy by the name of Earl Kettler. Earl was a Major and a Chaplain, who happened to be a Lutheran like myself. We became good friends. His job was to fly out to all of the Advisory Outposts and Special Forces sites and conduct services for the men. It was not an easy job. Most of the places he flew into were pretty hot and he got fired on a lot coming in and going out. I noticed that he carried a .45 caliber pistol with him, tucked inside his gym bag. He realized that if his helicopter got shot down, there would be no respect for his religion, or his position as a Chaplain, and he would have to fight his way out, like the rest. The troops in the field loved him. He was their kind of guy.

In the days that followed, I often drove over to the Binh Hoa Air Force Base Officers Club. It was a club run by the American Air Force for the Advisors who served the Vietnamese Air Force. There was a gang of them, about 20 in all, and all volunteers. They called themselves "X-ray Air Force." Their job was to teach the Vietnamese how to fly the A1E "Skyraider" and they were all crazy. They wore long white scarves, around their necks, that reached all the way down to their shoes.

I liked to go over there and have a beer with them and just sit around and talk. I also liked to go over there, because every night for supper they had a choice of steak, chicken, or shrimp, and a wonderful salad bar, not to mention delicious Filipino beer. Every night they would sit around and talk about their exploits of the day. They talked of how they dived down, rolled out and looked back (up side down) at the exploding bombs, all the while

124

gesturing gracefully with their hands. Because the VC had attacked this Air Base (South Vietnam's largest and most important Air Base) the Vietnamese Government had decided to retaliate by bombing North Vietnam.

What was not known was that these U.S. Advisors were going along for the ride. It was supposed to be an all Vietnamese effort, but in many cases, the Americans had even been leading the raids. They had to. There were simply not enough trained Vietnamese pilots to do the job. In some cases, only a Vietnamese trainee pilot followed off their wing.

One night, one of the Captains invited me to go along with him, on a bombing mission to North Vietnam. He said I could fly in the back seat, the "greenhouse," as they called it. I thought about it for a minute. It would have been a lot of fun and exciting. But then I started to think about what would have happened if I got shot down over North Vietnam. Maybe I could walk out. I didn't know. It would have been extremely difficult. I'm positive I could have avoided capture and worked my way out to the seacoast. But who would have picked me up? There was no U.S. Navy there and I couldn't have possibly walked from North Vietnam to South Vietnam along the beach. There were just too many enemy villages and towns along the way. Another thing I had to consider was that if I were shot down over North Vietnam, I would have been technically AWOL (absent without leave). That's a big offense in the Army. I could have been tried and court-martialed for leaving my battalion without permission. So, I turned the Captain's proposal down. But for a while, with a couple beers in me, it sounded like a heck of an idea.

The next day Dai Uy and I decided to look for housing for the families. We looked at what the Vietnamese Army had to offer. It was not much but, it was a lot better than what they had. All the Government could provide was huts made out of plywood, with a sheet metal roof overhead. Each family would have to live in one big room, but at least it would get them out of the rain. Then we drove around to see how they were making out. Many didn't have those huts yet and were sleeping along side some other person's shack, underneath a roof overhang, or something like that, just to get out of the rain. As I walked around, I saw lots of babies on their mother's hips and toddlers squatting on the ground without any clothes on. The wives cooked outdoors over a small charcoal fire squatting Vietnamese style. They poured cooking oil in a wok, added some vegetables and a few pieces of chicken and then stir fried the whole thing. That's what they called home. They slept outside and cooked outside. It was really bad. I made a mental note to get some help for those people soon.

The Formaldehyde Foot Incident

One night after supper, I decided to go over to our club in Train Compound to have a beer. I had eaten late, so when I arrived at the club there was already a number of people there. I saw 10 or 12 men gathered around a piano. Colonel Wilson was there, too. I had not met him yet but he was my new boss (the famous Colonel "Jap" Wilson, who was in charge of all the Advisors in III Corps). He was a real tough hombre. He was known to be a very mean man when he wanted to be.

I walked over to the group and joined in. I noticed a rectangular shaped fish bowl sitting on top of the piano. It was filled with formaldehyde. Inside was a human foot. The foot had been neatly cut off above the ankle. Colonel Wilson had found it after a battle. It belonged to some hapless VC who lost it in the fighting. Artillery had severed the foot as neatly as a surgeon's knife. Colonel Wilson had picked it up off the battle field and brought it back to Train Compound, where he dropped it in this fish bowl. Then, every night after dinner, the Advisors would gather around the piano and sing *"Tramp, Tramp, Tramp, The Boys Are Marching."* This always turned out to be a hilarious event, with everybody laughing and giggling, fit to die.

I knew there was a tremendous danger here, too. There were many Vietnamese working for us in Train Compound. They cleaned the area, cooked the food, trimmed the lawn, etc. One of them was bound to be VC. If word got back to the VC that a part of one of their boys was floating in a jar of formaldehyde in our Officer's Club,

126

we would all end up dead men some night. They would eventually attack that place with a ferocity that would be hard to believe. I personally believed they would storm the gates and walls at any cost, to rectify that problem. So the next day I talked to Colonel Wilson about it. I did not make a formal appointment. I just ran into him, spoke to him in the most respectful way about it, telling him that if the VC ever found out about the foot, they would pull out all the stops to attack Train Compound. He said nothing, but a few weeks later, when I came back from an operation, I noticed that the foot was gone.

Every day that the battalion was not out on an operation, the Vietnamese officers usually met for breakfast. A popular place was a road side restaurant, located at a major intersection in Binh Hoa. I always sat with Dai Uy. Every morning we ordered the same thing; "Pho." It was very difficult to pronounce, because it has a special phonetic ring to it. I never could get it right, so I would just point at what the others were having and the waiter would bring that. Pho was a soup. The Vietnamese usually had tea for breakfast, maybe a cookie or two, and then this soup.

It was so nice sitting around outside. The area was spotted with card tables, picnic tables, and benches. Lots of fun. I used to stroll inside and watch them cook the soup. They had many customers, maybe a hundred or more, so they cooked the soup in huge pots. The pots just boiled away, turning over exotic Chinese vegetables such as water chestnuts, bamboo shoots and noodles.

Later, I sat outside and watched the traffic go by. It was great to watch the parade of peaceful life pass, the people of Binh Hoa going to work; noisy motor scooters and motorcyclos, cars beeping their horns, and heavy trucks hauling their loads. It was fun to see the noise and life and bustle of the city. This place was really different from Tay Ninh City. And the soup was delicious. The smell of soy sauce was everywhere. They brought the soup to your table along with a set of chopsticks. What you did was grab the soup bowl in your left hand, dig out the noodles with your chopsticks and then drink the remainder of the soup right out of the bowl, by tilting it up to your lips. All very acceptable behavior.

The next day a chopper arrived and Dai Uy and I got on. We were told to come to a planning meeting in Tan Uyen. The ship lifted off and we climbed slowly to the north, following the Saigon River. Later, the Saigon River took a huge bend to the right. At that point, I could see a small town up ahead. It was Tan Uyen. As we flew towards this area, I noticed a road along the way that connected Tan Uyen with civilization. Tan Uyen was the last outpost between Saigon and War Zone D. It was on the rim of the jungle and was not very large. An Army camp was located on the jungle side of town, facing War Zone D. As we approached, I peered beyond into War Zone D. I hadn't been up there yet. Prior to this, all my operations had been along the Cambodian border, the Ho Bo Woods, or the Michelin rubber plantations, but never War Zone D. I had heard a lot about this place. There were many tunnels and caves in this area, and it was allegedly the contact point between the VC in the jungle and the VC in Saigon. We landed. Some advisors and Vietnamese came to meet us and walked us over to their planning room. We would be going on a joint operation with them. The 48th Infantry based there would strike North. We would fly on ahead, land deep in War Zone D and push back south toward them. The operation was for the following day, November 10th.

The next day arrived and it was time for takeoff. There was not enough helicopters to take us all in at the same time, so we would have to fly in three lifts. There's normally about 10 choppers to a lift, and we usually put about 10 Vietnamese on each helicopter, so the initial landing force normally had about a hundred men in it. I would be going in with the first wave.

My job would be to secure the landing zone for the guys who followed. The first wave was going to fly into the jungle clearing, unload, and then wait for the choppers to fly back all the way to Binh Hoa to pick up the second load, and then wait again a third time, until the whole battalion was finally landed. I didn't like it. We were going in "piece meal," and would be standing around too long in one place. If "Charlie" did decide to hit us all split up like that, we would be dead meat. Or, if he chose not to fight, he certainly would get the message well in advance and take off before the rest arrived.

It was time to go..."ours is not to reason why." The chopper hovered, poked its nose forward and started to run down the vegetable fields on the outskirts of Ninh Hoa, picking up speed, it began a slow climb. As I looked off to my right, I could see the insane asylum, a large building where the mentally insane were kept. They looked up at us through the bars on their windows. As we passed by, I could see some of them looking right at me. I couldn't help but laugh inwardly and think that it was we who were the crazy ones.

We climbed north. I didn't like it. It was dark. A dark and cloudy day. The jungle ahead appeared ominous and dangerous. I was scared. Later, we started our descent. The helicopter blades made that flat popping noise as we dropped further and further. Then the helicopters all lined up, one behind the other, ready to land in the clearing ahead. I wondered if it was going to be a "hot" LZ. (An LZ is where the enemy knows in advance that you are coming and is all lined up on both sides waiting to gun you down.) It's hairy and scary, because you never know.

My heart pounded wildly. We were down to about 100 feet, I was in the lead helicopter. I got out of my seat, scooted across the floor and put my feet on the landing runner. With my carbine in my right hand and my left hand holding on to the door frame, I stood outside the helicopter. Boy, it was breezy out there. I was going to be the first guy in. If that LZ was hot, I wanted to make a run for it and get as far away from the helicopter as I could.

We were about ten feet off the ground when the helicopter stopped its forward movement, hovered and started to let itself down. At the same time, I jumped off and hit the ground running. The pilot must have been shocked to see a human being race by in front of him before he'd even landed his ship, but he had his job and I had mine. I was on my way to a decent fighting position. But it was also safer for the pilot, too. The sooner he could get out of there, the less chance he had of being hit. I ran out about 50 yards and lay down. Other Rangers jumped

129

off quickly, too, and we formed a circle, rifles pointed outward toward the jungle. The choppers pulled up and out. In a moment they were gone and it was now deathly quiet.

I looked around. My eyes peered intently into the jungle's edge ahead of me, my rifle was at the shoulder, cocked and ready to fire. I looked down the barrel at every leaf and bush. I checked for movement. Was anyone out there? Would they open fire? Chances are it wasn't going to happen because too much time had now gone by. They usually try to catch the choppers while they are down. However, on rare occasion they do wait until the choppers leave and then "hose down" the infantry. But it stayed quiet. All eyes continued to search the jungle. Nothing. Now it was time to secure the clearing. Orders were given, commands were barked out in Vietnamese and everybody jumped up and made a run for it. I did, too. We ran straight for the jungle, rifles cocked, ready to fire. Finally I made it. Out of breath I plunged into the jungle. I stopped and looked around. Everyone else was doing the same thing. I saw Rangers to the left and right of me. After a quick check of the immediate area, we all moved in a hundred yards or so further into the jungle, to see if any enemy was hiding that far back. There was none. It was all clear. We moved back to the clearing leaving some people behind for early warning. The rest of us would wait along the edge of the LZ for the remainder of the troops to arrive.

After what seemed to be an interminably long period of time, we finally heard helicopter blades popping. The second lift was on the way. They descended into the landing area and Rangers jumped off and fanned out. Of course, this group knew it was safe. We were "holding down the fort" for them. The helicopters took off and climbed skyward, and we waited again. I didn't like all this waiting. We had been in this same spot for over an hour and had now told the enemy twice where we were. This was their country and it was real "bear country." There were thousands of them out there. If they found out what was going on, they'd come over and clean our clocks before the rest arrived. We were in a very precarious position spread out like that. Finally, after another long wait and with great relief, I heard the third lift coming. They landed, Rangers jumped out and the ships took off. We organized quickly into combat patrols and plunged south into the jungle.

About ten minutes later, I heard rifle fire up to my front. It was sporadic fire. Then it was over. I wondered what they saw. We moved south again. We moved single file through the dense jungle. I just followed the Ranger in front of me. Five minutes later, we had sporadic firing again. This time about ten rifles opened up. They fired about ten rounds apiece, and then there was silence again. I surmised that they were firing at someone who just took off and ran away.

We continued south. My heart pounded as rifles popped off to our front again. I could tell it was our Rangers firing. Just a few rounds. Then silence again. We moved out. Finally, the fourth time, they opened up with a huge volume of fire for about one full minute and then ceased. The battalion halted and stood still in the bush. I wondered, "what's going on up front," so I moved forward. They had overrun a VC base camp. All that firing had chased the VC out the other side. I entered the base camp and looked around. It consisted of nothing more than a few bamboo huts with thatched roofs. There were still a couple of fires burning. We found a pot of rice. It was still hot and cooking. It appeared to be one of those temporary base camps that they used for about a week and then moved on.

The Rangers had captured a woman. She was wearing black pajamas and had no shoes on. She was carrying lots of documents, VC papers, and letters on her. She paid no attention to me. She simply stared straight ahead; impassively, showing no expression whatsoever. She knew she'd "had it," and accepted her fate. Their faces never showed anything; no fear, no hatred, no bravery, nothing. Just a blank stare.

The camp turned out to be a miniature supply dump. It had bags of rice in it and some medical supplies. We searched around the area for about 15 minutes, and then headed south again. My radio operator, Chan, normally walked right behind me. But since I could hear voices on the Advisors Channel, I asked him to get in front of me, so that I could hold the handset up to my ear, and follow along on what was being said. It was the advisors of the 48th Infantry to our south. They were calling in a helicopter gunship, because they had heard noises to their front, and wanted to put a gunship strike on it. I began to piece two and two together. They were south, hearing noises and we were north, making them. They wanted to call in a gunship strike on us. I immediately got on the radio and told the gunship pilot that I intended to halt our battalion and "pop smoke" on our position, so he could check to see if that strike was being called in on us. Maybe it was for some other place, but I had to be sure. Then I shouted over to the Dai Uy, "Halt the battalion."

I then tossed a red smoke grenade onto the ground. It made a popping sound and then began to pour out an effusion of red smoke. Gradually the red smoke rose to tree top level and then out through the trees above. The pilots saw it and asked, "What color did you throw?"

I replied, "Red."

He then told me that I was standing on the exact same position he was told to hit. The Advisors to our south were calling in a strike on us. Why were they doing this? Didn't they know any better? This was supposed to be a coordinated effort. They knew we were north of them. Why would they do such a thing? If I hadn't accidentally overheard the request we would have been hit and suffered serious casualties.

We moved out again. For some unknown reason, we were now not going to link up with the 48th to our south. Possibly, it was because of the danger we faced in running into each other in the jungle. We were told to move out in one direction and they were told to go another. Our new mission was to work our way down to a position a few miles east of Tan Uyen. There was a large clearing down there, a rice paddy. We were to head there.

We arrived later without incident. I wondered to myself, "Who owns this rice paddy? Were the communists farming it from the jungle side, or were the people coming out from Tan Uyen?" I had a feeling it was the communists. It was just too far out to be a "friendly" paddy.

We moved into the open. The Rangers secured the paddy and broke down into helicopter loads. It would be my job to fly out with the last lift. The first group of helicopters arrived. The Rangers were well organized. Each man knew where to go and what to do. They jumped on board quickly and the helicopters took off. We waited. This time the wait would be much shorter, as we were much closer to Binh Hoa.

The second lift came back, loaded up and took off. We waited again. My job was to stay there with the last lift and call in gunship strikes in the event we got hit before the helicopters came back. But finally they arrived. What a feeling of relief. I climbed on board, sat facing out, rifle pointed towards the jungle. The helicopter hovered, pointed its nose forward and began to climb. I aimed my carbine at the jungle now flashing by to my front. There was no fire. We were safe. And I was happy to be out of there.

CHAPTER 13

12 November

We ran an operation near Di An. Di An was flat farm country, with patches of jungle here and there. It was located between Saigon and Binh Hoa Air Force Base. It was a very peaceful area, open country, pastures, cows grazing, farmers working in vegetable gardens. A very enjoyable, pleasant, pretty area. This would be an easy operation in terms of walking and in terms of the enemy. As we pushed off in the morning, one sniper fired at us, but we didn't even hear the crack of his bullet, because he fired at such a great distance. He probably just wanted to let us know that he lived in this area. But there was definitely no threat of a large enemy force being there. It would just be a pleasant walk in the sun.

We stopped for lunch around 12 o'clock. There was a little thatched roof hut up ahead, alongside a dirt road, with two card tables inside. It was a roadside beer stand. The Dai Uy and his staff officers went inside and sat down. The troops fanned out in a large perimeter around the area and ate their lunch. The Dai Uy asked me to join him. The owner brought us some large plastic drinking glasses, with long slivers of ice in them, opened several bottles of Biere LaRue, and put them on the table. We picked them up and poured them into our glasses. Dai Uy noticed a jar of pickled pigs feet up on the counter and ordered some of them. We sat there eating pigs feet and drinking beer. It was a lot of fun and I enjoyed it.

After lunch, we continued our patrol. As I suspected,

it turned out to be nothing more than a nice walk in the sun through some very beautiful Vietnamese countryside.

About 4:00 p.m. we settled in for the night. It appeared that we were on a pacification mission (an operation where you just sit on top of the property, protect the people, and allow them to live normal, peaceful lives, courtesy of their government). Since the area was fairly safe and the battalion wouldn't need me for an air strike, I radioed for my jeep. I had another job to do, something very important.

Tau showed up on a dirt road near by. I hopped in and headed for Corps Headquarters. I wanted to see Colonel Plummer, the G-3 (Operations) Advisor for III Corps, and now my boss. Our battalion had been working directly for III Corps ever since we had moved to Binh Hoa Air Force Base. I walked into his office. He was a tall fellow, built like an athlete, with slightly graying hair. He was a very distinguished looking officer and a good man by reputation.

I told him the reason I had driven in from the field was to talk to him about the problems the families of the battalion were having. I described the move down from Tay Ninh City and how the families could only follow along by taking the next bus out of town and how they were now living out in the open. I told him how the Vietnamese Army did not provide housing for dependents (like our Army did) and how the families had to sleep in tar paper shacks or whatever else they could find. In addition, another problem had cropped up. Something had gone wrong with the food rationing system and the families were not receiving their normal allotment of rice and cooking oil. I also told him that the battalion needed a rest. It had been on operation after operation for a period of three months now and cracks in morale were starting to show. The men were just plain tired. They dragged their weapons and stared straight ahead. Their state of combat readiness was pitiful and they hadn't had so much as a single day of training. Many couldn't fire their weapons accurately and I saw many other problems. We needed time off to settle families and time to train.

After pleading with Colonel Plummer over these problems, he told me that he would push for five days rest. I thanked him from the bottom of my heart. Then I walked outside, hopped into my jeep and headed for the battalion. It was about dark when I got back. The ambush patrols were starting to move out. They would have no success tonight. There was no enemy out there.

Morning came and we moved out again. We got on line and swept across the ground looking for "spider holes" (camouflage tunnels), or anything else that the enemy might be hiding in. But it was clean. It turned out to be a very lazy, slow moving day. About 2:00 p.m. we reached the end of our search line and stopped. Trucks were supposed to be waiting for us there but they were not. So we sat out in the hot sun for another two and a half hours waiting for them. Finally they did arrive and we headed back to Train Compound and the air base.

The next day our battalion was going out again. This time they split up the battalion, so we would not be going out as one unit. It was the first time they had ever done this to us. Each one of our four companies had been parceled out to the surrounding districts and would be working directly for the district chiefs. The districts screwed this up horribly. They failed to establish control. There was no command post, no radio contact, nothing. Our troops were just out there thrashing around without supervision. And the districts sent them out into the worst possible areas imaginable since they were afraid to go out there themselves. I didn't like it.

I saw LTC Plummer later that night. I told him again that the troops needed time off, time to train, time to rest and time to get their families squared away. Since we had moved from Tay Ninh City, we now had six men AWOL. This was a bad sign. I was beginning to get concerned about morale. LTC Plummer listened sympathetically and promised to do the best he could.

The next day I drove into Saigon to get maps. Since the battalion was starting to operate all over III Corps, we would need maps of the entire area. While there, I ran into John Ramsey. He had a jeep full of his local "ruff puff" with him, grins all over their faces. It was good to see him

136

again. It was good to know John was out there doing a great job, and his village forces were, too. They were the secret to this war. John said he was going home soon, too, to an ROTC job, at Westminster College in Fulton, Missouri. What a wonderful soldier...absolutely fearless.

The battalion staff was finally getting a home. They were given some offices at III Corp headquarters. The rooms were extremely large, French style, just like we had in Tay Ninh City. It was a nice place for the staff officers to hang their hats and do their work. The Vietnamese supply system was starting to work, too, providing some materials for housing, such as lumber, plywood, and corrugated sheeting for the roofs. Now the men could build little shelters for their families. Also, one company was alerted today for a possible helicopter assault, north to Men Cat. The men sat out back of the insane asylum all day waiting to be airlifted, but the mission was called off.

Later, we heard that Bear Cat had been assaulted by thousands of VC and had been overrun. There was talk of flying our battalion up there, into the only landing strip in town, a soccer field right in the center of everything. But it would have been a suicide mission. The whole town had been overrun and we would have been mowed down from every side. I think somebody finally figured that out. That's why the mission was called off. Yet, you never know when some bozo may decide to send you in anyway. That was the hairy part about the job. But, in the end, they decided to attack over land with tanks and infantry, and it worked. They drove the VC out, and put Bear Cat back on solid footing again.

We got the word to move north to Phu Cuong for a big operation. Our job was to "stand by" as corps reserve. Many battalions from all over Vietnam were going to helicopter assault into the Boi Loi and Ho Bo Woods (a fanatical VC stronghold). We were designated as corps reserve, and would fly in if things got too hot. So we convoyed up to an old abandoned Japanese airfield outside of town. It was nothing more than a long gravel strip out, in a big flat field. Off to the side was an old French building. It had been an old French office or something like that. Dai Uy selected it as our CP, and we hung up our hammocks. The troops fanned out around the airfield and set up a perimeter defense. The next morning we would be ready to fly out, if needed.

The following day Dai Uy got word that he and I should leave the airstrip and drive into town about ten miles away. So we did. We each took our own jeep and headed down the highway. Phu Cuong was a large town, but was completely isolated. There was jungle all the way around it. The VC owned the area north of the town. Everything south of town was okay by day, because the road led to Saigon. We arrived at a large government building, in which the command post had been set up. As I walked in, I could see large maps on easels all over the place, and heard radios crackling. I looked around and spotted General Khanh, the President of Vietnam. He had taken over through a coup. Dai Uy and I walked over to the maps. LTC Plummer spotted us and gave us a hasty briefing as to what was going on. It was an extremely large operation, the largest to date. Vietnamese Marines, Rangers, Paratroopers and the entire Fifth Division were operating in an area called the Iron Triangle. The Iron Triangle was owned, lock, stock and barrel by, the VC. The Ho Bo and Boi Loi Woods composed the northern part of this area. It, too, had been in VC hands for years.

I spent the day monitoring the operation, sitting in a chair listening to the radios on the various frequencies. They were taking heavy casualties out there. Seventy killed and wounded every day. I heard the advisors call in requests for "dust off" (Medical Evacuation Helicopters). Sometimes the word was passed to the Vietnamese, and they would send out an H34. Other times when the H34s couldn't go in (or wouldn't go in, because the Vietnamese pilot refuses to fly the mission) they would ask for an American pilot, and he would go in and pick up the wounded. One of the Advisors came on the air and reported that a Vietnamese H34, loaded with wounded, had just exploded in midair. He said it just exploded into a fireball and disappeared. There was a Saigon staff officer sitting next to me, sent out from Headquarters, sitting there in his immaculately starched khakis. He turned to me and said, "It's just like listening to a Saturday afternoon football game, isn't it?"

I didn't say a thing back to him or start any trouble. But it wasn't a football game out there. It was a life and death struggle, and that had been the end of those guys. He wouldn't have said something like that if he had ever been close to the situation, and seen the torn limbs, the burned ships, and the dead bodies. He was just so typical of so many people, who didn't understand what was going on.

It was getting late. We decided to drive back to the air strip. As I walked out to my jeep, I noticed an artillery unit down the street; six canons poking their snouts into the air. They were New Zealanders. Why not drop by and say hello to the "Kiwis!" So I did. They were not advisors, but are real live combat troops, a whole battery of gunners and officers from New Zealand, about 150 of them. I didn't know New Zealand had sent combat troops to Vietnam. The U.S. sure hadn't. The Kiwis were very friendly and showed me around. After a brief visit, I hopped back into my jeep and headed for the abandoned Japanese airfield, to spend the night.

The next morning, we got word that the road to Phu Cuong had been cleared by the local forces and we were to head into town again. This time we took three jeeps. The heavy dew was still on the grass. As we got closer to Phu Cuong, I could see the thatched roof huts of the outlying villages. Eventually, we arrived in town and passed through the heavily defended town gate. We spent the day in a nervous posture, sitting on the edge of our chairs at Corps Operations Center, waiting for somebody to come over and tell us that the situation was so hot and desperate that they had to throw us in. It was just one of those things that wore you down, sitting there all day worrying about it. How bad could it be before they threw in the reserves? You knew the best were out there; the Rangers, the Paratroopers, and the Marines. The cream of the crop. If they couldn't handle it, who could? What difference would we make? It would mean very heavy casualties. So we just sat in fear and waited.

Finally, the end of the day came. Good news! The

operation was finished, and the troops were going home. It was all over. We would not be flying into some VC trap after all.

There was a big party over at the District Compound that night, and everybody was going to be there. It was a farewell bash for Major "D" Flannigan, a former advisor to the 35th Rangers. He was an old friend of John Ramsey, and a man that I had met from time to time, a very flamboyant fellow, and a darned good infantryman. He was going home after a year in Vietnam. He had been an advisor to the 35th Rangers, but a few months before he was to go home, they transferred him to district to keep him out of combat (that was a standard policy in Vietnam.) It turned out to be a large party. Many people were there, both advisors and Vietnamese. It was very crowded. There must have been 50 people there. Of course, Dai Uy went with me. He was drinking scotch and I was drinking martinis "Air Force style" (Beefeater's Gin poured over ice, followed by a three minute waiting period).

After a while, I was feeling pretty mellow and Dai Uy was feeling pretty mellow too. Since I had been with him for a long time now, I felt that it was a good time to bring up something about the battalion that I didn't like. I felt we had come to a point in our relationship where I could talk to him directly about a problem, and he would not get angry or lose face. We were very close. We had shared a lot together, dodged a lot of bullets together, we were like brothers. So, it was time to bring the subject up. Sitting off to the side at a table all by ourselves, oblivious to the party going on around us, I said, "Dai Uy, I want to bring up one thing with you, about the battalion that I don't like. It's about when we cross the rice paddies. We are getting worse and worse. We no longer fan out. We walk on the dikes. We cross rice paddy after rice paddy, walking one behind the other. We walk right down the middle of the dike, three hundred men in a straight line. One of these days there's going to be a machine gun at the other end of that dike, and it's going to kill everyone of us. Why do the Rangers do that? Why don't they do what they are trained to do? Why don't they get out in the knee deep slop and fan out, rather than walking one behind the

140

other on top of the dike?"

Then Dai Uy, now feeling very melancholy, and perhaps a little drunk, looked directly at me and replied in a very slow and sad voice, "Because we all going to die. Maybe not today, but tomorrow, or the next day. All Rangers die. So what is difference?" And then, after a long pause, he said, "Besides, it is easier to walk on the dike."

I sat there stunned, absolutely stunned. I couldn't answer him a word. I knew he was right. What he just told me was the truth. I knew, too, it was just a matter of time, for him and for me and for all the guys in the 33rd. At that moment I stopped being the aggressive, fire eating American Advisor who came to win the war in one day. At that moment, I became Vietnamese.

It was 10:00 p.m., and time to go home. We had to get back to the airstrip that night yet. So we walked out onto the front porch. "D" Flannigan and some of the advisors were out there. As we walked out into the night air, we heard firing to the north, on the north edge of town. The VC were attacking that particular area. Since we didn't hear any firing directly to the east, (the direction in which we were going), we got ready to hop into our jeeps and take off for the Japanese airstrip. I knew it was stupid to drive home that late at night, especially through all that jungle, but my job was to stay with Dai Uy, and that's what I intended to do. I had to follow him. If I didn't, I would never be able to walk another foot with him again in Vietnam. At that moment, the advisors started pleading with Dai Uy not to go. "Don't drive out into the darkness," they said, "you'll run into an ambush. There's VC all around the town tonight. They'll kill you."

But their pleas fell on deaf ears. Dai Uy had to spend the night at the airstrip with his troops. A jeep loaded with some of our Ranger officers tore out first. Dai Uy and I remained behind, as the advisors continued to try to convince him not to go. They spend about five more minutes talking to him, but it was to no avail. His Vietnamese boss would crucify him, if something happened to his battalion and he was not there. So, he hopped into the jeep and roared out.

Tau and I followed. We departed the town and hit the

141

open road. I saw thatched roofs ahead in the moonlight, a few scattered huts here and there. Then after a while, nothing. Nothing but the white moonlit road winding through the darkness. We caught up with Dai Uy and followed right behind him. We might as well. There was no sense letting him go through an ambush first, and me later. Maybe if we went through together, guns blasting, we could make it. My hair stood on end. We crested a hill and sped straight down a long gentle slope, plunging into jungle, and then out again into an open rice paddy. This was insane. There was a curve up ahead. As we sped around it, we came upon a jeep lying on its side, lights stabbing grotesquely into the night air. Two men appeared to be dead on the concrete, another was stumbling around, hurt. I told Tau "ambush," grabbed my carbine and got ready to fire. But Dai Uy, in front of us, had already stopped his jeep. He had determined that this was not an ambush. The guys in the first jeep had simply been driving too fast and had turned their jeep over, going around the curve. We quickly loaded them into our jeeps and sped off into the darkness, leaving the disabled vehicle behind. Finally, I saw the Japanese airstrip ahead. We pulled in by the old French house. We were safe. We turned the injured over to the medics, and went to bed.

The next morning we got word to head back to Binh Hoa. All the units, that had participated in the operation, were pulling out and going home. We were told the road had been cleared, all the way back to our headquarters. This time we would not be going back in convoy, but in separate vehicles. Tau said he knew a short cut, so we decided to take it. We headed south from the old Japanese airstrip toward Binh Hoa. It was a beautiful area. The sun was shining, and I could see rice paddies and palm trees everywhere. We drove for about half an hour down old French blacktop roads. As we approached a rubber plantation to our front I heard firing off to our right. It sounded like it was about 300 yards off to our side. Not really close but close enough to be scary. That was the weird thing about Vietnam. The sun could be shining. It could be so bright. You could see life and green all around you. Then, suddenly, shots are fired and a man is dead, blood running out of his nostrils, eyes frozen wide open. It was all so macabre. Tau jarred me from my thoughts by flooring the accelerator. He believed that it was an ambush, and that they were firing at us.

A few moments later, down the road, directly in front of us, I started to pick up some figures, people in black pajamas, five of them. They were all facing the opposite direction, but they turned around when they heard us coming. Who were they? VC? We had just heard shots off to our right flank. Now this. Men in black pajamas to our front. I grabbed my carbine and pointed it straight ahead, barrel resting on the dash. (The windshield had been previously folded down and there was now nothing in the way.) It was time to kill all five of them. But what was I to do? Shoot them in the back before they shot me? Or, were they just friendly local forces out patrolling the road? I had no way of knowing. Not one of them had a weapon up yet. None of them looked threatening.

At that point, one of the men who was walking backwards looking at us, turned around and began to walk straight ahead. I took it as a good sign. It led me to believe that they were local forces and not interested in me, but I kept my rifle pointed right at them, anyway. As we roared by at 50 miles per hour, I kept my gun barrel pointed at them, carbine on full automatic, ready to spray them down at the twitch of a finger. But nothing happened. They made no false moves. We sped past. Who were they? VC caught out in the open "with their pants down," so to speak, as we roared up behind them so unexpectedly? Or local forces out patrolling in black pajamas? I would never know. But I came within a hair's breadth of killing all five of them. Even if they had been VC, I would have felt bad about gunning them down in the back like that, without a warning. The memory would have haunted me the rest of my life.

LTC Plummer told me that the 33rd Ranger Battalion was now to become permanent Corps Reserve, and would be trained in helicopter assault tactics. Instead of guarding Binh Hoa Air Force Base, or going on small operations here and there or being parceled out to the districts, we were going to become the reserve attack force for the entire corps, an area which stretched from Saigon to the Cambodian border, and included all of War Zone D and the famous Iron Triangle. It covered an awful lot of area, and an awful lot of hot spots. Being in reserve simply meant that we would be "on call," to be thrown in when the local or regular infantry battalions couldn't handle it anymore. We started training immediately, in the pasture land around Thu Duc. It was so peaceful in this area. Pastoral is a better world. It was located off to the side of a super highway that ran between Saigon and Binh Hoa. There were large, flat, open grass fields there, ideal for helicopter training. So we began training, coordinating with the pilots and practicing for a full week. We learned how to break down into loads, jump on board, exit the aircraft, assemble, etc.

There were lots of things to know about heliborne operations. For example, don't put all your radio men on one helicopter, because if that helicopter goes down, you won't have any communications when you land. Another one is not to put all your officers on one helicopter, or you'll have no leadership on the ground if you lose that chopper. Safety was another big factor. You had to stay away from the tail rotor. It would cut your head off. And, never run toward the helicopter with your radio antenna sticking up. It will smack the blades and damage the helicopter, as well as injure you. There were just hundreds of things to know, and we covered them all with the troops, in classes and in actual training.

While waiting for the helicopters one day, I mentioned to Dai Uy that I thought being trained in the helicopters was a good idea. I expressed this out of naivete, simply because I thought that riding helicopters would be fun. But Dai Uy said that he had prior experience with them and he didn't think they were "fun to ride." He proceeded to tell me about a time, in the old days, when his former unit was using the H19 helicopters (a helicopter that looked like a flying banana). He was down in the Delta then. They had been flown into a position along the sea coast. His battalion was down there, all alone, when the VC got wind of it, and marshalled thousands of men, and completely surrounded him. Dai Uy and his men were

144

trapped with their back to the sea. They fought all day and all night and were in a terrible predicament until finally rescued by naval forces. I think what Dai Uy was trying to tell me was, you can fly out "too far" with these helicopters. You can fly yourself into a trap. It was an ominous warning.

Colonel Wilson
That night after training, I ate supper alone in Train Compound. It was late. Afterwards, I decided to walk over to the club. As I walked through the entrance of the club, I noticed that it was extremely quiet, even though there were about 20 people inside. They were all gathered at the bar, standing around Colonel Wilson. As I came through the door, I heard him say, "Who's the meanest son of a bitch in Vietnam? Who?"

He kept saying it over and over again. He was drunk, very, very drunk. He could hardly stand up. His head was bobbing back and forth. The men were terrified of him. He was in an extremely ugly mood. They didn't know what to answer, but he kept on asking them anyway, getting angrier all the time. Suddenly, he spotted me standing over by the door. He threw his arm out wildly, beckoning me to come over. I walked over to him. He looked me right in the eye and, with the meanest look I have ever seen on anybody anywhere, asked me, "Who's the meanest son of a bitch in Vietnam, Behnke? Huh? Who? Who?"

After a long pause I looked him right back in the eye and said, "You are, Sir."

He immediately replied, "You're god damned right I am."

Everybody tittered, and then broke into laughter. Eventually, things went back to normal. I sat down next to Colonel Wilson, and ordered a San Miguel beer. We began to talk. I found out the reason he was so upset. There had been a coup that day, staged against General Khanh. In fact, it was still going on. Colonel Wilson didn't like it for two reasons. Number one, it probably signaled the start of many more coups to come. Now, anytime anyone didn't like what was going on, they would simply overthrow the government. He felt the original coup against Diem was necessary, because of the corruption of the Diem family. But if they were going to have coup after coup in the future, there would be no stability in the government. Secondly, he was upset because General Khanh was his best friend. Khanh had been the commander of II Corps in the north, before the first coup, and Colonel Wilson had been his advisor up there. During that period, they became quite close. When General Khanh took over in Saigon, he naturally brought Colonel Wilson along with him. Colonel Wilson became the Senior Advisor to III Corps, an area which included the Capitol (Saigon) and everything around it.

Colonel Wilson then told me that General Khanh was, at that very moment, surrounded by coup forces in Saigon, but was still holding out in the National Palace. He told me the building had a flat roof on it. He then asked me, in a very serious manner, if I would get the 33rd Ranger Battalion together along with some American helicopter pilots, and lead a raid on Saigon to save the General. He wanted me to land on the roof and rescue Khanh. And he meant it. Even though he was drunk, I knew he meant it. But it was just something I couldn't do. It would have meant involving the United States in a very new and serious way in Vietnam. It would have meant that the U.S. was now running the war. And I couldn't do that. It was their war. They were going to have to run it for themselves. I let the conversation run its course. I think Colonel Wilson sensed that I was not picking up on his idea, or perhaps he was having second thoughts about it himself. But, for a moment I had an opportunity to be a part of history.

There was a road between Binh Hoa in the north and Vung Tau in the south, which ran along side a mountain. There were lots of VC on this mountain, and they used to come down to the road and ambush the columns all the time. Then they would run back up into the mountain, where we couldn't find them. This "cat and mouse" game had been going on for some time. One of the Corps Advisors came up with a plan to "ambush the ambushers." His idea was to have a bunch of trucks go down the road, with dummies tied to the back seats (they would take uniforms and stuff them full of straw, to make it look like soldiers were riding in the back). This phony convoy would be backed up with hundreds of tubes of artillery, ready to fire into the area. In addition, A1E Skyraiders would loiter out of sight, loaded with napalm and bombs, and helicopter gunships would be ready to fly in, too. Tear gas would also be used to blind the enemy. Right behind this phony convoy would be our battalion, the 33rd Rangers, mounted in helicopters, ready to drop in on a moment's notice. When the ambush "popped," we would gas and blind them. Then the aircraft would come in to bomb and strafe them. Following that, the Rangers would drop right in on top of them and finish them off.

This was an American idea, and the U.S. Corps Staff Advisors decided to brief Major Nha on it right after siesta one day. Major Nha was the Vietnamese Corps G-3 (plans and operations officer), and would have to approve the plan. So at 3:00 p.m. one afternoon, the Vietnamese opened up the large wooden doors to their offices, and the American officers filed in and sat down around the conference table with this hot idea. They explained it in great detail to Major Nha, who listened stoically and with great patience. Finally, when they got all done, they asked Major Nha his opinion. Major Nha who was a bit overweight and looked like Budda personified, turned to the Americans and said, "You have very good plan. Only one problem. Where you get drivers for trucks?"

It was a night off for the battalion. One of the platoon leaders (a Lieutenant in the battalion) was getting married, and they were having a bachelor party for him. The restaurant was located in Thu Duc, halfway between Saigon and Binh Hoa. The total distance between those two towns was about 30 miles. Saigon was a very large city. It sprawled way out. Beyond that, there was what you might call suburbs, and beyond that rice paddies and then the city of Thu Duc again. Then beyond Thu Duc, there were lots of open farm country and then Binh Hoa. The whole area was considered to be one big defensive area, "the Binh Hoa/Thu Duc/Saigon defensive zone." One was about as safe as the other, except that Binh Hoa was located closer to the jungle, and could be mortared from that side. There was no danger of any large scale VC attack in these areas, but there were individual guerrillas who could throw grenades and assassinate people. I arrived at the restaurant with Dai Uy Duong, and we sat down. The restaurant was rectangular shaped, about 20 feet wide and 60 feet long. It had wooden tables scattered all around inside, with straight back chairs. Like most restaurants in Vietnam, it was not very fancy. The building was French style. It had very thick walls with arches, and the ceiling and walls were painted white. They had a head table up front, for the Lieutenant and the Dai Uy. I was invited to sit up there, too, out of courtesy to my rank. All of the officers were there, walking around from table to table, laughing, having a good time, and drinking Biere LaRue. Later we ate. They served Chinese style food: bamboo shoots and beef slivers in sauce. It was really delicious. It was so good to see the officers relaxing and smiling, having a good time. It seemed impossible that there was a war on. The war seemed to be so far away at that moment.

After a while, I went to the bathroom and, since there was no indoor plumbing in the restaurant, I had to go out back. I pushed open the back door and walked out into the darkness. I waited a minute for my eyes to get adjusted to the darkness. The restaurant was surrounded by many tall bushes and plants. I moved forward, away from the restaurant about 20 feet, and began to "take a leak." Standing there, looking out into the darkness, my eyes became accustomed to what little moonlight there was. Suddenly, I noticed a man standing out there in the dark to my front. My heart skipped a beat. I quickly finished my job and buttoned up my pants. Was he friend or foe? I noticed that he was wearing a beret. That probably meant he was a Vietnamese soldier. Then I spotted the outline of a weapon. A thousand thoughts raced through my mind. What should I do? Go for my pistol, tucked under my left arm in a shoulder holster? While I was trying to make up my mind he spoke to me in Vietnamese. "Chau Dai Uy, Dai Uy Manh Gio?" (Hi Captain, how are you?)

As he approached, I noticed that he was carrying a

Thompson Submachine gun. I could now tell that he was one of our guys, a Ranger. But what a spooky event. I found out later that Dai Uy Duong had put the man (and others) out there to guard the building. Dai Uy realized that, once reservations were made at the restaurant, word might leak out to the enemy. It would have been easy for one of them to have sneaked up through the bushes, while we were all inside partying, and have thrown a grenade through the window, blowing us all to kingdom come. It would not have been the first time something like that had happened. But Dai Uy had the foresight to put sentries out back, and I felt good about that.

Corps, for some unknown reason, had now put us under the OP CON (operational control) of district. This meant that they could employ us anytime and any place they wanted to. They usually took advantage of the situation, by employing us in the very worst possible locations. If they had an area that they didn't like to go into, one where they might take heavy casualties or where there were mines, booby traps, and panji sticks, they usually left the area alone, until they could get a Ranger Battalion to clean it up. Naturally, we ended up in some really bad places. The district had an operation planned for us in the Rung Sat area, but the spot we were going into was not typically Rung Sat. The Rung Sat area was normally all canals and swamp. We were going into the northern part, where there was lots of open fields and jungle.

We took off from behind the insane asylum, climbed out and headed south. We passed over vegetable fields and villages and jungle. Down below, I could see a large river winding around like a silvery snake, the reflection of the river hemmed in on both sides by the dark jungle. We were getting closer to the LZ now. I could hear the blades pop as we started to descend. The helicopter banked and I could see it up ahead. There was the landing zone. A green smoke grenade was burning on it, marking the place for us to land. A reconnaissance helicopter had done this for us. (They usually flew over the landing zone first, to make sure no enemy was sitting on it. Then they would throw a green smoke grenade on it to let us know that everything was okay. Green meant "GO." Red meant "DANGER.") It also conveniently marked the landing zone for us, so we didn't land in the wrong field by mistake. Suddenly, I saw puffs of white smoke exploding along the edge of the field. I recognized what this was right away. Rockets were being fired into it from the gunships. I couldn't spot the gunships as yet. Then I picked up their red tracer rounds stitching up the area. Then I saw them, strafing and making passes up and down the LZ. I asked the door gunner, "What's going on?" (He had a headset on, and could listen to the pilots.)

He turned to me and said, "The LZ is hot."

A quiver of excitement ran through me. This meant that the enemy was on the LZ. It was time to land. We came in slow. The front of the ship tilted back. As we approached the LZ at this agonizing speed, the door gunner grabbed his machine gun and started firing. He was right next to me and it was extremely noisy. He was firing tracers and he was firing like crazy, stitching bullets all over the field. I stepped out onto the runner. When we were about five feet off the ground, I jumped off, raced out 50 yards to my left front, and hit the dirt. I looked around. I couldn't see any enemy and I couldn't hear anything being fired at us either. I looked back. Troops were still pouring out of the trail choppers. When the last chopper unloaded, they pulled up and flew out together, climbing to the right. Suddenly they were gone. It was all quiet, not a sound. Chan was next to me. I grabbed the radio and asked Playboy (the gunship commander), "Is this LZ hot?"

"Negative," he replied, "it's not."

"Then why did they fire?" I asked myself.

We stood up and moved around. Some of the Rangers began to scout the area. While walking across the LZ to find Dai Uy, I saw a bunch of Rangers gathered around a dead body. It was a farmer. He looked to be about 50 years old. He had been shot dead by the helicopters. Why, I don't know. There was no enemy. We were not receiving any fire. So why then did they open up? For what reason? Who killed this farmer? It was just one of those terrible things about war. A big mistake had been made, and this man had paid the price. The battalion formed into three columns and slipped into the jungle. About half an hour later, I heard firing to our front. It was sporadic. Then it stopped. Word got back to Dai Uy that a platoon of VC were sighted, but they bugged off. We continued south. Suddenly, our command group came up on a group of Rangers standing around. It was the lead element of our battalion. They had hit tunnels. I looked down one. They were freshly made. The VC used them as hiding places from the government, and to store ammunition and supplies inside. Since none of the Rangers had dropped down inside to explore the tunnels yet, I decided to do so myself.

I let myself down by holding on to the sides of the hole with my elbows, and gradually eased myself down to the bottom, about eight feet below. Once on the floor, the tunnel cut sharply to the right. I couldn't see very far. It was too dark. But it was clean and well used. At that particular moment, I wished we could put mustard gas in those tunnels. Not the aerosol type that ruins people's lungs, but the paste type that you could spread on the walls, just to keep people from using them. It would burn their hands and feet if they chose to hop down inside. Mustard paste was the one thing that would have kept them out. It didn't do any good to blow up tunnels like these, with explosives. They would just come right back and rebuild them again. Besides, we didn't carry a lot of explosives with us.

We continued moving south for the rest of the day. Late in the afternoon we came upon a village. We moved in. We were going to spend the night there. Naturally, there were no men in the village. They were all VC and were hiding in the jungle. We saw only women, and they ignored us. They continued to look down at their work, or walk around staring straight ahead, as if we didn't exist. The children hid behind buildings and were afraid of us, as usual, but by the time darkness had fallen, they were all gathered around me, laughing and giggling. We had made friends once again. I ate supper with the Dai Uy. We sat around a large picnic table. We did not bother the women of this village to cook for us. Dai Uy's Cowboy cooked up some rice, and we opened some canned Spam for the occasion, and we called that supper. Later that evening, just prior to darkness, the District Chief from the local district and his advisor tried to fly into the village, but they took sniper fire as they approached, so they returned home. Evidently there were VC all around us. It was time to "circle wagons" and get some sleep for the night. I put up my hammock and sacked out. Later that night, around midnight, one of our far out ambushes blew. I heard a Claymore mine going off, followed by some firing. What was it? Who was it? We wouldn't know until morning. Meanwhile, it meant sleeping with one eye open.

Morning came, and it was time to move out. After a breakfast of cold rice balls and hot tea, we moved down the road. We would move back east, toward a blacktop highway, and be picked up there by trucks. To our left was jungle, and to our right was rice paddies. We put men out on both sides of the road and ahead of us. We made it about 100 yards, when a sniper opened fire on us. The Rangers dropped and looked around. He had fired at our lead element, and they were now maneuvering against him. Then he took off. We continued walking down the road.

Just ahead of me, sitting out in the middle of the road, was an old kilometer marker (mile marker) made out of stone, about the size of a concrete building block. The French used them in the old days, to let people know how far down the road they had come. Someone had picked this one up and placed it in the middle of the road. I knew this was a VC trick for sure. As usual, they had probably put a huge explosive device underneath it. If someone now tried to pick it up or move it, it would blow him to kingdom come. Surely, none of our Rangers would be so stupid as to try to kick it, or push it over. They all knew better than that. But as we walked along, the man right in front of me suddenly moved over to the middle of the road, put his foot up against the mile marker, and pushed it over. There was not time for me to do anything, but to wait for the horrible blast that would take me to eternity.

152

But nothing happened. The marker just toppled over. It wasn't booby trapped. But what a dumb stunt. I felt like clubbing the man with my carbine.

We continued east and hit the blacktop. The road had been secured up to this point by Regional Forces. We loaded up and went home. I wasn't happy with this operation. There was no artillery support, or radio communication with the District Forces.

The battalion was still not under the operational control of III Corps, but continued to work directly for individual District Chiefs who continued to employ them in the worst manner possible. We were working for Binh Hoa District, when one night I decided to go by the District Advisor's house. I pulled my jeep in up front. There was a party going on inside. All the Advisors were standing around the bar talking. Some of their Vietnamese counterparts were there, too. I had a beer with them, and then later "moseyed" around the house, walking upstairs into the operations room. Inside, I saw a Second Lieutenant planning an operation on a map. The operation that he was working on was the same one that we were to go on the next day. I watched for a while. I could tell he didn't know what he was doing. He was completely unfamiliar with tactics and map symbols. But there you had it, a Second Lieutenant planning a combat operation, that I and the rest of the Rangers would have to carry out the next day. (Where this guy came from, I don't know. He must have been the only Second Lieutenant in Vietnam. Normally, advisors were experienced people.) I couldn't go downstairs to the Senior Advisor, and tell him to get up there and plan the operation himself. That was not the way things were done in the Army.

The next day we moved out. It was to an area west of Bear Cat. Bear Cat was an abandoned air field, formerly used by the Japanese. It was about a third of the way down between Binh Hoa and Vung Tau. The road was usually clear to that point. Many times on weekends people drove all the way down this highway, to the beach at Vung Tau, but the road south of here tended to be bad country. The trucks stopped just short of Bear Cat, and we disembarked.

At first the Rangers all milled around, but then scouts were sent out. Finally, the companies got organized into formations and we moved out. Initially, it was rubber. Then we hit jungle. The thick vegetation forced us to walk in single file. Then we found ourselves walking downhill. We wound our way down this hill, and pooped out into some rice paddies. We crossed the rice paddies and then turned south. There was a hill to our front. I didn't like the situation, because we were crossing in open rice paddy, with high ground to our front. But nothing happened. We hit the hill and began to climb up. It was not extremely thick, sort of like the woods back home. We were, about halfway up the hill, when suddenly the enemy opened fire to our front. I couldn't tell how many there were but it was a high volume of fire. It could be a lot of them and a few of us firing back, or a few of them and a lot of us firing back. I didn't know. But I could hear the sharp crack of bullets overhead. I immediately hit the dirt. There were definitely lots of bullets coming our way.

Tree leaves, snapped off by bullets above me, floated gently to the ground. The whole situation seemed eerie. Here we had bullets cracking along at a thousand feet per second, along with a tremendous volume of noise from the weapons, and yet these leaves were floating peacefully to the ground.

Suddenly, I heard yelling. The Rangers were yelling at the top of their voices. They were screaming at the enemy. They grabbed their rifles and charged forward, mad as hell. They overran the enemy and forced then down a tunnel. Again, the VC employed their usual tactic. They didn't stand and fight, but ran away. Their tunnel probably had a back exit some 300 yards away in the bush. Some Rangers jumped down inside the tunnel to chase after them, but nobody was there. We captured a few documents, and that was about it.

From this point, we cut left and headed back towards the Vung Tau highway. It was suspenseful, because we figured we might run into the retreating enemy at any moment. But chances were slim that they were headed our way. We eventually hit the blacktop. Dai Uy got on the radio and asked for the trucks. About 30 minutes later they appeared, and we hopped on and rode back to the battalion headquarters in Binh Hoa. I got off and got in my jeep, and then drove back to Train Compound, where I lived.

I was very angry about this operation. It was completely fouled up! The local advisors were not clued in on what was going on, and they were not in contact with us, and they were the ones who had requested us to work the area. We were doing it for them. We were out there risking our lives for them, and they weren't even in radio contact with us. Furthermore, we had no communications with the L-19 spotter plane. Normally, I had an L-19 airplane above me, who kept in contact with higher headquarters when we operated so far out that our radios wouldn't reach back. But no such plane was requested. I was very angry about that. If I had been shot there would have been no way for Dai Uy to have summoned a helicopter to take me to the hospital.

Another problem was that we were also out of artillery range. No artillery had been preplanned or provided for us. Suppose we had run into a large VC force? What would we have done then? Also, I found out later that we had been operating in an area that belonged to Special Forces. It was their private battle zone, and they had authorization to kill anybody they saw in that area. Yet here we were, walking around in their area, and no one had told them we were there. To make matters worse, I also found out that the area was a "free fire" zone. That meant that the Air Force considered it a bad area (and in coordination with Special Forces, who routinely patrolled it) they could kill anything they saw moving in it. They, too, had not been informed we were there. Lastly, I found out that it was also a "drop bomb" zone. That meant that when Air Force fighters came back from missions, with unused bombs hanging on their wings they would jettison them in this area, just before landing at Binh Hoa Air Base. So we might have been hit by one of our own friendly aircraft as well. I was furious with all of this. I went to see Colonel Plummer, the G-3, and made a formal complaint about it.

We were now attached to Binh Hoa Special Zone, and

would be going on an operation for them. We headed south out of Binh Hoa. I saw RVN soldiers along the road and, later, local forces in their rag-tag clothing and mixed uniforms. They grinned as we sped by. We traveled south, past the area of our last operation (where we ran into those VC on top of that hill). This time we were going to turn left and operate to the east. It turned out to be really rough country, the worst jungle I had seen so far. It was extremely thick. But still, the Rangers didn't use their machetes. In some places, we had to get down on our hands and knees and crawl under the vines, and then stand up again, but we never had to chop our way through anything.

At midpoint in the afternoon we came to a ravine. Walking down to the bottom of the ravine, I spotted a small stream. It was damp and cool. There was not too much vegetation down there. It was kind of clear, although there was still a jungle canopy above. When we moved up and out of the ravine, and got back on higher ground, the battalion stopped. I wondered why. Then I noticed all the Rangers pulling up their trouser legs, and I spotted leeches all over their legs. (A leech is a big fat worm about two inches long, with a big fat head. It attaches itself to your leg, and then sucks the blood out of your body.) I took off my own boots and pants, and found one hanging on my leg, too. One of the Rangers came over to me with a lighted cigarette butt. He touched the end of the leech with the hot ember, and immediately the leech squiggled loose and fell to the ground. (It was the only way to get rid of them.)

We moved out again. Later, about dark, we came to a hamlet. Again, we "circled wagons" for the night. The Dai Uy got together with the officers, and divided the village into four pieces of pie. Each company took a piece of the pie, guns pointing outward toward the jungle with their backs to the village. These were very friendly people, Catholics living way out there all by themselves. They were refugees who had escaped communism in the north, and were now trying to hack out a living in the bush. I felt sorry for them.

The next day we moved out again. We moved fourteen

kilometers due east toward Xuan Loc. Occasionally to my front, through the jungle, I could see a high hill (or maybe it was a small mountain). We eventually struck the bottom of this mountain and began to climb up. We climbed to 1,150 feet. Finally, we got to the top. There was not much vegetation up there, and a good stiff breeze was blowing, so it felt really comfortable. Since it was very high up, about the altitude of an airplane, I decided to try and call my old headquarters in Tay Ninh City, to see if I could reach any of my old friends there. I switched over to the frequency used by Tay Ninh City, and began my transmission. To my amazement, the RTO in Tay Ninh City responded, and we got in a conversation. Later LTC Tansey came to the radio, and we talked for a little while. It was a fun break. I was absolutely amazed that the radio could reach that far.

At the same time, Dai Uy Duong got on his radio, too. He was using the AN/GRC44, an old World War II radio. It was not light and compact, like mine, but very heavy and bulky. My radio was about two feet long and six inches wide, with a battery located in the bottom. I talked through it via a microphone, attached by a long flexible cord. It was light and easy to carry, and could reach for miles.

The Vietnamese had a similar backpack radio, too, the old PRC 10, but it didn't have as good a range. So when they needed to reach out to a greater distance, they used this AN/GRC44. It was about the size of a case of canned beer and was just as heavy. It didn't use batteries, but had a hand crank generator. The generator was mounted on a tripod, and had bicycle pedals sticking out each side of it. A man would bend over this generator and crank the pedals with his hands, while the other man tapped out a message in Morse code. This radio had an extremely long range, around the world in fact, and Dai Uy was able to keep in contact with our headquarters, all the way back in Binh Hoa this way.

After Dai Uy had sent his transmission, we moved down off the mountain and broke into rubber. In the middle of the rubber was a French plantation. It was very beautiful, but also kind of eerie. There were rows and rows of white buildings, where they processed and stored the rubber. Off to the side was a landing strip. Later, I spotted an old fashioned French car near the main building. There was also a Frenchman standing there. He was dressed in a white short sleeved shirt, white Bermuda shorts, white calf length socks, and white shoes. His whole outfit was white, white, white. He looked like he had stepped off the pages of some story book. They say he owned and managed the place. As I passed by, I looked at him with a jaundice eye. I knew I couldn't trust that guy. Nobody could live out there all alone, surrounded by the VC, without paying taxes to them, without being in contact with them, and without working for them. I didn't trust him any further than I could throw a freight train.

We followed the rubber plantation road back out to a government road. When we got there, we set up security and waited for the trucks. Eventually, the trucks did arrive, along with a jeep carrying a very effervescent, bubbly, District Chief. He was a typical politician, with a big grin on his face. But he did something very unusual. He had a big box of money with him, and he went around from Ranger to Ranger, paying them in cash. I thought to myself, "What a wonderful thing to do."

Most politicians were corrupt and kept the money for themselves. But this man risked his life coming out to the field to give it directly to the men. It was his way of saying "thanks" for coming into his area and taking on the VC for him. There wasn't a Ranger around who wasn't smiling broadly and extremely grateful for their gift.

When I got back to Binh Hoa I went immediately to see Colonel Plummer. I told him that we needed time off. The men were being pushed too hard. We still didn't have housing for the families. And, I told him I had to have a communication link in the field. I couldn't keep going out there, day after day, with no radio contact with higher headquarters. Sooner or later, something disastrous was going to happen, and I wouldn't be able to summon help.

Tau, my Jeep driver.

Crossing a rice paddy.

In the jungle.

In the rubber trees.

Dai Uy Duong coming off patrol.

Loading the helicopters.

Break time on patrol.

Lift off.

Map check with Dai Uy.

Enroute to objective (no safety belts).

Walking on the dike.

163

Coming in for a landing on the objective.

Coming in the back door of Cu Chi Ba.

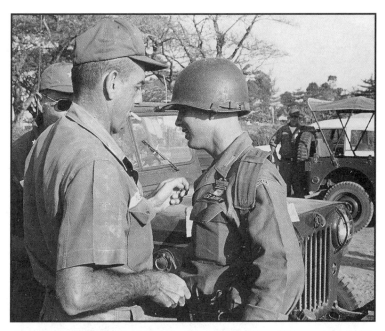

Getting the "CIB" at Binh Gia, (Col. Jap Wilson on left).

My Vietnamese "girlfriend" at Binh Gia.

165

This photo appeared in every major newspaper in the United States in December 1964. (Captioned: Wartime Buddies—Lt. James Behnke of St. Louis, Mo., has no trouble making friends with this receptive Vietnamese girl in South Viet Nam village of Binh Gia. Behnke is a U.S. Adviser for the 30th Ranger Battalion which defended the village against heavy enemy attack this month.)

166

The USMC Sergeant Advisor who servived the ambush at Binh Gia and who hid all night in a rice paddy as the VC shot all his wounded Vietnamese Marine friends in the head.

Downtown Saigon.

*The good life in Saigon, out on a date with
"Dee" Buchalter at the Crazy Cow Rstaurant.*

The good life in Saigon, reading the Sunday morning paper at the Rex Hotel.

General Throckmorton, commander of all Advisors in Vietnam, awards Captain Behnke with the Soldier's Medal (the Nation's highest award for valor not involving direct contact with the enemy) for rescuing helicopter crewman from burning aircraft at Binh Gia.

169

CHAPTER 14

Binh Gia I

The next morning, I got called over to III Corp Headquarters. Dai Uy was there. He looked a little scared. He had been told that a village by the name of Binh Gia had been overrun by the VC. There wasn't much information. They had received a message from the village that morning, but then nothing more. It would take some time to figure it out. In the meantime, we were to stand by. It was always very hard on the nerves to sit around and "stand by." At first, we kept busy getting organized and breaking down into helicopter loads. But later, we just sat under a shade tree and thought about what was ahead. Neither of us spoke. We both knew what was on our mind. There was heavy fighting somewhere, and we were going to be thrown into it.

Finally, after lunch, we got the word to go. The helicopters arrived, and we quickly hopped on board. I sat down on the edge of the floor facing outward, feet dangling into space. The chopper lifted off, and away we went. I was sitting on the right hand side of the aircraft as we headed south. As we gained altitude, I could look out and see the outskirts of Saigon and Thu Duc to the west. I had a commanding view of Vietnam below; jungle, swamp, a river here and there snaking along through the green. Then we banked left and headed east. We crossed the Vung Tau Highway and headed for real jungle country.

After about a half hour flight, I heard the helicopter

blades begin to pop. We were starting our descent. I looked ahead and saw a village, with a large field to the north of it. That would be the LZ. The choppers landed and I hopped off. The Rangers raced out and lay on the ground. The air was noisy with the helicopters lifting off, but as soon as they were gone it got quiet again. We listened. Nothing, not a sound, only an occasional bird chirping.

We moved out. The Rangers were about 100 yards ahead of me, headed for the village. They were well dispersed, well spread out. Suddenly a Thompson opened fire, followed by the crack of a bullet overhead. Sporadic firing. What was it? An enemy outpost? How many were there? Again, more sporadic firing, a Thompson fired, a carbine cracked. Then we got word on the radio that the VC were running away. They were fleeing the village. My heart leaped with joy, and I breathed a sigh of relief. I had been expecting the worst, a well dug in enemy ready to fight to the last round.

We moved through the village. It was full of little thatched roof houses with bamboo walls. A very neat village. It was shaped like a Velveeta Cheese box, and was divided into three different sections. Each section was called a hamlet, with the center hamlet being the heart of the village. That's where the life of the village, took place; markets, the church, the town square. There was a main street running through the middle of the village with little side streets running parallel to that. None of them were paved. Just sandy trails. All throughout the village were banana trees and bushes growing everywhere. It was a beautiful village. The Rangers were very cautious, carbines at the shoulder, darting here, looking there, checking everything out. It was getting dark. I heard more firing off in the distance. The people were smiling at us and looked happy. It indicated to me that we had taken the village, and the VC were gone.

Since the VC fled east, we naturally headed that way. We walked along, methodically clearing the whole village. The enemy was not to be found. We set up our CP in a school house on the edge of a soccer field. The school was made out of concrete, with walls up to about the height of a man's chest. Above that was a big gap (for windows), and above that, a thatched roof mounted on poles. The gap between the walls and the roof allowed the breeze to pass through the school to cool the kids. A neat idea. We made it our command post for the night.

It was almost dark. The S-2 had been walking around the village talking to the people. Then he came up to me, and told me that the people had told him that the VC had said that they would come back that night to kill us. I asked him how many VC there were. He replied, "Too many, too many."

I then corrected his grammar (because the Vietnamese always said "too many" when they meant "very many." I told him that there were "very many VC" but not "too many VC."

He agreed, "Very many VC, very many VC."

Either way it was not very encouraging.

10:00 p.m. Dai Uy and I checked the lines. It was quiet, except for the fact that I could hear a Vietnamese soldier, one of our own Rangers, moaning. It was a rare occurrence when you heard a Vietnamese cry. They never cried out or screamed when they were wounded. They just lay there and took it. Usually they just sat off to the side and stared straight ahead, glassy eyed. But this man was unconscious, and was moaning in his unconscious state. He was hurt, and he was hurt bad. There were bandages all over him. I don't know what had happened to him. He probably got hit in all that sporadic firing when we first landed. He was not going to last very long, because he was very severely wounded.

Dai Uy had the AN/GRC44 up, and had been calling for the last two hours for a Vietnamese H34 Helicopter to come in and pick him up, but so far none had arrived. (The H34 is an older model helicopter with a gasoline engine, and was used by the Vietnamese Army as a "flying ambulance.") It was the job of the Vietnamese pilots to come out and pick him up, but they wouldn't come. We called and called, but to no avail. Finally, Dai Uy came up to me and admitted that they were not coming. He knew they didn't like to fly in the dark. They very seldom came out at night. They thought it was too risky, at least with the type aircraft they were flying. The Americans had newer and better helicopters that didn't explode when hit by gunfire. So, he asked me if there was anything I could do. Could I get an American helicopter to come out?

The Americans did fly at night. There was only one problem. They were not supposed to pick up Vietnamese, only Americans. I told him I would try. I got on my radio and told the folks back at headquarters that we had a wounded Vietnamese Ranger, and that the H34s were not coming, and that if they didn't come the man would die. The operator instructed me to wait. After a few minutes he called back and said, "Roger, a chopper is on the way."

Now it would be my job to guide him to my location. I immediately started to mull over in my mind the best way to bring him in. I knew the VC had run out to the east, but I didn't know exactly where they were. I was positive they were no longer in the village, and I was pretty confident that they were still out to the east, so my plan was to bring the chopper in from the north. That way he wouldn't have to fly over the VC. (They did shoot at flying ambulances even, though they were marked with a red cross.) Later my radio crackled. It was the pilot on the radio. He was enroute to our location, about 15 minutes out. I told him to turn on his landing lights. Then I peered skyward. I picked him up at a very high altitude, maybe at 3000 feet, and many miles away. His landing lights were extremely powerful, so it was easy to spot him. He looked like a star moving across the sky. I shot a compass azimuth to the chopper, and gave him the "back azimuth" to my location, so he could fly directly toward us. Then he snapped off his landing lights.

On his way to the village, I steered him towards us by telling him to bank left or bank right, depending on which way he was headed. Finally, he arrived overhead. At this time I turned on my strobe light. He picked it up, and then knew exactly where we were. However, from his position high in the sky, all he could see was a little white light blinking in the inky darkness below. How would he get down? How would he approach? Where were the trees? That part was my job...to talk him down. I told him to fly in a circular pattern north of the village and to drop altitude with each circle. So he started doing lazy circles in the sky, dropping with each turn. I told him not to worry about crashing into anything because there was nothing out there, no mountains or trees. He was, of course, putting his life in my hands. If I made a mistake, or there was a hill out there, he was a dead man. I knew he couldn't see a thing in that inky darkness. So he kept on dropping the helicopter. Finally, he got down to about 500 feet. It was time to bring him in. I would have to talk him in every step of the way now. He was about a mile north of the village.

I lined him up on our position by vectoring him left or right. Finally, I got him lined up, coming right at me. We kept up a constant conversation on the radio. "Drop lower, lower, keep coming at me. Lower, lower."

He was in a sea of blackness, flying slowly toward me, as slowly as he could, yet all the while dropping altitude and lining up with my flashing strobe light. Finally, I had him down to about 75 feet. When he got past the edge of the village, and safe from enemy fire, I yelled "Lights on."

He flipped on his powerful landing lights. A huge beam of light stabbed out into the darkness. Now he could see. The light illuminated the soccer field to his front. However, the soccer field was extremely small so he had to rear the helicopter way back, in order to land. He almost crashed the tail section into the ground. The ship shuddered, leveled out and settled down. I gestured for him to move to the end of the field where we could load. He hovered the helicopter again, walked it down to the end of the field, and turned it around. He then positioned the tail of the helicopter as far back against the end of the field as he could. He knew he would need every inch of space to get out of there again.

I yelled for the Dai Uy to get the wounded man on board. The carrying party was ready. They picked him up gently and carried him over to the helicopter. I took this opportunity to go over and talk to the pilot. I walked up to his window. He had it open. I stuck my head inside so he could hear me above the noise of the engine. I looked up into his face. He was a black officer. I told him, "I wouldn't want your job tonight."

He looked at the jungle all around us, eyes like a hawk, gleaming white against his dark skin and said, "I wouldn't want yours, either."

The wounded man was now loaded and the crew chief gave the thumbs up. Time to take off. I backed away from the chopper. I heard the blades turn faster and faster as the whine of the engine increased. He hovered and started to move forward. The search light was on again. He moved down the soccer field and suddenly up. Then he was gone, lights off. He was out there, somewhere in the night sky, headed for Saigon. We stood in silence listening to the noise of the blades fade far away in the distance. I whispered to myself, "God bless you, Sir. Have a safe trip home." Then I walked back to the schoolhouse.

Later, Chan motioned for me to get on the radio. It was our L-19 pilot. He was over my area now. Although I couldn't hear his engine, I knew he was off somewhere high and to the west, between me and Saigon. He told me he would be up all night. That was his job, to take care of me. He would be my relay. With him above, I could get a message back to headquarters immediately. It was comforting to know that he would be up there all night. Normally, infantry on the ground make radio contact every hour on the hour with the guy in the air, but since I was all alone, that meant I would never get any sleep. So I told him not to expect any "commo checks" from me. I was going to bed. If I needed him, I'd holler. He rogered my message, and told me he'd be standing by.

I was fast asleep. Suddenly, I was awakened by horribly loud explosions. Boom. Boom. Boom. They were just terrible, extremely loud and frightening, and they came in, one right after the other. Boom. Boom. Boom. I jumped up, wide eyed. Everybody else was wide eyed, too, looking around in fear. What was it? Suddenly, it all stopped as quickly as it started. Probably 30 or 40 rounds had been fired.

We soon learned what had happened. Dai Uy received word that a small Vietnamese Army outpost, located on the west end of the village, had been mortared. So that's what those explosions were all about! I wondered why they hadn't shelled us. Then I realized it was not their style. They didn't mortar villages, because that's where the people lived. They only mortared Army outposts, or something like that. So, we all went back to sleep.

The next day, December 7th. We were happy to see tanks and armored personnel carriers (APCs) moving into the village. I met the American Captain who was the advisor to the squadron. His name was Captain White, a black officer, kind of heavy set and a real nice guy. We became good buddies. We did a little coordinating about defending the village. His APCs would take a certain part and I the other. We would reinforce the areas most likely to be attacked with his tanks. It looked like we were all going to stay and help protect the village for a few days.

Later that day, trouble. I was hanging around the town square when word reached me to get over to Dai Uy. I grabbed my radio and ran to his location. He was on the north edge of the village. Some of the Rangers had been patrolling that area, when they received word from the villagers that some VC were holed up in a banana grove to the northeast. It was quite close to the village. Actually, the area north of the village was all open fields for about half a mile. This banana grove was in the middle of that field.

Dai Uy asked me to put a gunship strike into this area. I called for one, but while waiting for the chopper to arrive, I had my doubts about this request. Something inside me told me it was all wrong. That banana grove was out in the middle of a flat farm field. Why would VC be hiding there? Of course, they *could* be. But there might be some villagers in there, too. It was just too darn close to the village to smell right to me. I asked the Dai Uy to confirm, to make absolutely sure that no innocent people were in the banana grove. He sent for some village elders. The elders arrived and assured us that no one was in there. "VC, VC," they kept saying.

About this time, the gunships came on station. I oriented them on the target. The first ship made his attack from south to north, guns blazing. I heard the staccato of his machine guns as he made his pass. He was doing a marvelous job. Not one bullet was missing the target. The banana grove was being chewed to bits. What a professional pilot. Suddenly, horror. People came running out of the banana trees, yelling and screaming.

"Villagers," I hollered to myself. I grabbed the radio hand mike and yelled for the pilot to "cease fire."

The chopper immediately stopped firing and banked left. What a sad scene. Villagers streamed out of the banana trees terrified and crying. We ran to meet them. As I approached the group, I saw one man carrying a young boy in his arms. The young man appeared to be dead. His arms hung lifeless, his head tilted back. He had been shot four times. There two bullet holes in his arms and two in his chest. What a bloody mess. I immediately called for the gunship, the same one that hit him, to take him to the hospital. They landed and we put the boy on board. As the chopper lifted skyward, tears welled up in my eyes.

I was furious with myself, with the world, with the war. I tore off my helmet and threw it a million miles away. Then I took my carbine in both hands and drew back to give it a massive heave, too. But something inside stopped me. I stood there, like a statue, arms back motionless. In spite of my overpowering grief, I knew deep down inside me I would need that rifle again. I grabbed my carbine at the middle and began to run back to the village, tears streaming down my face. I had just killed an innocent little boy. All the anger and frustration and pain of five months poured out of me in uncontrollable sobs. Crying, crying, I ran to the village square and then into the back of the church, pausing only to lean my rifle against the back wall. Sitting in the very last pew, I sobbed uncontrollably. "What am I supposed to do, God?," I asked myself. "Quit? Go home? Keep fighting?"

I was so torn. I had once studied for the ministry. Now this...a little boy dead. And at my hands. What was I to do? Quit and go back to the Seminary? I asked God to forgive me and to stop the war, to stop this endless killing of what seemed to be everybody in Vietnam. But as terrible as I felt at the moment, I did not make a decision to quit and go back to the Seminary. I had made God too many promises in the past. I just said, "God, you do with me what you want."

After a few minutes, emptied of tears, I walked to the back of the church, picked up my rifle, and with slow, purposeful steps walked back to the battalion. My place was still with them.

The next day was a day of rest. It was fun to walk around the village, to talk to the people and see the way they lived. I really enjoyed that. I savored every moment. It was a very relaxing day, a time to forget the horror of war.

The next day we got orders to move out. We were going to search the area east of Binh Gia, the direction in which the enemy took off. It would be a combined operation, with Captain White's tanks and APCs assisting us. The morning sun was bright and gleaming to our front. We took a little sniper fire moving east of the village, a shot or two, but nothing really serious. The enemy was not about to take on tanks and armored personnel carriers in open terrain.

Later, the armored personnel carriers reported that they had captured a local VC. I couldn't figure that one out, because there were no other villages around there except this one and all the people there were quite friendly to us. But they reported that they had captured a VC. In the middle of all this, Captain White got word to leave Binh Gia and head back to Vung Tau. It was all very mysterious, because we haven't swept all the way to the end of the open farm fields yet. So we scrapped the operation and headed back to the village. For our part, we were ordered to remain in the village. Captain White would hit the black top west of town and then head south for the coast. We waved good-bye to each other and he took off, his noisy tanks clanking west.

About a half hour later, in the very far distance, we heard explosions. Dai Uy and I looked at each other. It was gun fire. We were too far away to pick up the rattle of rifles, but we could hear the distant thump, thump, of a .50 caliber machine gun, and we could hear explosions. It was a Viet Cong 57 millimeter recoilless rifle, and we both knew it. It could only mean one thing. Captain White was being ambushed. We looked at each other helplessly. What were we to do? By the time we moved cross country, on foot, through all that jungle, it would be over. I stood there, frustrated. I knew what we were supposed to do. We were supposed to go over and help him. I wanted to go, but at the same time, I didn't want to go because they had surely set up a trap for us, too, and we would be playing right into their hands. I stood there frustrated and ashamed. But it was not my decision to make. It was up to the Vietnamese. And they weren't going. Maybe they had been ordered to stay and defend the village regardless of the situation. I never did find out.

Later we got word that Captain White had escaped the ambush. He had been in the middle of a column and should have been killed, but he jammed the accelerator of his jeep to the floor, and drove by all the burning tanks and APCs and got out safe. Not one bullet hit him. Some tanks and tracks made it out too. We later learned that six tracks had been destroyed, seven men were killed, 20 wounded, and 14 had turned up missing. One of the missing was his American Sergeant. The guy just disappeared. It had all happened so quick. Within a few minutes it was all over. After the ambush, Captain White picked up the survivors and headed south. Later the Vietnamese Air Force came over. We could see them off in the distance strafing and bombing. But it was too late. Captain White was headed for Vung Tau, and the VC were headed for home.

The Saigon High Command now ordered Dai Uy Duong to stay in Binh Gia for a few days and protect it. The people were Catholics, and had fled the North and Communism when the Geneva Accords were signed in 1954. That agreement partitioned Vietnam. North Vietnam was to be Communist, and the South was to be Democratic. Since these people did not want to live under Communism, they moved all their possessions and families south in oxcarts and hacked out a new home there in the middle of nowhere. They literally moved an entire village from north to south. All they were seeking was a peaceful life. But once again the Communists, and the war caught up with them.

This would be a good break for me, and a good break for the battalion. No helicopter flights to unknown places, from which we might never return. All we had to do was to get up every morning and protect our own village. I liked that. The village had become home to me. The Dai Uy had arranged for me to live with a family. They lived in what you might call a four room house. It was located right next to the town square. The Dai Uy was located in the house next to mine, so we were right next to each other, and in the heart of the village should they need us.

My new home was owned by a Mr. Sung and his wife and two children. They looked to be about 35 years old, although the wife appeared to be much older, because some of her teeth were missing, and her teeth were black from chewing beetle nut gum. The husband was a very kind man and distinguished looking also. He was a farmer. They had a beautiful five year old daughter that I dearly loved. She was so cute. This was my new home.

My daily routine included getting up early in the morning and walking across the town square to the Catholic Church to attend mass. Everyone in the entire village went to mass every morning at 6:00 a.m. It was wonderful. I sat in the back pew. No one seemed to notice me. Although I was Lutheran, and they were Catholic, I could follow the service pretty well, because our liturgies were somewhat similar. Mostly though, I just worshipped privately in the back, praying and reading my New Testament, while they worshipped up front. I wanted these villagers to know that I was a fellow Christian, and that I was one with them. The service was a little bit different from the Catholic mass back in the states. The people here seemed to participate more. There seemed to be more responses by the people and more singing. It was fun to go there every day. And it was a great way to start the day.

After mass I would usually take a walk around the village, carbine slung over my shoulder. As I walked down the sandy streets, I could see women washing clothes, and men with hoes slung over their shoulders on their way to work, oxcarts being driven by men sitting on their haunches, going out to the fields for the day. Little kids were running around after each other, playing tag and laughing, and pointing their finger at me and giggling.

As I passed by the center of the village, I noticed a mortar crew working out. The Dai Uy had taken some of our Rangers, and one of our mortars, and was giving the local people training on how to use it. This might help them in the future.

I walked over to the market place. It was bustling with activity. The market building had a large sheet metal roof over it and was open on all sides. There were about 15 to 20 large wooden tables set up underneath, with people selling various items. They sold trinkets and cheap little dime store rings, toilet paper, flashlights, batteries, notebook paper, ball point pens, etc. One little stand sold crucifixes. They were beautiful, made of black wood, with a silver figure of Christ mounted on them. I bought one.

Later, I arrived at the meat tables. There were two men there selling meat. Both of them were in the same business, although separately. They coordinated their activities daily, so as not too have too much meat on hand on any one day. The town had no refrigeration, so the butcher killed the cow the night before, and it was sold early the next morning. The village was large enough to support two butchers, so they butchered two cows every day. When the market opened at dawn, they would set their meat out on these wooden tables. They did not set it out on clean pieces of paper, or wrap it in Saran wrap. The meat just sat there on a dirty table, flies and all. Occasionally the butcher would brush the flies away with a miniature broom. The meat was sold in chunks. It was hacked into pieces and sold in one or two pound squares. There was no such thing as ground hamburger, filet mignon, or the various cuts of meat that we are accustomed to. Everything was just hacked into chunks and sold that way. The butchers were usually finished selling by 11:00 a.m. and then took the rest of the day off.

The people later cooked the meat by slicing it into very thin slices, and then fried it in a wok with vegetable oil and soy sauce. A t-bone steak or pot roast was unknown to them.

They also sold the head of the cow. It looked funny lying there, chopped off at the neck, lips curled back, teeth barred, eyeballs staring straight ahead. I suppose

181

somebody would buy the head, scrape the brains out and eat those. The whole scene was a bit grotesque, with chunks of meat sitting on a dirty wooden table, and a cow's head with bulging eyeballs, and flies everywhere.

I found out more and more that Binh Gia was not as isolated as I thought it was. It was connected to Vung Tau by a paved road located about a mile away. This black top highway ran from Xuan Loc, to the north, to Vung Tau in the south. The road wasn't used very much, due to guerrilla activity. However, this did not stop enterprising salesmen from bringing things up from Vung Tau on motorcyclos. The driver rode up front, like on a regular motorcycle, and had a large cargo box mounted on two wheels behind him. The items they brought up for sale included bolts of cloth, ice, beer, and soft drinks. So, a market flourished daily in Binh Gia.

While I was "downtown," I decided to get a haircut. There was a barber shop located on "main street." It consisted of a canvas tarpaulin hung between some poles for shade, a straight back chair, and a barber, with a pair of scissors and comb. That's all he needed. I leaned my carbine up against a tree, (no danger there, the village was perfectly safe), sat down in his wooden chair and told him "Hoc toc," (haircut). I took off my fatigue jacket and he started trimming away. He did a very good job with just the scissors. There were no electric clippers, because there was no electricity in the village.

Meals were great fun too, especially the evening meal. Every day I walked over to the marketplace and bought a chunk of meat. That was my contribution to the family. Vietnamese usually did not eat beef every day. They couldn't afford it. (But they did have pork, chicken, and fish.) So I bought beef for the family daily, and brought it to the lady of the house for preparation for the evening meal. The family, in turn, provided fresh vegetables from their garden, or whatever else they might bring from the market place.

Eating with this family was like going to a Chinese restaurant every night. They had a large, wooden table sitting in the middle of the room. I always sat next to my little girlfriend (their cute little daughter). The wife would then place a large bowl in the center of the table. In this bowl were the thin slices of stir-fried beef in soy sauce. Off to the left would be a large bowl of rice, and to the other side a bowl of vegetables. Each of us had a small bowl in front of us. We would scoop some rice in our bowls and then flavor it by pouring in some "nuoc mam." (Nuoc mam is a fish sauce that was made from compressing dead fish together in a barrel. The sauce that came out the bottom smelled horrible, but tasted delicious.) They also sprinkled soy sauce over the rice. Then we would hold the small rice bowl up to our mouths and shovel the rice in with our chopsticks. Meat and vegetables were eaten directly "out of the pot." You just stuck your chopsticks in, pulled out a piece of meat and transferred it to your mouth. It helped to hold your small rice bowl under your mouth as you chewed, because sometimes the meat slipped off your chopsticks.

If the main dish was chicken, you would find that it was prepared quite differently than in the States. They took a perfectly good piece of chicken (like a leg), and chopped it into four of five pieces with a meat cleaver. There was, of course, always a piece of bone left in the middle of the meat. I often wondered what to do about that until one day I saw someone spit the bone out of their mouth and onto the floor, and a dog came along and carried it off.

After every evening meal, the father and I would play a game of sorts with the kids. The children had to memorize a portion of their Catholic Catechism every day, and so we decided to let them recite it to me every night. Of course, I didn't know Vietnamese well enough to catch any errors on their part. But if they did a good job, the father would signal me with a slight smile or nod of the head while the children weren't watching. I, in turn, would tell them they had done a good job and would praise them in Vietnamese, and then give them a big handshake. They were just tickled pink to be able to recite their Catechism to me. And it was lots of fun for me too. I enjoyed sitting there every night. Sometimes the recitations went along for two full minutes. The Catholics taught them well.

After dinner I would walk around town with Father Thuy, one of the three Catholic Priests. He was a very young man, probably about 30 years old. He had been educated in Switzerland and spoke fluent English. The other two Priests in this village were much older men and served the other two chapels. (There was a total of three churches in the town; the main church in the center of the village, and two smaller chapels on either end.) Every evening Father Thuy and I would go for a walk around the village, smoking our cigars and talking. I enjoyed those walks very much.

I learned a lot from him, about the treatment of the Church under Communism, and life in North Vietnam. It was not good. We walked slowly and casually through the deserted streets, puffing on our cigars. It was so quiet and beautiful in Binh Gia at night. No traffic. No automobiles. Nothing. Not a sound. Not even a bird. Just a beautiful Vietnamese evening. Down the street a kerosene lamp would flicker inside a home. Nothing else disturbed the black beauty of the evening. I loved the village and the life it offered.

The first night I stayed in Mr. Sung's home I had a problem. I wanted to sleep in my hammock, but as their guest of honor they wanted me to sleep in their bed. They insisted that they sleep in their hammocks. There was only one problem. A Vietnamese bed had no springs or mattresses. It was nothing more than flat boards laid end to end. In reality, it was just like sleeping on top of a picnic table, very, very hard. They did lay a thin straw mat on top of the boards, but that didn't make much difference. So that first night they insisted that I sleep on their bed. I knew, of course, that if I did not accept, I would be insulting them, because the Vietnamese have some very strict rules about being a good host. So rather than offend them, I acquiesced to their persistent demands. That night I laid down to sleep on their bed, but I could not fall asleep. It was like sleeping on top of a flat rock. I tossed and turned all night long, and felt miserable the next day. My bones ached terribly.

The next night they insisted again that I sleep in their bed. I still couldn't tell them no, because I still didn't want to offend them. So I walked over to Dai Uy's house and got a small bottle of rice wine (white lightening) and sipped it all down. That made me sleepy and I was able to doze off in that "gawd awful" bed. But again the next morning, when I awoke, my joints ached something awful. I just couldn't stand it. It was time to have a polite conversation with the man of the house.

So the next day I convinced him, in as diplomatic a way as possible, that I should sleep in my hammock, and that he should sleep in his bed. Since we had both done the very best we could, protocol had been satisfied. I honored them by being a good guest, and they honored me by being a good host, and everyone lived happily ever after. I noticed that when they did go to bed in the evening they used no covers. The man slept in his boxer shorts and the lady in her pajamas. They didn't use pillows either. They just lay their head down on that hard bed. They did take something that appeared to be a small, round pillow, and placed it between their legs. That roll, about nine inches thick, allowed air to pass between their legs at night and kept them cool.

One of the things I had to do every day, of course, was take a shower. But how do you take a shower, when you live in a house which has no bathroom? The answer was "the well" out back. I did the same thing that everybody else did. I headed for the well, stripped off my clothes (down to my boxer shorts), threw an empty bucket down the well with a rope, pulled it up, poured the water over my head and then soaped myself down from head to foot. When finished, I simply threw the bucket down the well again and poured three to four more buckets of fresh water over my head, until I was all rinsed off. It made for a very refreshing bath.

One day while I was in the village, Colonel Wilson flew in. He had a couple of men with him. One was Brigadier General Throckmorton, and the other a photographer. Colonel Wilson asked me, "Did you get shot at today?"

I replied "No."

He said, "Did you get shot at yesterday?"

Again I answered "No."

Then he said, "Did you get shot at last week?"

I said, "Yes."

Then he said, "Here's your CIB," and he pinned it on me.

A CIB is the Combat Infantryman's Badge. It's a blue badge with a silver rifle on it, and is given to infantrymen who have been in combat for 30 days or more. I had earned this badge almost five months before but by the time the paperwork had been processed through Saigon, here I was receiving it at a later date. But I was happy to get it. It was a badge of great honor and respect among all American infantrymen, and I had finally earned mine. I was very proud of it. We posed for a picture and then Colonel Wilson flew off again.

While living in the village I had to purify my water every day. I noticed that the Vietnamese did not purify theirs. It is incorrect to say that the natives get accustomed to the water, and never get yellow jaundice or hepatitis. They get just as sick as anybody else. These poor folks just didn't have any tablets. They were simply not available. I, for my part, had received very strict instructions from the American Army not to drink any water from any well, or any other source, even though it looked perfectly clear and clean. So every day I filled my canteen with water and then threw in two small iodine tablets, and let them dissolve for 20 minutes. After that, the water was okay to drink. I did know that I had ingested some bad water from time to time, by eating in Vietnamese homes, because they washed their vegetables in contaminated water. But I hoped that by the time they steamed and fried the vegetables, it would kill most of the germs.

Another thing I did healthwise was to take a malaria tablet once a week. It was a very, very large tablet, rather like a horse tablet. It was so large that it was actually difficult to swallow. I didn't like the tablet, because it left a bad taste in my mouth for about five hours, and gave me a terrible case of diarrhea. But I also knew that if I didn't take the tablet I was going to get malaria. I could remember back when I was grade school that one of my teachers, a Mr. Peitsch, had malaria. He had contracted it while fighting in the South Pacific. I vividly remember how he used to turn yellow and pale, and then start shaking uncontrollably in front of our class. I told myself I wasn't going to let that happen to me. So I took my tablet faithfully.

Later a helicopter came in and dropped off a six pack of beer, my mail and some newspapers. I was surprised to see my picture in the *Stars and Stripes.* It depicted Colonel Wilson giving me my combat badge. I would have to save this copy and mail it home.

After a few days of this wonderful village life, it was time to go home. Dai Uy got word that the battalion was to move out. The road back to Binh Hoa had been cleared, and we were returning to become Corps Reserve again. It was a sad time for me, as I had to leave the village, and I could see that is was sad for the Rangers, also. They too, were sorry to go. They had made many good friends there and there were many good-byes to be said.

As I walked down the street and out of the village toward the trucks, an old man came up to me and started telling me something in Vietnamese. I couldn't understand him, so I waited for Dai Uy to catch up. Then I turned around and asked the Dai Uy what the old man was saying. He talked to the man for a moment and replied, "He wants your grenades." (I had two hand grenades, one hanging on either side of my harness.)

At first I thought he wanted my smoke grenades, which were hanging on my harness, just below the hand grenades. But no, he wanted my hand grenades, the kind that explode and kill people. So I asked the Dai Uy why he wanted my hand grenades. The Dai Uy talked to him for a moment and then turned back to me and said, "This man says that when you leave, the VC will come back and cause much trouble. He says, 'I am too old to fight, but I can throw grenades in the dark.'"

What a testimony to a simple people who just want to defend their own way of life. I gave him my grenades, moved down the street, got into my jeep and drove away.

We headed straight west out of the village down a dirt road until we came to the Vietnamese Army outpost (the one that had been mortared). What a mishmash of barbed wire, piled up dirt, and old shacks. It didn't look like a fort at all. But there it was, out in the middle of nowhere. I

187

wondered how long it would be before it was overrun. We hit the blacktop and turned left. Later, we passed by all of Captain White's burned out vehicles. All along the road security was now posted for us; Vietnamese infantry, some local forces, and occasionally an armored personnel carrier. The road was clear all the way down to Vung Tau. And I was glad of it. We headed south. The road ran downhill for a long way, but gradually it leveled out, and we left the jungle behind us. We then entered marshy country. Ahead of us, I could see the South China Sea. We bore to the right and took a bypass around Vung Tau. It was all safe in this area. I saw vegetable stands along the road, kids playing, so many other signs of normal life.

We headed north again, toward Binh Hoa and "ambush alley." I was a little bit scared, because if the VC did come off of the mountain, we would never know it until they hit us, and that section of road got hit at least once a month. My heart pounded every mile of the way and with each curve in the road. But finally, we made it safely past "ambush alley" and then continued our trek north.

Eventually, we began to see more and more villages and finally Bear Cat. We were just south of Binh Hoa now. I was so thankful to be back safe again that I began to sing *"Praise God From Whom All Blessings Flow"* at the top of my lungs. The words reverberated around the inside of the truck cab. The Vietnamese truck driver sitting to my left didn't know what to make of it, but he knew I was happy, and he started laughing and grinning too. We were both glad to be safe and home again.

CHAPTER 15

When I got back to Train Compound I found out that a new Advisor had been assigned to the battalion. His name was Bennet—a Sergeant. He had been assigned to me under some rather unusual circumstances. It seems he had been in Special Forces up north, but had been kicked out of the unit, because he had punched an officer in the face. Now that's a very serious charge in the Army, striking an officer. However, in this case, there were some extenuating circumstances. He had known the man before he had become an officer. They were old enlisted buddies. Later, after the man had graduated from OCS, they both happened to end up in the same unit. Somehow or another they got into an argument and then a fight. So, instead of court-martialing him, they transferred him to a Ranger Battalion. I took that as an ominous sign, a sort of "back door punishment." They were going to pay him back by putting him in an outfit that took heavy casualties.

The next day we got another man. His name was Craft. His rank was Private. I couldn't believe we were getting this man. He was a very young kid, barely 18 years old. Somebody told me that a new man had been assigned to my unit, so I went looking for him. I found him lying down, resting on top of a table out of doors. When I approached, he snapped to attention. The only problem was, he snapped to attention lying down. An experienced soldier knew better than that. Then he saluted me lying down. I knew right away that he was very, very green, because you always stood up when an officer approached you. To snap to attention and salute lying down was really funny.

I talked to him for a while and found out that he had never volunteered to come to Vietnam. Everyone assigned to Vietnam was supposed to be a volunteer. Furthermore, he had never been to Ranger School, nor had he received any kind of commando training. He had absolutely no experience. Yet there he was, a brand new recruit, fresh out of advanced training, assigned to a highly elite, all volunteer, combat unit. The only reason he got the assignment was that there was a vacant slot for an English speaking radio operator in my Battalion. The poor guy didn't know a thing about combat or the infantry. All he got after basic training was a short course on how to run a backpack radio and then off to Vietnam.

Knowing this, I went to Corps Headquarters and talked to the Personnel Officer. I told him that I liked the kid (he really was a nice person), but I just felt he was too "green," and that something might happen to him. He was either going to get killed or captured. The Personnel Officer agreed with me. He said he had a young Buck Sergeant with field experience, who was presently serving as the Corps radio operator, and he could switch the two over in a couple of weeks. The switch would take place on the first of January. Could I wait until then? (It was the 15th of December.) I said, "Fine, I'll keep him two weeks and then we'll make the switch."

The next day, the Corps Sergeant Major came to see me while I was eating lunch. He asked if he could talk to me privately outside. I told him "Of course" and met him a few minutes later out by the big shade tree.

He looked very concerned. He then told me that Sergeant Bennet had gotten into an argument with him the previous night in the bar and had socked him in the mouth. Now this is something you just didn't do in the Army. You are not supposed to fight in a club, and above all, you're not supposed to hit a superior non-commissioned officer, much less the Corps Sergeant Major. He then told me that he had received promotion orders on Bennet, promoting him to the next higher rank, but as the Corp. Sergeant Major, he was also duty bound to court-martial Bennet for hitting him. So, he said, "Let's make a

190

deal. I won't court-martial Bennet if you agree we don't promote him."

I replied, "You got a deal."

So, he tore up Sergeant Bennet's promotion orders right there in front of me, and that was the end of that.

For about two weeks we had been following some information on three captured pilots. We had received word that three American pilots had been shot down in separate incidents, but were now together in a POW camp near the Cambodian Border. Corps had begun planning a rescue mission to try and free them. I was included in on all the planning sessions. I looked at the target area on the map. It was right next to the Cambodian border, no more than 1000 yards from the line, but still inside Vietnam. The area involved was nothing but trackless jungle. It was hard to say where Cambodia began and Vietnam ended.

Right along side the camp was a small, dry, lake bed. Some reports said that the Americans were held in this camp in cages, while other reports said they were held in tunnels. Since this was going to be a surprise attack, Corps had issued an order that absolutely no one would fly over the area, so as not to tip our hand. (One of the quickest ways to let the enemy know that you are coming is to increase air activity over his "house." First an Artillery Officer usually flies up and look at it. Then an Operations Officer. Next the Air Force. Then the helicopter pilots, and finally, the infantry assault troop commander. It doesn't take long for a guy on the ground to look up and figure out why all those people up there are looking down on him. So Colonel Wilson put out the word, "There will be no overflights of this area. Absolutely none." And he meant it. This would be a top secret operation. Of course, we could get photos of the area from high altitude aircraft (ones that flew at extremely high altitudes, like the U-2). It would be impossible for the enemy to see or hear them. And they took very good pictures indeed. With photos like these we were able to examine the jungle, the dry lake bed and the place where we thought the camp was.

A part of the plan called for the use of CS/CN and tear

191

gas. That was my idea. Tear gas made you cry and CS/CN made you "throw up." My idea was to dump all kinds of tear and choking gas on the enemy. Then they wouldn't be able to see or breath as we came down on top of them. As soon as the gas dissipated, they would be "healthy as a horse" again, and we would be long gone. It was all very simple, and it wouldn't harm anyone. Corps agreed with my idea.

We began training for the mission, using gas as one of the elements to the attack plan. We drew gas masks. They were brand new, very good ones, with a black face, not like the old fashioned models that had a little hose running out the side. These fit flush up against our faces and had large eye pieces. We would have to practice wearing them if we were to use them well and practice under every conceivable condition possible; on patrol, loading the helicopters, jumping off, talking on the radio, drinking water, etc. We simply had to find out if we could fight and wear them at the same time. The helicopter pilots started practicing with them, too.

Finally, the day came that we married up for a practice together. We were to fly to the airstrip at Bear Cat, dismount, execute a fake raid, rescue prisoners, get back to the air field, call in the choppers and fly out ... all wearing gas masks. The plan was the same as the real raid now scheduled for Christmas Day.

There were lines of Rangers standing around wearing gas masks, looking like something out of a space war. Then the helicopters came in and landed. I noticed that they came in kind of "raggedy." We climbed on board and took off. I looked up in the cockpit. The pilots were wearing gas masks, too. (I had heard that the gas mask lens distorted the pilots depth perception because they were made out of plastic. This really concerned me because it could be very dangerous. We could run into each other up there in the sky.)

The time came for the landing at Bear Cat. I noticed that the pilots hovered very, very high above the ground. I could only assume that they were having depth perception problems. Finally, they set down. We hopped out and they took off. The next lift came in right behind us. As they landed, the lead chopper hit the ground too hard and pitched forward on its runners. It pitched so far forward that I thought the blades were going to strike the ground and wreck the aircraft, but it rocked safely back to earth. It was all very scary and proved to me that the pilots were having great depth perception problems with their masks.

It made me very anxious about the raid. All it would take was for one of those blades to clang together at 2000 feet and we would all fall to a horrible death. I didn't like it at all. Also, I was having second thoughts about how effective the tear gas was. Tear gas dissipates very rapidly. I was afraid it would blow away too quickly, leaving us all exposed to the enemy. In addition, I was worried that the tear gas would not penetrate the jungle and consequently the VC beneath the thick trees might not be effected by it at all.

The Corps staff insisted I was wrong. In any event, I knew we would need "tons" of tear gas to get the job done, so I convinced them to use heavy Air Force cargo planes (C-123) to do the spraying. In addition, Army helicopters would drop hundreds of tear gas hand grenades directly on top of the target. Even so, I still wasn't convinced. Something told me it just wasn't going to be that easy. In the end, I feared it was going to be "too much jungle and too little gas." It was a big world out there.

I came up with another idea. I knew of another type of gas that would fit our plans much better and I hoped we could use it. At the time it was a classified "secret." This gas was like LSD. One pass over the enemy and, bam, he went "blitzo." One sniff, and the enemy would be walking around like zombies, dazed and unable to do anything for hours. I knew in my heart that this was what we really should be using. We could spray it on them a half hour before the operation. Because the gas was colorless and had no odor, they would never know what hit them. Within a half an hour they would all be walking around like zombies. All we would have to do is fly in with one helicopter and pick up the prisoners. It would be as simple as that. I pushed very hard for this plan, because I did not want to take a chance that we might lose a single prisoner, nor did I want to land in a veritable hornets nest. I was fully convinced in my own mind, the tear gas would not work. The G-3 went along with my new idea, and Saigon concurred too. They took it all the way to Pacific Headquarters in Hawaii and they agreed. Eventually, the request went all the way back to President Johnson, who denied it. I was told that he said that it was "too controversial." We would have to go in using tear gas and CS/CN only.

I looked at the lake on the map. It was too small to bring in all the choppers at one time. Consequently, we would be forced to land about 1000 yards away, at a larger clearing, and then work our way toward the camp. I quickly calculated that by the time we worked our way over to the camp from this LZ, the tear gas in the air would have dissipated and the enemy would have grabbed the prisoners and ran. It would take us at least a good half hour to get through all the jungle. So, I decided to send one chopper in, all alone, directly on top of the enemy in the dry lake bed next to the POW camp. If all went well, if surprise were on our side, if the POWs were lightly guarded, if the tear gas worked, then one chopper loaded with ten Rangers could get the job done. But there were a lot of "ifs" to the plan. The lone helicopter mission soon picked up the name "suicide chopper." We all sort of joked about it while working on the map. To my surprise, Sergeant Bennet walked up and volunteered to take the "suicide chopper" in. In a way I was not surprised. He was a very brave man. We also asked for ten Ranger volunteers and immediately got them. I made a mental note to give Sergeant Bennet my best radio, the PRC-25. I would take in the old PRC-10. The PRC-25 would give him instantaneous and powerful contact with the support forces above, in the event he needed help.

December 25th. It was time to go in. We moved out to the area in back of the insane asylum and lined up in loads. The choppers came in. We hopped on board and took off. We had three squadrons of helicopters, enough to lift the whole battalion at once, so we would all be landing at the same time. No one put on their mask. It was too early. About five minutes out from the objective we started masking. The pilots did the same.

I looked out to my front. I could see the objective. The C-123s had already sprayed the area and now the helicopters were moving back and forth dropping tear gas containers. White clouds sprouted up all over the area. It looked pretty thick. But I just knew it was not going to last. Now it was time to get scared. We were at 1500 feet and the helicopters started tightening up their formation. They got so close together that it seemed like their blades were intertwined. Pop, pop, pop. We began our descent. I just prayed to God that one of them wouldn't hit the other and take us to a falling, screaming death. Suddenly, the "suicide chopper" peeled off and headed for the lake. We continued straight ahead. The helicopters flared and we landed.

We all raced for the jungle. We quickly got organized and pushed off. There was no contact. We wormed our way through the jungle as quickly as we could, pushing aside bushes, moving by compass azimuth towards the unseen dry lake ahead. After a few minutes we got a call from Bennet on the radio. Nobody was there. The camp was empty. The whole operation was now useless. But we would have to push on through to check things out.

One Vietnamese soldier took off his mask and began sniffing around. Then he giggled. He knew the gas had dissipated long ago. The gas had been completely worthless. It hadn't worked at all. So we took off our masks and pressed forward. Finally, we arrived at the dry lake. Sergeant Bennet was there with his commando squad. The area was secure.

I checked out the lake bed. It looked like we could only bring in one chopper at a time for the lift out. Now for a decision. We could all walk back through the jungle to the original LZ and lift out of there all at one time, or we could pull out from where we were, one ship at a time. Since it was Christmas Day, and there was no point in dragging out the operation any longer than necessary, I recommended to Dai Uy Duong that we lift out one at a time. He could go with the first lift and monitor the operation from above. I would fly out with the last helicopter. I also insisted Sergeant Bennet fly out on the first helicopter. He deserved a break. Dai Uy agreed with my plan so we

195

called in the ships, one at a time.

It took a long time to get the whole battalion out. Finally, it was my turn. I told the last helicopter to keep on circling and to land in exactly three minutes. This would give our security scouts time to make it back to the LZ. I signaled to the Vietnamese Lieutenant in charge of the scouts to get his men in. He hollered at them across the LZ and they all came running. We quickly lined up on the edge of the jungle. The chopper landed and we raced out and hopped on board. The chopper hovered, nosed forward and started moving down field. We all brought our rifles up to our shoulders, fingers on the trigger, ready to fire. We swept forward like an eagle skimming the ground, then up and over the edge of the jungle. Nobody fired at us. We headed back home for Christmas.

After landing back at Binh Hoa, Tau met me with the jeep, and I returned to Train Compound for a turkey dinner. Although it was past 1:00 p.m. and the mess was closed, there was still some leftovers with gravy and stuffing and all the trimmings. So I got to have a great Christmas dinner after all. It was so good to be back.

I had just finished eating when the G-3, LTC Plummer, walked in and asked me where the G-5 was. (The G-5 was an American Army Captain who worked with the Corps Public Information Office. They did public information, propaganda, announcements, brochures, that sort of thing.) I told him I didn't know, and respectfully inquired why he was asking me about him. He then told me that this Captain had gone along with us on the operation that morning. At the last minute they had gotten their own chopper and tagged along in the formation as the last ship. The G-5 had taken along his RVN propaganda team; two Vietnamese with a portable PA set. Their mission was to set up a loud speaker and ask the VC not to resist, but to surrender to the landing forces.

I told him I knew nothing about it. Then I told him we did not come out the same LZ that we had landed in. The full impact of that statement hit us both at the same time. The American Captain and his little propaganda team were probably still out there in the jungle broadcasting to the enemy.

196

LTC Plummer quickly summoned a helicopter to pick them up. I didn't go along. No one went along. A pilot who had been on the operation knew where to go. He flew out there. Sure enough, there was a team of three men standing down there in the middle of a jungle clearing, speakers on full volume, telling the enemy to "come out with their hands up." I assume that the only reason these three guys didn't end up as prisoners of war was that, either there were no VC out there at all, or the VC heard their loud speakers and wrongfully deduced that there must be thousands of them out there and left them alone. In any event, the chopper came in and picked them up. Boy, were they ever lucky. It was one of those ridiculously funny things that could only happen in a war.

The next day at Train Compound I received a telephone call from "Mirth 6." (He was the Major in charge of the helicopters that hauled us into battle.) He told me that the Filipino nurses from Tay Ninh were in Saigon and that we both had dates for the evening. He told me that he'd pick me up over at the chopper pad at Binh Hoa Air Base at 6:00 p.m. So Tau drove me over to the base, I hopped on board his helicopter and we headed for Saigon. Flying along the four lane highway, I could see the lights of the trucks and cars below, blinking and moving along in a regular pattern as if there was no war at all.

We landed at Tan San Nhut Airport. He had a jeep parked there. We hopped in and drove over to pick up the girls. They were staying at the Filipino Ambassador's house. I got in the back seat with my date, and he got in the front seat with his, and we headed for a French restaurant. It was all very nice. We had a glass of wine, some delicious French food, French bread, and later dessert which consisted of a slice of cheese, followed by more wine. Then we just drove around town.

Since the curfew was about to take effect, it was time to get the girls home. As we pulled up in front of the house, we made a date with them for the next day to take them to the Saigon Zoo. Then we headed back to the Air Field.

When we got back, a message was waiting for us. We were going on an operation in the morning. A Vietnamese

Paratroop Battalion was in deep trouble. Captain Throckmorton, their Advisor, had been shot through the stomach. He landed in a hot LZ and got hit the moment he stepped off the chopper. They threw him right back on the same helicopter that he came out on. He was now in serious condition in a hospital in Saigon. (His father was General Throckmorton, the Commanding General of all Advisors in Vietnam.)

We would be flying out in the morning to help the rest. Back at Train Compound I lay down on my bunk. I was scared! I knew one of our guys got it real bad, and a lot of paratroopers were out there hurt and wounded, and we would have to fly out to the same spot tomorrow morning. Overhead I heard a chopper passing by. I knew that very soon I would hear those blades again, calling for me, calling to carry me into battle. As I lay on my bunk I asked myself, "Will I get mine tomorrow?"

I opened up my pocket New Testament and read from the Psalms. One Psalm, in particular, gave me great comfort. It was the 139th Psalm. *"Whither shall I go or whither shall I flee from Thy presence. If I ascend up into heaven, Thou art there. If I make my bed in hell, behold Thou art there. If I take the wings of the morning, and dwell in the uttermost parts of the sea, even there shall Thy hand lead me, and Thy right hand shall hold me."* I closed the New Testament, put it back in my fatigue pocket and fell fast asleep.

Morning came. The Rangers were all lined up. It was a quiet morning with a bright sun. There was a heavy feeling in the air. Mirth 6 came in with his choppers, and we hopped on and took off. Initially we followed the Vung Tau Highway south, but then we veered east and began to lose altitude. Up ahead I could see smoke on the LZ. We landed, and I leaped off and made a run for it. The choppers took off again.

There was no contact. I didn't know where the Paratroop Battalion was. In fact, I didn't know anything about this operation except that I was on it. I hadn't been briefed. I had gotten in too late the night before. But Dai Uy knew, of course. We moved off the LZ. Dai Uy then told me that we hadn't landed on top of the paratroopers, but a few miles away and to the side. Our job would be to look for the VC, and to move cross country after them. We headed east. The chopper blades faded in the distance. It was all quiet. Then began a very long, monotonous, but scary walk through the jungle. Would we run into the VC, or would this be just another hot day? I bounced back between boredom and sheer terror.

After about an hour I heard the blades of a single helicopter popping overhead. They became louder and louder. Suddenly, my radio crackled. I picked up the hand mike and listened. It was Mirth 6. He was in the chopper directly over me. He knew it was hot and steamy down there where I was, so after he got his ships safely home, he had decided to come back and have a little fun with me. The radio cackled with his voice, "Boy, it's cold up here with the window down. In fact, it's so cold that I'm going to have to close my window because I'm freezing to death."

Then he burst into mock laughter. He just kept it up, taunting me. Then he closed with, "Well, I have to fly back to Saigon now. I have a date with two pretty Filipino nurses. See you later. Have a nice day ground pounder, you hear me?"

Again, laughter reverberated across the airwaves. Zap! He got me real bad. The chopper turned and headed northwest. I laughed out loud. What a funny guy!

We continued patrolling into the next day. We were now north of Vung Tau, near ambush alley. The battalion had had it. They had seen too much combat, too much action, too many days of walking. The men were bone tired. Chan, my radio operator, could no longer keep up with me. I had to pull him along by the microphone cord. Suddenly, there was a fire fight to our front. Bullets snapped and crackled over my head. I lay down. It was another one of a hundred, endless battles. I wondered to myself, "Will we be overrun this time? Will I get mine?"

I was so tired of waiting to be killed. I was tired of walking in terror, day after day, step by step, wondering when I was going to be killed. Of course, I didn't want to die. I wanted to live. But, I could close my eyes and see myself in a flag draped coffin. My brother and dad were crying over me. I knew how sad it would be for them but I just couldn't take it anymore. All I wanted to do at that moment was die. I wanted the suspense, the agony, the fear of not knowing when, what step, what day, what hour....I wanted it all to end. I wanted peace. I hoped that a bullet would come at that very moment and finish me off while I was ready for it. I was going to get it anyway. Better now than later. Better now at this moment while I was waiting, while I was ready. I closed my eyes. I could feel death around me. Its present in the jungle like a mist. I could almost reach out and touch it. I spoke these words penned by myself to Bach's immortal tune, *"Come Sweet Death."*

Come sweet death,
Thy soft wings gently my soul enfold.
Lift now this pain scarred heart,
From earth, to heaven above,
Where verdant pastures grow,
And I shall dwell in peace forever more.

I noticed too, that of late, I was starting to get the "one thousand yard stare." Lots of combat vets in the Pacific in World War II had it. They just stared straight ahead and thought about other things. I too, daydreamed to leave my situation. It was an escape mechanism. I simply was not there. I put myself into a state of nothingness. A person just could not be out there, day after day, and think only of dying. It would drive you crazy. So I escaped. I put my mind in a mental blank and stared straight ahead. The fire fight ended and we got up and moved out, alive again.

The next day we were still on patrol. The men were so exhausted. It was worthless for us to be out there. They were all like walking mummies. I had never seen it so bad. They were just completely gone. Right then and there, I made a decision that I was going to call in a chopper, and head back to Corps and demand that they pull the whole battalion back in. I promised Dai Uy that I was going to get the battalion out. I gave him my solemn word, right out there in the jungle, that even if I had to resign, quit or whatever, I would get the battalion out. The abuse by the Vietnamese Command had gone on too long.

We shot an azimuth to the nearest clearing where a helicopter could land and moved toward it. By the time we got there, the chopper I had previously ordered, was already circling. It landed, and I hopped on board and rode back to Corps. Passing over friendly villages I knew I was safe again. What a great feeling it was to leave the jungle and to come back to peace and tranquility.

I landed on the Corps chopper pad and walked right into Headquarters without taking off my combat gear. I couldn't help but notice what a clean, immaculate place it was. In contrast, I was covered with mud and slop, wearing a dirty uniform with two live grenades hanging from my shoulder harness, carrying ammunition, a rifle and needed a shave real bad. The Corps Staff Officer, an Army Major (and kind of a wimpy guy) was sitting behind his desk. He yelled at me not to bring my grenades inside. He began to lecture me that this was against Corps policy.

I strode right past him and into LTC Plummer's office. I sat down and spilled out the whole story. I told him that the battalion was exhausted. I told him about the fact that all they have had to eat was rice, and Vietnamese can't live on rice alone. They get too emaciated. They just go into a zombie state and drag their rifles on the ground. The battalion was completely combat ineffective now. I also told him about the problems we had been having with the districts; that there was no artillery, that we patrolled in restricted zones where aircraft routinely jettison their "left over" bombs, that we patrolled in Special Forces ambush areas without informing Special Forces, and that we have no radio contact with our higher headquarters, and worst of all no medevac. No nothing. The situation was ridiculous and very dangerous. I told him too, that since we had moved down from Tay Ninh to Binh Hoa, the men had had no time off with their families. They had no housing. Their families were literally living out in the streets. I told him that, in no uncertain terms the battalion had to come out, and it had to come out now. Then I told him in a very calm but measured voice, "I'm not going back out until they get the word to come back in."

The Colonel drew back and thought for a moment. He

201

knew the situation was desperate. Even though the decision was not his to make, he agreed with me and gave me his solemn promise, "The battalion will be brought back. I'll talk to the Vietnamese immediately."

I thanked him from the bottom of my heart and headed back for the chopper. I flew back out to the battalion. Dai Uy was waiting for me in the landing zone. I could see the look of anticipation on his face. I smiled and told him, "We're going home."

He grinned from ear to ear. At that moment I felt like we had become brothers. It was a very emotional moment, because he knew that I loved the battalion as much as he did. An inexplicable bond had been established between us, forged by war and difficult times.

It was time to move out again. We continued to patrol. Later, Dai Uy received a message to cancel the operation and return to Binh Hoa. We both looked at each other knowingly. Then we turned west and headed down a jungle trail for the Vung Tau Highway. Suddenly a sniper opened up, just as we came to a dirt road crossing. Everybody got down. If we tried to "take him out," it would be the usual story. We would lose five men and in the end the sniper would take off running. So, we all took turns running across the intersection. Sometimes one man would cover the other with a burst of submachine gun fire. Other times, they would just leap across the road as fast as they could, counting on surprise to deceive the enemy. The sniper didn't seem to have an accurate shot at us, but he was bringing bullets into the road junction. I got the feeling he knew where we were, but he couldn't get a good bead on us.

Nevertheless, we each had to take our chance crossing the road. Soon it was my turn. I grabbed my carbine at the middle, lowered my head and charged across. I plunged safely into the jungle on the other side. But I was angry, angry at this sniper and angry at the situation. I wanted to pay this guy back for all the fear and inconvenience he had caused me. So I walked up to Dai Uy and told him that I wanted "time on target" on the road junction, just as soon as we got past. (Time on target meant that all the canons from all over the area would fire in such a way that all of their shells would land on the enemy at the same time. In some cases, depending on how much artillery support you had, up to one hundred shells could impact on the same spot instantly and without warning.) And that's what I wanted for this guy. We passed safely by the intersection and Dai Uy placed the order on the radio. Then I heard the thump, thump, thump of distant canon far away. Then the shrieking of 105, 155, and 8 inch shells overhead. The exact area from where the sniper fire came erupted with tremendous violence. The earth shook with terrible explosions and noise. Black smoke and pieces of jungle cascaded into the sky. I could only hope that at the precise moment when all that artillery impacted, the sniper had stood up wondering where we all had gone, and the shrapnel had cut him into a thousand pieces. I was beginning to want revenge.

CHAPTER 16

December 29th. A day that will live in infinity, at least for me. We got the word to assemble at Corps Headquarters. Things were going badly at Binh Gia, the same village we had rescued before. There was heavy fighting down there. It was all very sketchy. There was some talk of the village having been overrun, other talk of a Ranger Battalion blocked on the west end of the village. Nobody knew anything for sure, except there was big trouble. We would be flying in to clear the village.

Dai Uy and I did a hasty map study while waiting for the choppers to come in. He planned to land south of the village in two separate groups and then head north. One LZ would be at the extreme end of the village with Companies One and Two going in there. Sgt. Bennet and Pvt. Craft would accompany this group. I planned to give them my best radio. I would go in with the Dai Uy and Companies Three and Four, just south and center of the village. Then when everyone had landed, we would attack north together. Bennet and Craft went in on the first wave, but their group waited on the ground until the helicopters came back and picked us up, so we could all attack together.

The first lift arrived and Bennet's group took off. We waited for what seemed to be hours. Then the helicopters returned. I climbed on board and sat down facing out the door, legs dangling, waiting for take off. Suddenly, the Vietnamese Corp G-3 arrived and ran up to my chopper and shouted above the roar of the blades, "Be careful, I think maybe ambush."

In the same instant we lifted off. How nice! An ambush. But it was too late now. We were on our way. Enroute we got word from Sgt. Bennet, who was already on the ground, that everything was all quiet. Also, we would have gunships scouting our LZ prior to arrival. They would find out if there was a reception party waiting for us or not. After about a 30 minute flight, we peeled off to the left and started downward. I could see the village and fields up ahead. Off to the south, gunships raced up and down the LZ at ground level ready to fire at anything that moved. Evidently, the LZ was not hot.

We landed. I raced off as usual and lay down. The choppers picked up and left. Now it was all quiet. Nothing but a bright, shiny day. It scared me. We moved out. We got about half way to the village when all hell broke loose. Mortar rounds started falling. There was a tremendous volume of rifle and machine gun fire to our front and it was all heading our way. Bullets were flying everywhere, cracking all around us. But no one got down. We continued to walk forward, using marching fire (firing from the shoulder as we walked). I got a call from someone in the air, probably a chopper pilot. He said to be on the lookout for another Ranger Battalion in the area and not to get in a fire fight with them. I shouted this over to Dai Uy. He shouted back over the din of the battle, "Not Ranger, this VC."

We approached a banana tree grove growing in the middle of all these farm fields. A bullet sawed off a large banana tree leaf to my front. It spiraled downward in slow motion. I was mesmerized by this oddity. Suddenly my trance was broken by a huge explosion to my left, not more than 15 yards away. And what an explosion! Black smoke and dust everywhere. A shell had just exploded. It was probably an enemy 82mm mortar or maybe even a recoilless rifle shell. Miraculously, I was not hurt. Why wasn't I cut into a hundred pieces by the shrapnel? Strange! Probably, the half of the shell facing me failed to explode into tiny fragments, as it was supposed to and flew past me in one big chunk. It was my lucky day. But I didn't have time to dwell on the subject.

We moved forward again. There was a terrible fire

fight going on, lots of noise and bullets everywhere. But nobody was lying down. Nobody was running away. Everyone was just walking forward, firing their rifles from the shoulder as they went. I was about 20 yards from the banana trees, when some men stepped out of them to my front. They had on Ranger uniforms and steel helmets with a black panther face painted on the front. (Our battalion didn't use that helmet, but most of the other Ranger Battalions did.) Suddenly it all came to me. We had run into another Ranger Battalion and were in a terrible fire fight with them, killing each other. What a mess. I looked to my left. One of our .30 calibre machine gun teams was lying there firing away. I shouted to them in Vietnamese, "Ngung lai, ngung lai," (stop firing, stop firing).

Then I looked back to my front. At this time one of those men directly to my front shouldered his rifle and fired dead straight at me. I heard the loud thump of a bullet hitting a body behind me and air being expelled from someone's lungs. He had missed me and killed the Medic standing to my right. I saw the medic fall as I dove for the ground. I immediately realized that these were Viet Cong dressed in Ranger uniforms. I glanced up and tried to bring my rifle up to my shoulder when another bullet hit the ground just a few inches from my face and threw sand into my eyes. I blinked and shouldered my carbine.

The man who fired at me had now disappeared. For some unknown reason I uttered the words, "Bad day at Black Rock." I knew he had jumped back somewhere in those leaves. No time to panic I told myself, "Remember what they taught you at Ft. Benning. No John Wayne stuff, blasting away on full burst, wasting all your ammo. Use fire distribution, single shots fired quickly but calmly at the enemy's stomach level all across your front."

So I started working the area, left to right. Bang, bang, bang, spacing my shots about a foot apart. I was surprised at how calm I was. Bang, bang, bang. I fired all the way to the right. Then back left again. Bang, bang, bang, always at stomach level. Suddenly my vision was blurred by a big piece of metal close to my eyes. It was the bolt of my carbine automatically locking back telling me that I was out of ammo. Quickly, I inserted another 30 round clip and started firing again. I saturated the area to my front with stomach level rifle fire. If he was in there, I got him.

I stopped firing. It was quiet all around me, although I could hear firing to my distant front. But now I couldn't find the Dai Uy. He had been off to my front, but now he was gone. Gone, too, was the machine gun crew that was to my left. All that was left was me, Chan, and two Rangers whom I did not know and both of them were wounded, shot through the arms. They just stood there looking at me, with those silly grins on their faces. I could tell they wanted to hang in with me. There was no time to bandage their wounds now. Too many VC around. What should I do? The enemy was everywhere and wearing our uniforms and I had lost contact with my own battalion. What was I suppose to do now? What should I do when I saw another Ranger now? Obviously, I couldn't shoot first. It might be one of our own men. But if I didn't shoot first then he would have the drop on me. It would be a case of the "quick and the dead." I thought about it for a moment.

There was only one thing I could do. Call in a chopper, fly over to Sergeant Bennet and bring his group to the rescue. So I got on the radio and tried to make contact but I couldn't get through. There were too many gunship pilots talking to each other and my radio was too weak to push through to interrupt, but I kept trying. I kept calling and telling them I had an emergency. Finally, one pilot shouted into his radio, "Shut up everybody, there's a grunt on the ground in trouble."

Quickly, I told him my problem and that I wanted a chopper to come in take me over to Sergeant Bennet's position. A gunship pilot told me to "pop smoke" and he'd come in. The problem was, I didn't have any smoke grenades on my harness. Why? I don't know. I always carried two. But now I had none. I must had forgotten them. Quickly, I explained to Chan and the Vietnamese with me that I needed a smoke grenade. One of the wounded said he had one buried in his pack. We tore it open to find it. It turned out to be a white smoke grenade.

If only it were another color. You always see white smoke on a battle field. But not red or green. But no matter. It was all we had. I pulled the pin and threw it. It popped, but didn't go off. It put out a small puff of white smoke, but it didn't billow into a huge, white cloud like it was supposed to. It was a dud. I got on the horn and told the gunship pilot my problem. He asked, "Did it pop and make a small white plume?"

I answered "yes."

He said he saw it and knew where I was. He also said that there were VC all around me and they too were throwing smoke grenades in order to sucker him into their position. (They must have been monitoring our frequency.) But he had noticed the small white plume and would now come in and land.

We didn't have much room for him. A helicopter can't climb straight in and out like most people believe they can. They need a little bit of a run to land and to take off. He came in nose high, flaring wildly and put it down. There was no time to back up and get more runway space. He would just have to fly it out of there as best he could. He told me to get on as fast as possible and yelled, "There's VC all over the place."

The two wounded and Chan had already scrambled on, fear in their eyes. The pilot, Captain Johnson, asked me, "What's going on?"

Then he explained to me that he could not take all four but only two of us. The aircraft couldn't handle it. He insisted and Chan and I get on first. Maybe another ship would come in and pick up the others. But I knew it wouldn't be right for me to get on and leave those two wounded Rangers behind. The sight would haunt me for the rest of my days. It would be the supreme act of cowardice. Also, I doubted if I could pull them off even if I tried. They were terrified. They knew they were surrounded and they were wounded. They would probably fight to stay on the chopper and I didn't have time to explain things to them. So I shouted through the window to Captain Johnson to take off. "Take these two. Send somebody else for me later."

He looked around at the jungle. Then he shouted

back, "Get on. You won't be here when we get back."

I guess he knew what he was talking about so I hopped on. I sure hoped the thing could take off. It was a gunship, heavily loaded with ammunition. It was not supposed to carry any extra weight, much less four men from a clearing the size of a postage stamp. The engines whined to fever pitch. We edged forward, then up. As we got to the end of the clearing the bottom of the ship sailed through a banana tree. Luckily we didn't strike the trunk. Miraculously we were airborne.

As we gained altitude, a sister ship came along side to give us cover. I was sitting in the door, feet dangling, carbine in my lap, looking out at the other helicopter flying along side of us. Then I noticed a very thin trail of white smoke start to come out of the engine exhaust. I didn't think much of it. It was hardly visible. But the plume got wider and wider. Then it turned to black smoke. Suddenly, the whole back of the helicopter burst into flame. Fire belched out of the engine compartment engulfing the whole tail section. They didn't seem to know they were on fire.

I couldn't get the attention of our pilot to tell him because he couldn't hear me shouting above the wind and the noise. So I grabbed an iron bar lying on the floor and start banging on the back of his seat. He immediately thought he was taking hits on the aircraft. I banged again. This time he glanced back at me. I pointed wildly at the chopper off to our side. He immediately barked out a warning to them on the radio. But it was too late. They were going down.

We followed them in. The pilot still seemed to have control. It looked like he was going to glide it in and attempt a crash landing at about 50 miles an hour. At the exact moment of impact we veered left and I lost sight of the chopper. Captain Johnson turned our ship around and headed back to the crash site. He landed as close as he could, about 300 yards away. I hopped off the chopper and took off in a dead run. Any VC here? I didn't know and I didn't care. I had to get to that chopper and help the injured crewmen before they burnt up. I saw the chopper ahead of me.

It had landed in a large hole in the upright position. Only the tail section was burning. I saw the two pilots lying on the grass in front of the chopper. They were badly hurt and were all cut up and moaning. How did they get there? Did they crash through the windshield or did they climb out of the cockpit and then fall there exhausted? I couldn't tell.

My attention was diverted to a man lying inside the helicopter, in the back portion. It was the door gunner. He was lying inside, unconscious. What a big guy. He was the size of a pro-football player, maybe 240 pounds I jumped inside the chopper and tried to pull him out. But I couldn't. He was all dead weight. I couldn't budge him. I heard ammo exploding in the flames next to me. At this point I felt ashamed, for having left my battalion, for having left my buddies on the ground. I didn't care if ammo was popping off all around me. I would do anything to make up for that. I couldn't run from this injured man. It was the least I could do. I was going to get that man out of there even if I died trying. I tugged and pulled. Through super human strength I dragged him out of the aircraft. We were now at the edge of the wall that ran around the hole. But, I couldn't lift him over. He was too heavy. We were still right next to the burning helicopter, only two yards away. "When it explodes," I told myself, "it will take us all with it."

Suddenly voices. Men. The other pilots and crew members who had landed now joined us at the crash scene. They jumped in and helped me. We carried the wounded to the waiting helicopters and then took off. Captain Johnson had left his ship too, blades turning and all, to come over and help. Airborne we headed for the airstrip at Vung Tau. Enroute I felt ashamed. I was flying away from the battle, away from my friends. I was overwhelmed by guilt. I spotted the beautiful South China Sea ahead. We landed on a black top runway. There was lots of activity going on, lots of helicopters, lots of whirling blades.

I spotted Mirth 6. Major Stewart was patching up his helicopter with green masking tape. I counted over 30 bullet holes in the tail section of his helicopter. He was refueling and rearming, getting ready to fly back to Binh Gia. I told him that I had to go with him, that I must get back to the battalion, that I must find the other half of the battalion and Sgt. Bennet and salvage what I could. He then informed me that Sgt. Bennet had been captured, at least someone had monitored a transmission to that effect. He said Bennet kept talking on the radio right up to the very end. Bennet reported that there were dead Rangers all around him and hardly anyone left. Only he and Pvt. Craft and a few others. Sgt. Bennet described how the VC were advancing toward him and how he was about to be captured. He kept talking and describing what was happening right up to the moment when the VC took the microphone out of his hand.

Mirth 6 then looked me in the face and said, "Don't go back. It's useless. The situation is too fluid. The Battalion has been overrun and nobody knows where anybody else is."

I insisted on going. I just couldn't stay on the runway in Vung Tau while all this was happening 40 miles away. So he told me and Chan to hop on board his gunship. I noticed another guy in the back of the chopper, a Vietnamese. He was required to be there by the Geneva Convention. American gunships were not allowed to go into combat without a Vietnamese observer on board. But in this case he was just extra baggage. He couldn't see a thing out of the back seat and he couldn't read a map and he was scared silly.

I put the head set on and talked to Mirth 6 on the way back to Binh Gia. He said there was a .50 calibre machine gun near the village, firing at the helicopters and he intended to take it out. We approached the target zone. The co-pilot would fly it in and Mirth 6 would operate the guns. Boom. Boom. There were horrible explosions right outside the door. It was our own rockets being fired, going off in the pod like sticks of dynamite and then arching their way downward. Then our machine guns opened up. It was deafening. It felt like the ship itself was being torn apart. The Vietnamese next to me was terrified. Then we broke left.

Mirth 6 screamed into his microphone. He cursed the

211

co-pilot and called him every name in the book, including coward. He was absolutely furious. He accused the co-pilot of breaking off too soon. "The next time," he screamed, "we ride it all the way down."

What a nut, attacking anti-aircraft guns with a heli-copter. Round and round we went, pass after pass, the horrible explosion of the rockets being launched, the deafening noise of the machine guns. I was terrified. I didn't like it up there. It was not my kind of war. I wanted to get back on the ground. Finally, Mirth 6 ran out of ammo.

He told me that there was no contact with anyone down there, and Bennet and Craft had definitely been captured. He then volunteered to let me off at the Viet-namese Army Compound, just west of town, and asked if that's what I wanted to do. I told him "Yes, that's about all we can do."

We landed and I got off. As he took off to the south headed back to Vung Tau I looked around at my sur-roundings. It was not much, one of the rattiest looking outposts I'd ever seen. Very small and not very well organized. Just sand bags flung here and there, with the whole thing ringed together by a mish mash of barbed wire. There were only a few soldiers. If the VC came for us tonight it would be "Custer's last stand." But at least I could fight it out there.

At dusk, Vietnamese Skyraiders arrived to join the attack. I didn't know who was directing them. It was not the Dai Uy. We were on his frequency and I couldn't pick him up. (Most times the pilots knew what to do without being told anyway. They had an uncanny ability to pick out targets from the air.) They were attacking a .50 calibre machine gun, perhaps the same one Mirth 6 tried to take out earlier. I was mesmerized by the scene. High in the sky, the Vietnamese Skyraider rolled over and plunged straight down. Then the VC .50 calibre would open up. Tracers stabbed upward through the darkening sky like a liquid fire hose. The Vietnamese Skyraider seemed to ride this hose down. Downward, downward he plunged, into that never ending stream of tracers. The bullets seem to come up into the aircraft and pass right out the back.

Then I saw the bombs break loose off their racks. At the same time the aircraft pulled out and the bombs continued to fall straight down. There was a huge explosion. Dirt, branches, pieces of trees flew up into the air. I cheered quietly. Then another Skyraider would take his turn. He rolled over and he too began his downward plunge. To my amazement the VC machine gun would open up again. Evidently, the first plane hadn't taken it out. Again the red stream of bullets arched skyward and the Skyraider rode the red stream down. Again the bombs released and the ground erupted with violence.

This went on for what seemed to be half an hour. Plane after plane rolled in and attacked and each time the machine gun fired back again. Were they dug in that well? Or was there more than one gun? Finally, the air battle was over. The planes went home. Twilight had called the contest.

I started to feel ashamed again. All of my friends were out there scattered, and here I was safe in this compound. Darkness, my old friend, had arrived. I could now move cross country and rejoin Dai Uy. It was the least I could do. At least I could try. If I ran into VC, then I'd just head south to the ocean to avoid capture. If we did run into the enemy, I knew I could evade successfully until I got there. But after much though I changed my mind. It finally occurred to me that it just wouldn't work. Suppose I was lucky enough to run into my own Rangers. How would I identify myself to them in the dark? I didn't speak Vietnamese that well. And how could I tell the difference between them and the VC? The last time I saw them they were all wearing the same uniform. It was all so hopeless. But I felt so ashamed about it. I wanted to walk out and find Dai Uy and yet, I knew in my heart, I was just going to have to sit it out.

Later that night Chan awakened me. He was very excited. He had Dai Uy on the radio. I put the headset up to my ear and talked. It was Dai Uy all right. I recognized his voice. He informed me that he was cut off with a small group of Rangers and needed a gunship strike. I was elated to hear from him. I told him, "Roger."

I then switched to the Advisors "push" to contact the

L-19 circling above. He forwarded the request. Later, he called me back and said, "Help is on the way."

When the choppers arrived overhead, I contacted Dai Uy and told him to turn on a light. I would act as a "go between" for him and the pilot. The pilot located Dai Uy's position and I told him where the target was from there. Then he came in guns blazing. Suddenly Dai Uy called me up very excitedly and told me that the first pass was way off target. I relayed the adjustment to the gunships. The next time they came right in on target. I could tell the Dai Uy was elated. He thanked me profusely. I continued to help Dai Uy all night with gunship strikes and flare ship requests. The sky over Binh Gia was filled with floating parachute flares. I continued to hear sporadic firing. Dai Uy was continuing the fight, getting small groups of Rangers organized. Later he informed me on the radio that the VC were pulling out of town. It grew quiet again. After a long lull I decided to go to sleep.

Morning dawned. I got word from my headquarters that reinforcements were on the way and that Colonel Wilson was coming to see me. Later, choppers flooded the sky as a whole battalion of Vietnamese Marines landed south of town, in the same spot we did. About this time, Dai Uy called me on the radio to tell me that the people were saying that the VC had pulled out of the village last night at 3:00 a.m. Then a lone chopper approached my location. It was Colonel Wilson. I went to meet him. He landed and we walked off to the side and I began to brief him on what happened. Suddenly, I burst into tears. I told him of how ashamed I was, of how I had left my Battalion, of how I hadn't meant to desert them, and how Bennet and the other half of the battalion had been overrun, and how the gunship took me to Vung Tau and back again, and how badly I felt that they had to fight all night without my help. I wept uncontrollably. I told him he had every right to "fire" me.

But to my surprise, Colonel Wilson put his arm on my shoulder and told me not to worry. He told me that I had done a wonderful job with the battalion and that he had every confidence in me. I didn't know what to say. He was a tough old bird. Somehow there was a bond between us, a bond forged by his own experience in combat, in the many bitter campaigns and battles he has seen in his own life. Nothing more needed to be said. I could tell he understood. And more than that, at that moment we became like father and son. The silence was broken as he said, "Come on, let's join the battalion."

We took off in his chopper and I told Dai Uy to pop smoke on his location and we'd land there. He was at the south edge of the village. We landed and I spotted Dai Uy. It was so good to see him. I ran up to him and we hugged each other unashamedly. He was grinning from ear to ear. We were both so happy to see each other and to be alive.

Dai Uy told me about his own encounter. He said in the course of the fighting he had run into eight VC, all who had the drop on him and had ordered him to surrender. For some unknown reason, and acting on some insane impulse, he started screaming, charging and firing at them at the same time. Somehow or another he charged right past them and escaped. But his opium smoking bat boy didn't make it. He was never seen again. The XO had also been killed. A great loss. All in all, the battalion suffered 30 killed, 75 wounded, and 40 missing.

Sergeant Bennet's group was evidently wiped out in the first ten minutes. They were caught in a murderous cross fire. Only eight men were left standing when the VC charged them and took them prisoner. We later learned that we were fighting two North Vietnamese Regiments, four thousand men dug in with commo wire, machine guns, recoilless rifles and mortars. A "classic defense" against lightly armed Rangers in the open. Half our Battalion had been lost in one afternoon.

Colonel Wilson wanted to check out the village, and asked me to go along. We joined the Marines who were now starting to move out on line to clear the east end of the village. They were moving in the direction the enemy had last been seen. The Marines moved stealthily, peering behind every bush and house, guns at the ready. To my surprise, Colonel Wilson took the point. He pulled out his 9mm automatic pistol, cocked a round in the chamber, and started striding down a narrow road that ran through the middle of the village. Soon he was out in front of the Marines. Quietly I told myself that this was not smart. He was going to be the first full Colonel captured in this war. But Colonel Wilson strode on, unafraid. I walked beside him, hair bristling, carbine at the ready. The Marines followed. After about 30 minutes, we came to the end of the village. We could see open fields ahead. Colonel Wilson turned around, his job was done. He was one lucky dog. He now knew that there were no VC in the village. The Marines stopped too. Later, they pushed out into the open fields after the VC.

On our way back to the chopper we passed by the field in which Sergeant Bennet's element had been ambushed. The whole field was covered with bodies. The hot sun had done its work. The bodies were bloated and yellow. Flies rested on their faces. Some of them had died with their eyes open, frozen in shock. They stared hauntingly out into space. Blood ran out of their nostrils. Arms were frozen in grotesque shapes. It was a sad sight. A whole field of dead men, like some macabre scene from an ancient battlefield. It was "wall to wall" bodies. It probably would have made the most spectacular photograph of the war but I did not take my camera out. Something inside told me not to disturb these valiant men.

We returned to the village square and the church. By this time the press had arrived. That Saigon Commando who previously had visited me in Tay Ninh was with them. I didn't like any of them. They acted like ghouls. "Look over here," yelled one, "a dead body." Then they would all run over and start taking pictures.

Colonel Wilson gave me the job of taking them around the battlefield. I did so reluctantly, and purposely steered them away from the field with all the dead bodies in it. I would not have these newsmen jumping up and down with glee over one of the saddest scenes of the war. These fallen soldiers must rest in peace. I did take them around to other areas, however. A body here, a gun position there, they got a picture of what had happened. A large force had been dug in and the 33rd got hosed down.

Later, we returned to the village square. I struck up a conversation with one of the photographers, a decent sort of guy, I think his name was Peter Arnett. I showed him where I lived with a Vietnamese family from my previous stay there. Their little girl ran up to me and I snatched her up in my arms. Both of us were grinning as Arnett snapped a photo. Later it would be published in every major newspaper in the United States.

Before the reporters left I asked Arnett to do me a favor. I told him that my dad was sure to have read about the 33rd being hit hard with two of its Advisors being captured and that he would naturally assume that I had been captured. Could he do me a favor and send a telegram to my father and date it the day after the battle and put in the words, "Happy New Year, see you this year." That way my father would know I was still alive. He said he would. (Later I found out my plan hadn't worked so well. My dad did read about the 33rd being decimated all right but when the Western Union messenger arrived at the door with the telegram he naturally assumed that it was to inform him that I had been killed in action. The time between his seeing the telegram in the messengers hands and reading it was one of the saddest moments of his life. He just knew his son had been killed. Why else would he get a telegram? My good intentions had back-fired.)

It was time for the "members of the press" to leave. Since Colonel Wilson's helicopter had been moved to the market place, he took off with the rest. I spent the remainder of the day calling in helicopters and evacuating the wounded. Dai Uy circulated around, talking to the men, finding out what we had left, reconstituting the battalion. Later on in the afternoon Mirth 6 arrived on the scene with a case of beer and my mail. He was a sight for sore eyes. The Marines were now east of the village pursuing the VC. It was about 5:00 p.m. The sun would set soon.

It was all quiet in the village and time for me to take a shower. It was the usual procedure; dress down to my boxer shorts, pour a bucket of water over my head and soap up. Half blind, and thoroughly covered with soap, people suddenly started running past me in panic. It was the villagers, running by and yelling. Little children were

217

screaming. I stopped one of the men and asked him what was happening? He gestured wildly behind him and said, "VC, VC."

I couldn't believe it. VC in the village. It couldn't be. There was a whole Marine battalion out there. But I had to believe what I was told. These villagers knew the area and were now terrified. It must be so. Instantly I grabbed my towel. There would be no time for a rinse. The VC might be right behind the next guy. So I wiped the soap off my face, grabbed my carbine and ammo, and ran back to Dai Uy and the Command Post.

Soon we started to see Vietnamese Marines running through the village. They were terrified. Most had no weapons. It was a full scale rout. I found Dai Uy and we quickly formed a defensive line to the east with our Rangers. We told the Ranger officers to stop the Marines as they ran through the village and to assemble them in the rear. Then we sent out patrols to our front to give us early warning as to when the VC would hit us and also to tell whatever Marines they ran into to head for our perimeter.

Two U.S. Marine Advisors showed up. One was LT Phil Brady. We soon learned the whole story. The entire Vietnamese Marine battalion, 500 men, had been wiped out, caught in a three sided ambush in an open field. He told me that his boss, a U.S. Marine Captain had his nose shot off and had been captured along with another U.S. Lieutenant. Also, their NCO was missing, and the VC were now headed our way. I told him to quickly reorganize the Marines. They would serve as a reserve and be rushed to the point of attack if needed. He did a marvelous job of collecting the stragglers, reorganizing them into a fighting unit and staying in touch with me. He was a very calm and cool guy. Our Rangers gave them ammo and weapons and redistributed what we had.

I moved forward to check the line with Dai Uy. The Rangers were out in front in an arc facing east and the Marines were in back of us ready to counter attack if necessary. There were only about 150 Marines left out of the entire battalion. At this time I noticed a ditch running out back of our position. I made a mental note of it. If we got overrun tonight I planned to escape down that ditch. The next half hour was like an eternity. Every eye watched the front. Every finger was on the trigger. It was getting dark. Our Ranger Patrols reported back by radio. They had swept forward all the way to the end of the village and could now look out into the open fields to their front. There were no VC. We could now relax a little. At least we'd get an early warning when they did come.

Darkness fell. Still no VC. We continued to wait. Minutes passed into hours. No VC. It was 10:00 p.m. Still no VC. Surely they would have hit us by now to take advantage of our situation. It was a tactical principle to pursue a retreating enemy and run him down before he stopped to get reorganized. My guess was they were not coming. Dai Uy confirmed this. Somehow or another he had learned that the VC had pulled out and were now on top of a hill 5 kilometers north east of the village and would spend the night there. He asked me to order a gun strike for this location. I did through the L-19 circling above. He forwarded my request.

Later I heard the drone of a multi-engine aircraft coming into the area. They contacted me and told me their call sign was, "Puff the magic dragon." They informed me that they were "something new" in Vietnam and that they couldn't tell me what, but I could watch the show. Then they requested the location of the VC. I oriented them on the radio and they flew off. I listened to them in the darkness following their engines, peering out to the northeast. Suddenly, the sky lit up as tracer bullets plunged downward from seemingly nowhere in the sky. It was like the USS Steel hour. Molten lava flowed downward from the heavens and all in complete silence. There was no noise. Nothing. Then, a few moments later, a howling noise, an eerie noise, piercing the sky. I learned that the noise had been caused by a rotating canon mounted in the door of a C-47 firing thousands of rounds per second. "Puff" saturated the area with "zillions" of bullets. A five second burst could cover an area the size of a football field. After 15 minutes of firing, he departed the area.

It was quiet again. It was New Year's Eve. Lt. Brady

and I and Dai Uy decide to have a party. We started opening up the cans of beer while Dai Uy drank rice wine. By 1:00 a.m. we were feeling pretty good. Suddenly a call came in from the L-19. He had a message for us from headquarters. We were to pull out and evacuate the village in the morning. I couldn't believe it. Give up the village after all we had been through. Both Brady and the Dai Uy agreed with me. We were not going to pull out. I knew in my heart that I was not the bravest man in the world but one thing I could not do was run. I couldn't run and leave all those faithful villagers behind. I grabbed the mike cord, and in a somewhat slurred speech, I told the L-19 pilot to inform Headquarters that we were not leaving. I told him to tell Corps that, "We refuse to obey the order."

The L-19 pilot could tell something was a little "screwy" down below but he said he would relay the message anyway. About an hour later he called back. "Stay where you are. Help is on he way."

We had one more beer and went to bed.

Dawn broke. The VC did not attack. The village was alive with sounds; chickens clucking, birds chirping, people moving back and forth in pursuit of their daily chores. Everything was back to normal. How can life jump from instant death to the routine at a moments notice? This never ceased to amaze me.

Dai Uy sent word for me to come to his hootch. When I got there I spotted a United States Marine Corps Sergeant seated on a bench. He was the one who had been reported missing the night before. I had never seen anyone so completely exhausted. He was completely fatigued and physically spent. He stared straight ahead, a cigarette smoldering between his fingers. Someone had graciously brought him a bottle of Biere Larue. He unfolded his story. He had been caught in an open field with the rest of the Marines. It was all over in a matter of minutes. Hundreds were killed and wounded. The rear element ran away in panic. He was caught in the open with the rest but pretended to be dead. Later that night he was able to crawl off and hide in a ditch. Then he spotted the VC moving around firing bullets into the heads of the surviving

Marines. They finished them off one by one. He lay there terrified, hoping they wouldn't find him. After the slaughter the VC left. He continued to remain in hiding until dawn and then came in.

Later that morning, the Airborne flew in with a whole brigade of Vietnamese Paratroopers, 1500 men. Our activities would be coordinated with them as we were going into combat again. They would move east, through the site where the Marine slaughter had taken place and push out after the VC. We in turn would move south along the Vung Tau Highway to open it up. At the same time armored forces would move up from Vung Tau to meet us. They would be escorting some trucks coming in to take out the bodies. The dead would be taken back to Binh Hoa for identification by their families and then buried.

It was time to move out. My heart was not in it. We had just come through a major battle with over half the battalion killed and wounded and now here it was time to pick up and go again. A great sadness came over me. I now knew that I was not going to make it home. I was going to be killed. And it would probably happen that day. Waiting for it was both agonizing and saddening. I'm sure the Rangers felt it too. But they all smiled as they got ready to move out. In fact, laughter rang out in the midst of their sing song chatter as they found something amusing here and there in their mundane preparations.

It was all so macabre. How could they laugh? How could they smile? For myself, I just wanted to quit. I didn't want to go to my death. But I had to. I had to go with these brave, smiling, little men. How could I desert them? How could I ever look at myself in the mirror again if I didn't? How could I be the first Ranger coward in history? So I picked up my carbine and stepped off with a heavy heart along side of them. At almost the same moment in Saigon, unknown to us, a coup was taking place. We didn't even know who we would be fighting for. Much worse, we didn't know who we would be dying for.

Dai Uy had a good plan. He wasn't stupid enough to go right down the middle of the road. That's what the VC expected. No, we would move 1 kilometer off to the side of the road with scouts out to our far flank. That way, if the

VC were setting up an ambush on the road, we could wheel around and come in from behind them. It was a good plan. It was all quiet for about the first 5 kilometers of our walk. Then, as we came down a long hill and started to cross a ditch at the bottom, a .50 calibre machine gun opened up from on top of a hill to our front. I recognized the slow, deep firing of a "fifty." It seemed to be out there all on its own. Nobody else seemed to be with it. There was no other firing. What was it? A VC flank guard?

The bullets wopped in around us. I crawled into a ditch. Some leaves floated down from on high to my front. I could tell he really didn't have a good bead on us. He was just throwing out lead, covering the area. I told Dai Uy to get some artillery in on it. He agreed and start jabbering into his radio. Suddenly, about one minute later a huge shell exploded right out in front of us. Now that's what I call instant artillery support. I laughed and congratulated the Dai Uy. But then he told me, "that not our artillery. Ours not fire yet."

Then what was it? It did sound like the explosion of a 105mm shell, one of our own shells. I was pretty sure of that. I didn't think it was coming from the VC. Then what is it? I began to think. There was a column coming up from the south. Maybe they were the ones who had called it in. The fact that it exploded at the same time as we requested ours could have been a coincidence.

I got on the radio and contacted the L-19 circling above. I told him to contact the unit pushing up from the south to ask them if they were firing any artillery to the north. If they were, they were to stop immediately as it was impacting in our area. Sure enough, within a minute he came back to me. Yes, the unit attacking from the south had been shooting at us. Quickly I gave him a "no-fire" line to pass on to the unit to the south. They could fire all the artillery they wanted south of this line and we could fire all we wanted north of it. That way we wouldn't fire into each other. We also agreed to meet on that line. Soon our own artillery started impacting into the hill to our front. After a few explosions, the machine gun stopped. We pushed up the hill carefully but there was no fire. Whoever it was had bugged out. I'm sure a larger force had been waiting in ambush for us but had bugged out when we attacked their flank. We continued south until we met the armor column. Then we turned around and headed back to Binh Gia.

There was a lot of activity in the village, lots of big whigs arriving to take a look. One who flew in was the Province Chief, he brought in his own body guard with him. A very scary guy, an evil looking dude, tall and thin with a pale yellow face. He looked just like Jack Palance, (the movie star villain in "Shane"). As the chopper landed, this man got off first to check the area for the Province Chief. He got off slowly, gracefully, like a cat, glancing around at the same time. The human personification of a stealthy leopard. A real killer.

Other things began to happen, too. Some of our Rangers previously captured were now showing up, turned loose by the VC. They had given them a propaganda lecture, told them not to fight again and then had set them free. The VC were kind to our wounded, too. They had bandaged them up and told them that they would later carry them over to a government highway and would lay them in the road where a government convoy would pick them up.

Why all this kindness to us? Why had they been so nice to us on the one hand but had shot all the Marines in the head on the other? In my heart, I knew the answer. At least, I thought I knew why they shot all the Marines. There had been no quarter shown by either side during this war, that is, between the Marines and the VC. I had heard lots of stories of torture and executions. Conversely, our own Ranger Battalion since last July, had begun a policy of being extremely fair to prisoners. They hadn't beaten them, but had given them food and water and medicine when captured. The enemy knew of this. They knew our record. I personally think they were simply returning the favor.

The returning Rangers also gave us word on Sgt. Bennet and Pvt. Craft. Both had been captured and were being held under very strict security by the VC. They were tightly bound and guarded 24 hours a day, with no chance of escape. Both were in good health, although someone had said that they thought Sergeant Bennet had been slightly wounded. They also reported on the captured U.S. Marines. Both were Captains. One had been wounded in the face. I reported this information to Headquarters right away because I knew by this time that Sergeant Bennet's mother had been sent a telegram informing her that her son was missing in action. I wanted her to know that he was definitely alive.

Now the gristly work of finding the bodies and loading them on the trucks took place. It was a wretched, putrefying scene. Carrying parties brought in the bodies on stretchers to the village center. It was all so grotesque. The bodies were bloated and yellow. Arms and legs were frozen in bizarre positions. When they arrived at the trucks they tried to slip the bodies into "body bags." (A large rubber bag with a zipper.) The smell was absolutely horrible. Men threw up everywhere. The bodies had been rotting for two days. It made you gag. I don't know how the carrying parties could stand it. Many wore gauze masks but it didn't stop the smell. After a while they ran out of body bags and just started throwing the bodies on the trucks. When they were finished, there was a total of twelve trucks stacked high with bodies. It was all so unbelievable. Such a macabre sight! The trucks pulled out of the village and headed for Saigon and the waiting families.

Later that day I monitored a news broadcast from AFN. The announcer said that an Admiral Sharp, the Commander in Chief of all Pacific Forces, had just said in Honolulu that, "Victory as we know it, will be achieved in Vietnam in six months."

Who was this man? How could there be such a great gulf between us? Didn't he know what's going on?

It was our turn to go home. We were being flown back. The choppers arrived and we lifted out, arching to the north and west and then toward Saigon. The battle of Binh Gia was over.

CHAPTER 17

Back in Train Compound

The Battalion is finally going to "stand down." This time they mean it. We are going to be "reconstituted," (that's an Army term that means your unit got all shot up and is going to be built up all over again from top to bottom). There would be no more operations during this period. Instead, we would receive new recruits and officers fresh from Ranger School and integrate them into the battalion. New officers would be assigned to fill the vacancies of those who had been killed. Fresh replacements would arrive to fill up the squads and we would spend this time getting to know each other. We would re-establish the chain of command, go through training and maneuvers so that people would know who's on their left and right, and in general, learn to work together as a team.

It was a good time for the families too. Lots of time off for the men. And they used it to good advantage finding housing for their wives and kids. Most built little hootches and then roofed it with sheet metal (which had finally been provided by the Vietnamese Army.) I spent this time checking on the families, walking around visiting them. It was great to see the Rangers laughing and playing with their kids, or seated around a wok eating lunch with their wives. I had never seen the men so happy. We continued to push the Vietnamese Army to give us more building supplies and back rations and it was paying off.

It was a big change for me, too, I was to get an entirely

new Advisory team, four new Americans, a real sharp Lieutenant, a Senior experienced Master Sergeant, a young Buck Sergeant weapons instructor, and an E-4 Radio Operator, all top quality people. I could tell they had all been hand picked, and they were all Ranger and parachute qualified. I don't know why they were "beefing me" up so well. I had never seen such a large advisory team before. Usually there were only two of us. These men were good for me. They brought a new spirit to the team, a new life, a new enthusiasm, the American "can do" attitude. I needed that. Every day they went for a two mile run and I joined them. It was fun to have someone to talk to in English, to run with, and to go with on operations. I was no longer alone.

During this time, more of our men who were captured at Binh Gia continued to be released by the VC and returned to us. They continued to give reports on Sgt. Bennet and Pvt. Craft. Evidently, Craft and Bennet spent the first night of their capture east of the village. The next day they were moved about 14 km (8 miles) northeast, and then later to a rubber plantation further east of that. There were about 50 prisoners at this later location, captured from various units at various times. Craft and Bennet were being well treated although Bennet had been wounded in the arm. One man said that they were given rice, a meat sandwich, salt, and a package of Bastos cigarettes. They were tied up all the time and kept under very strict security.

I sent all this information through the mail to Bennet's mother and Craft's family. All they knew from the Army was that their sons were "missing in action." I knew for certain that they were alive and in captivity. I thought their families should know that.

A funny incident happened at this time. That Sergeant on Captain White's advisory team, who had been in that armor ambush south of Binh Gia, began to tell people that he had seen Perry Mason at Train Compound, (the same Perry Mason of TV fame.) Of, course nobody believed him. We all thought he had gone "off the edge." After all, he had been through a lot; the ambush, missing in action, separated and alone in the jungle, and finally rescued by a passing helicopter only after he waved his white T-shirt at them. And now he was going around telling people he had seen Perry Mason. "Sure, sure," people would say and then walk away. But it was true. Perry Mason (Raymond Burr) had been to Train Compound. Evidently, nobody but this Sergeant had seen him. Perry Mason had been on some sort of "secret" tour of Vietnam at the time. There was no publicity and he seemed to have his own helicopter. I never did understand why he was there, but he definitely had visited Train Compound. The Sergeant wasn't crazy.

Hospital — Cong Hoa

During this period, I decided to visit LT Trinh, a friend of mine from the battalion, who had been wounded in the battle of Binh Gia. He was in Cong Hoa Army Hospital. Cong Hoa was the central hospital of Vietnam. It was their largest hospital and was located in Saigon so there was always a lot of road traffic out in front of it. It was surrounded by a white wall and had a long driveway through the center of it. There was an administration building up front and white buildings scattered around behind that. It was in this vast complex of white buildings (the wards), where the wounded lay.

The wards were not like those in an American hospital. Each ward was a separate building and had a red tile roof over it. The buildings were not completely enclosed. Each ward had a low wall around it, about the height of a man's waist. So, as you lay in your bed, the room had a concrete wall to your front, a concrete wall to your back, and a view to your left and right that led right out to the open...looking over the low wall to the out of doors. It was in fact a form of automatic air conditioning as it allowed the breeze to pass through the wards.

Outside each room was a small walk way or porch, about 10 feet wide sheltered by a roof. This is where the families "camped out." Meals were not furnished to the patients at the hospital so the families would bring a charcoal fire and wok and cook outside on the porch and then bring the food into the men. As I passed by I saw a woman squatting there cooking, little kids running around,

227

others just sitting in the rooms, looking at their husbands or talking to them. I thought that, at least for the moment, they had a salary. They could buy rice. They were being taken care of. But I wondered what would happen to them after they were discharged from the Army for wounds. Their salaries would then stop. What would they live on then?

As I walked through these wards, I saw all different kinds of wounded men. One area was filled with nothing but amputees, ward after ward after ward of them. Some were still confined to their beds, all bandaged up, with a leg gone, or an arm gone. Many were multiple amputees, both hands blown off or one arm and a leg missing. Others, patients who had been there for a while were sitting out on the porch in wheel chairs sunning their stumps. There were literally hundreds of them. It just staggered the imagination.

As I passed by some would look at me sullenly. These were probably the ones who had just lost their legs, the recent amputees who had just awakened only to find a flat sheet where their leg used to be. But others would grin. Some would call out, "Chau Dai Uy," (Hello Captain). I received a wide spectrum of responses as I walked by but I didn't know what to say to any of them in return. It was all too moving. After a long search I found LT Trinh's room. He was in a private room. He was lying flat on his back, sheets covering his legs. Standing next to his bed was his girlfriend, a beautiful Vietnamese girl. She was wearing the traditional Vietnamese clothing.

As I walked in he gave me a big grin. He always had a happy smile on his face. What a tremendous guy. We talked for a while. Later he told me that he couldn't feel his toes. I pulled up the bottom of his sheet and looked at his feet. I tickled them. He couldn't feel a thing. I touched and pinched him. He couldn't feel anything. He told me that an American Doctor had operated on him. It was a civilian doctor, some kind of a "guest surgeon" at the hospital. Could I go and talk to him and ask him why he couldn't feel anything in his legs? I told him I would try.

I left his room and went around the hospital asking for this "Bac si my" (American doctor). People would point here and there. Finally I found him. He was in an office. He looked to be about 45 years old, portly and a very friendly fellow. He said he knew LT Trinh, and yes, he was the one who had operated on him. He would be very happy to discuss his case with me. Then he took me over to another room and put up a X-ray up on a viewing screen. He showed me what LT Trinh's spine looked like when he came into the hospital. A .50 calibre bullet, about the size of a man's thumb, had hit him right in the middle of the back. The bullet had completely severed his spine. I could see the bullet wedged all the way across the bones of the spine. Then the doctor looked at me very seriously and said, "He's never going to walk again. The damage is too great. His spine is completely severed. There is nothing we can do."

I walked out of his room stunned. I didn't know what to say to this game little guy, this trooper who always had a smile on his face. I walked slowly and painfully back to his room. What should I say? I told him I had found the doctor. "No, no, nobody knows anything for sure."

It was all I could say. I couldn't tell him that he would never walk again. As we said good-bye, I shook his hand and looked down at him. I fought back the tears. He kept looking up at me smiling and grinning. It was a very painful moment for me. "Yes, old friend," I said, "I'll be back. It's a promise." And then I left.

Since I was in Saigon and had heard that there was a nice place to have a beer, opposite one of the American hotels in the Chinese section of Saigon, I decided to drive over there in my jeep. I parked out front. I had my carbine with me, so I took the carbine inside so I could keep an eye on it. This was perfectly permissible because we Advisors were hand picked to go to Vietnam. You didn't have to worry about Advisors getting drunk and shooting up the place. There were no such incidents in Vietnam. And I needed to keep that carbine with me wherever I went, and that included "beer time."

Once inside, I ordered up a Bierre LaRue. Immediately, girls came up to me and began asking me to buy them a Saigon tea. It was sort of expensive, about 70 cents a shot and was just that, tea. They didn't drink beer or whiskey

229

or anything like that. They just wanted to appear like they were. It was strictly a business proposition. Half the money for the tea went to the house and the other half to the girl. For the price of a tea she would talk to you. It was great conversation and most of them were quite beautiful. Since I wasn't married, it was somebody nice and pretty to talk to, and so, I bought lots of Saigon Tea.

In this particular bar there were no prostitutes. Most of these girls appeared to be from good homes believe it or not. Now, I won't say that was true of every bar in Saigon, but it was true of this bar. All the girls would leave at curfew and go home together and the American clientele didn't go with them either, so I knew there was no hanky-panky going on. They were simply hostesses and had nothing but conversation for sale. They really were funny, and had lots of personality. They would laugh and "carry on" and were great conversationalists. It was lots of fun and I really enjoyed it.

While there I met My Ly, for whom the bar was named. She was the daughter of the owner/bartender, a Vietnamese woman. Her mother had previously been married to a Japanese gentleman, but he died leaving her a widow. This combination of Vietnamese and Japanese made My Ly a very beautiful woman, in fact, a fantastically beautiful girl. She was kind of young, probably 18. Her mother liked me a great deal. I think her mother knew that I wasn't out to cause any trouble. She trusted me. She would even allow me to sit with My Ly and talk to her for hours. My Ly and I were very good friends and I liked her a great deal.

Later, I asked her mother (who was very, very protective of her) if I could take her out on a date. At first she said no, but later she relented. Later on, I found out why she was so wary of Americans. An Army Major had previously been living with her, even though the Major was married back home. The situation had gone on for six months. The Major spent entire nights there, sleeping upstairs with the mother, instead of going home like he was supposed to when the curfew went into effect. While he lived with My Ly's mother, he made all sorts of promises to her, and told her all sorts of lies. But when time came for him to go home, he left without a word. He never even said good-bye. Her mother was very sad about that and consequently trusted none of us. And I didn't blame her.

The night came for my big date with My Ly. It was my first "official" date with her. I told her mother that I would take her to the My-Khong Floating Restaurant. I arrived in a taxi and went into the bar. There was My Ly, looking absolutely beautiful as usual in her Ao Dai clothing. We walked outside and hopped in the waiting cab. It was one of those ultra-mini cabs, about half the size of a Volkswagen bug, a Peugot mini car made by the French. I told the driver to take us to the My-Khong Floating Restaurant.

We were about half way there when the engine died. The driver pulled over and then turned around and told us that there was something wrong with the engine, and then hopped out and went around to the back of the car to fix it. Since I had just heard about another American who had been blown to bits by a taxi driver who, claimed that he had engine trouble too, but actually went around to the back to pull the fuse on a bomb, I immediately hopped out with him. I had my pistol with me, my .38 caliber Combat Masterpiece, tucked under my left arm in a shoulder holster covered by my shirt. I watched him closely as he worked on the engine, ready to "plug him" if he tried anything funny, but he hopped back in the taxi and got the engine going again, delivering us without incident to our destination.

The restaurant was nothing more than a large barge floating in the river, moored to the bank. It was nicely decorated with tables and chairs. We got a table over by the far edge, on the river side. As I peered across the river, I could see jungle on the other side along with scattered hootches on the opposite bank. I noticed that there was a lot of brush and vegetation on the other side, too. It made me uneasy.

We had a very delicious meal. It was almost like being in a restaurant back home. The waiters wore white jackets. We looked out across the river into the darkness sipping a glass of wine and talking. From time to time, I could see water lilies floating by. The water of the Saigon

231

River was dark and muddy. I couldn't help but wonder if that area on the other side of the river was secure and whether or not we couldn't be fired on from the other side. Then I thought about the large leaves that floated by. How easy it would have been for the VC to float a large mine down the river and attach it to the barge and blow it up.

We finished the meal, I paid the bill and took My Ly home. One week later, I read in the newspaper that the VC had put a bomb in the restaurant and killed over 50 people. We had missed it by one week.

I received some good news, one of the Vietnamese Lieutenants, in our Battalion, told me that I would never have to worry about being hit. He said that all the Rangers would gladly risk their lives to save me. He said they would never leave me behind wounded in the jungle or run away. I took that as a supreme compliment. If someone is willing to risk their life for you, then you know there is a tremendous bond there. I guess they knew that I really did like them. It was not something you could fake. You either liked them or you didn't and it showed. And they knew that I really did care for them. I fought for their families, for more time off for the troops, for better food and visited the wounded in the hospital to make sure that they got the best of care. They could tell. Even though we were separated by the strangest language in the world, there was still a great, if unspoken, bond between us.

Binh Hoa scenes

I liked to shop in the Binh Hoa area. There was a very large market there. The women squatted around their mats selling vegetables. Little shops lined the streets. The buildings were French style and were made out of concrete. The buildings ran the whole length of the block, with lots of little shops located one beside the other. All were locked up at night, with those accordion type sliding gates.

While downtown, I heard a lot of noise coming down the street, it was a funeral procession. The funeral wagon was high and long and very ornate. It had dragons carved out of wood on it and all sorts of oriental designs. I could see a casket in the middle of the hearse. Behind that, moving at a very slow pace, were the wife and family and friends. They were all dressed in white. (The Vietnamese color for mourning.) As they walked past they cried out, flailing their arms in the air, beating their chests, all the time wailing loudly. They really let their emotions out (unlike Americans, who are very stoic at times like these). This particular wagon was being followed by a young widow with children, all of whom were crying pitifully. It was all so very sad. I assumed it was another young soldier who had been killed in the fighting.

After fooling around Binh Hoa for the afternoon, I decided to drive to the battalion CP. It was a Saturday, a day off. The place looked deserted. I walked into Battalion Headquarters, passed through the first room and then back into the second where the main offices were located. There I noticed a man lying on the floor, belly down, hands tied behind him. He was a young fellow, about 17 years old. He recognized me and started yelling at me in Vietnamese. He was crying, something I had never seen a Vietnamese do before. He was actually crying. At first I thought he was an enemy soldier whom the Rangers had captured and were now beating against my wishes. But as it turned out he was one of our own boys. He was pleading to me for help. About that time Dai Uy came around the corner. He had a long bamboo cane in his hand. It was a whipping cane.

Dai Uy briefed me on what was going on. It seemed like this young soldier went into a bar in Binh Hoa the night before, had gotten all liquored up and literally destroyed the bar. He had taken his rifle along too, and fired through the ceiling, shooting bottles off the bar, breaking glass and in general acting like a real bad boy. He had been arrested by the Military Police and taken back to Dai Uy. The punishment that Dai Uy had decided upon was 30 lashes across the buttocks. He had not yet administered the beating when I walked in.

I thought about it for a moment. How different their punishment was from our own. In the American Army we would have court-martialed the man, taken the stripes off his sleeve, busted him down to private, fined him a lot of money, and thrown him into prison for three to six months. In addition to being separated from his family he would have had no money with which to support his wife and kids. Our way just ruined a man. But here in Vietnam, the man received a swift beating and returned to duty, the incident forgotten. I wondered to myself who had the best system. I turned around, walked out of the office, and left Dai Uy to do what he had to do.

The next day Dai Uy told me that he wanted to talk to me privately. He picked me up in his jeep and we drove outside the city to one of those roadside beer stands. He picked one that had no one else in it. There was a little picnic table outside, so we sat down there. A little girl came over and we ordered two Biere LaRues. We let the ice chill the beer for a moment.

Dai Uy looked pensive. After a few minutes he began to talk. He told me that there was going to be a coup in Saigon. He said this coup was being sponsored by the young officers. He said they were tired of the old generals and old politicians running the war. What was needed was a change. The young officers believed their government could reflect the feelings of the people, and the men who actually did the fighting in the field, and they wanted Dai Uy to join their coup. The part he was to play was crucial. He was to seize General Vinh, the Commanding General of all of III Corps. That part would be easy. His men lived in the same compound with General Vinh. All he would have to do is take him prisoner. Once General Vinh was captured, the entire area around Saigon would be paralyzed and the young officers would win in a matter of minutes. Then Dai Uy did a strange thing. He looked me straight in the face and asked, "What should I do?"

He seemed genuinely troubled by this, really bothered. I could tell it was a heavy problem for him. I was, of course, flattered that he would ask me what he should do. Many times Vietnamese didn't tell their counterparts anything, much less their inner thoughts and secrets. I really felt honored. He and I had become very close over a period of time. I attributed it to the fact that I genuinely liked him and that we had faced death together day after day. We had become brothers. I didn't give an answer right away. I thought about it carefully, sipping my beer.

After much thought I told him I didn't think he should do it. I told him that if he participated in the coup and failed, General Vinh would punish him, probably have him shot or at least put in prison. However, on the other hand, if he did not participate in the coup and the young officers won, the most they could blame him for was being loyal to his Commanding Officer and that was not a particularly bad trait for a professional soldier.

I then vented my own personal opinion on him. I told him that if everybody in Vietnam would just obey orders, everything would be all right. The government would finally stabilize and people would know what to do. There might be continuity in the government, instead of this coup after coup stuff. The coups disrupted everything, from the highest level, down to the villages. It just ruined things. The government had been changing hands so many times, that the people didn't know who they are working for any more. Then I stopped talking.

We sat there in silence for a long time. Of course he didn't make a grand pronouncement about what he was going to do. That was not the Vietnamese way. But I could tell from the look on his face that he had marked my words. We finished our beers in silence and drove home.

The next day was a day off. I decided to drive into Saigon. Not much going on. I did a little touring and shopping and then ate lunch. On the way home, I ran into some excitement. As we approached Thu Duc (home of the Infantry School), we saw a road block ahead. It was manned by infantry and tanks. Tau confirmed what I had already surmised...a coup was on. The road block was being manned by the young officers who wanted to overthrow the government and it looked like they had the Infantry School on their side. This was a considerable force. Tank training was also conducted there, so they had not only tanks and armored personnel carriers, but several thousand officer candidates as well. That was enough to field two regiments.

Overhead I saw VNAF fighters circling around. These had remained loyal to the government and were enemies of the guys on the road block. I got a funny feeling that those attack planes might dive down any minute and wipe me out along with the road block and I didn't like it at all. So I told Tau to drive right through, but to do it slowly. As we came up to the road block, the tanks had their gun barrels pointed right at me. They meant business. We slowed down enough to show them that we were not going to run the road block, but we kept up enough speed to indicate that we wanted to keep going straight down the highway. They recognized me as an American Advisor and waved me through. Phew! Glad that was over. I would have hated to have been killed by two quarreling factions of the same government that I had come over to fight for.

We continued down the highway towards Binh Hoa. I told Tau to head for III Corps and General Vinh's compound. I was interested in seeing what Dai Uy's reaction was to all of this. As we approached the compound, I could see that it was surrounded by our own Rangers. A platoon of them was at the main gate, armed with submachine guns and carbines. They wouldn't let us pass even though they recognize Tau and me as one of their own. I hopped out and talked to the Lieutenant in charge. I asked him what was going on. "Why can't we drive into our own headquarters?"

He replied, "I have my orders. Absolutely no one is to pass. No one without the Dai Uy's permission."

Then he sent a man to get the Dai Uy and a couple minutes later he arrived. He gave me a big grin and waved me through. We stopped and talked. Dai Uy had remained loyal to General Vinh. That's why his Rangers were out front...to protect him, not to capture him. In a few hours the coup was over. The government remained in the same hands as before. And Dai Uy had chosen the right side.

The next day I was contacted by a man named Captain Sommerfield. I had known him back in the States at Ft. Benning. He was a very sharp officer and a good man. He came right to the point. He told me that he wanted my job. He had been in a safe job at the Infantry School in Thu Duc for the last six months and now wanted to go into combat. Would I be willing to switch places with him? After all, it was normal for Ranger Advisors to rotate jobs at the six month mark.

I told him I would agree to it only if it was okay with the Dai Uy. I knew I couldn't walk out on Dai Uy no matter what. I thought to myself that no matter how much I wanted to get away from the death and the killing that I could not leave Dai Uy out there alone. So, I had a private meeting with Dai Uy in his office. I told him about this opportunity to switch jobs, to leave the battalion, to go to a safe job, but that I wouldn't do it if he stayed on with the battalion. (I had previously heard a rumor that he might be moving. Maybe this would bring things out in the open.)

Dai Uy then told me that he too was leaving the battalion. He had been given an important staff job in Saigon. Things couldn't be working out better. The battalion would get a new Battalion Commander and a new Advisor at the same time. We both agreed that I should take the new job.

In a way I hated to go because I felt like a coward, leaving the rest of the men, the ordinary soldiers who couldn't switch, who would have to stay on until they were killed or wounded. I felt ashamed. Of course, it was normal for U.S. Advisors to rotate at the six month mark but still, I felt like a deserter. I felt like a man who was running out on his friends. It was a great personal conflict for me but at the same time I felt a great burden was being lifted from me too. It was as if I had been sentenced to death and now that sentence had been lifted and I was going to live. But at the same time I felt deeply ashamed to leave my fellow Rangers.

From a personal view I was very glad to see Dai Uy going to the General Staff. He had been in combat for so many years. He had once had a nervous breakdown and had been in an insane asylum. It had all just been too much for him...too much fear and too much terror for too many years. But he was a survivor. No one had earned the right to leave the battalion more than he. Now he would be safe. It was also heartening to see him go for another reason. Far too often "politicians" ended up on the General Staff, "politicking" officers who held safe jobs at the District or Province level, who knew some full Colonel or General, who got them moved them up to some plush job

237

in Saigon. Meanwhile, all the Captains out in the field who got up every morning and slopped through the rice paddies and fought for their country were forgotten. They went out every day, usually to their death or serious wounds, without recognition or reward, while the political types forged ahead. But now, finally, the high command had reached down and picked a real soldier. It was a thrill to see it happen.

The next day, I walked into Corps Headquarters. A big operation was being planned. Lots of Vietnamese and Americans were there. A huge map board had been set up. We all got seated and the G-3 announced that a gigantic operation was coming up involving Rangers, paratroops, and the regular Army, as well as local forces. It was going to take place northeast of Vung Tau, where they believed the enemy ran after the Battle of Binh Gia. Intelligence had reported some very large camps there. My heart began to pound because I knew this meant we would be in heavy fighting again. As a part of the overall plan I noticed that the 33rd would be in reserve in Vung Tau, a seacoast town. It was a place that had been built years ago under French rule and had lots of cabins along the beach. It was just like a resort in Florida. This is where we would be staying until the helicopters came to pick us up and fly us into the fighting if needed.

At the end of the briefing, Colonel Wilson got up. He talked about the operation, about some of the things he wanted to see done and how he wanted the operation to progress. Then at the very end he looked at me and said, "Behnke, since you're being transferred, you will not go out on this operation."

I nodded. Inwardly I was happy, but it did present a problem. If the battalion was committed before Captain Sommerfield joined them, then they would be sent into combat without an Advisor. I didn't know what Colonel Wilson wanted to do about that, but he was not the kind of man you argued with. So I just left it alone for the time being. I knew if the battalion was committed, I was going to go in with them, Colonel Wilson or not. They couldn't go in without an Advisor. They would need gunship strikes and helicopter support.

The next day. It was time to move out. The units that were going into the combat zone were flying in by helicopter. We would travel by vehicle in a large convoy of trucks composed not only of Rangers, but of lots of artillery as well. It was about this time that I saw a film crew from ABC television. It was composed of two Americans and a couple of Vietnamese cameramen. They stopped their vehicle and got out to talk to me. They asked me what was going on with our Battalion. I gave them the basics of the operation. Then they asked me if they could accompany us. (They had permission from Corps.) I said, "Fine."

I then told them that we would initially be going down to Vung Tau by vehicle but that later we might chopper in. I told them that if we came in by chopper it might get pretty hot and that I wanted them to know in advance what they were getting in to. They said, "Fine." They wanted to see some action.

I said, "Come along."

A little later we were just sitting there, in this long line of vehicles waiting to move out, when the American reporter from the film crew stood in front of my jeep and began his newscast. I could hear the cameras turning as he said very dramatically, "I'm standing here in front of the 33rd Ranger Battalion. In a few minutes these men will be locked in mortal combat. And we are going with them. But first a word from our sponsor." I did a double take and looked at Sergeant Wentzel (my new Senior NCO Advisor). We both rolled our eyes skyward. It was unbelievable.

Finally, we got the word to move out. We headed South. It was comforting to see the VNAF Skyraiders (that I had asked for) orbiting overhead as we sped south.

After a while, we left the safety of the village and hit scattered jungle and rubber plantations. The road there was protected by Regional Forces; rag-tag guys wearing civilian pants and Army shirts, holding old single shot rifles, standing along side the road. Eventually, we ran out of them and were on our own. I knew that the road from there on out had not been cleared.

Later I saw a large mountain to our front. I knew that Vung Tau and safety were just beyond that. But first we have to get around the base of the mountain and...ambush alley. The actual danger area was about 10 kilometers long. The VC lived up on the side of the mountain, and occasionally, came down to ambush the vehicles that passed by. They had been doing this on a regular basis lately. As we approached the ambush area, I didn't see any security posted anywhere. We would just have to run through it as fast as possible. I was scared because I knew that if a fight did break out, no one would know what to do, as there was no control, no organization. We were all split up. Different vehicles from different units were all mixed up in the same convoy. It was a mess. The Dai Uy was way out front and I was way in the back and nowhere near him. I didn't like it at all.

Suddenly, I saw a vehicle stopped along the road in front of me. It was broken down. Everybody else was driving by him like crazy. But I knew what would happen to him if the whole convoy passed him by. The driver and all the soldiers riding with him would be left alone in that God forsaken spot in the jungle and taken prisoner or shot. I just couldn't leave them stranded there. So I motioned to Tau to pull over. We got behind the truck. I looked over my shoulder for a maintenance vehicle but none was in sight. It was just truck after truck loaded with soldiers roaring by. Where was the tow truck that was supposed to be at the end of the convoy? It wasn't there. The last of the trucks sped by and out of sight down the road. Then it was all was quiet. Oppressively quiet. The convoy was gone, now we were all alone, just this one truck with eight soldiers, Tau and myself. I was scared. The VC could pop out at any time.

Tau went over and talked to the driver. They popped the truck hood. I could hear them talking in low voices, pointing. I looked at the jungle around me, rifle at the ready. It was hot, steamy and scary. We were definitely in "bear country". Tau continued to work on the vehicle. Then the Vietnamese driver hopped back in, hit the starter and the engine roared to life. Everybody gave a great sigh of relief. I didn't have to tell anybody what to do. They all scrambled back on board like crazy. The driver threw it in first gear and tore off like a "bat out of hell." We followed directly behind, gas pedal mashed to the floor. The jungle rushed by. We tore through the green foliage mile after mile. It was all one big blur. Finally we broke out of the jungle and hit flat coastal land. I could see Vung Tau ahead. We were safe.

Vung Tau.

A beautiful town, a seacoast town, a seafood town. It had white beaches, sandy roads and kids playing happily and safely in front of their homes. The South China Sea lapped gently against its shore. The jungle was miles away. The battalion would set up on the air field. That way the helicopters could pick us up quickly if they had to. We turned on our radios so we could monitor the units already in the field. We tuned to the company level frequencies and could actually hear the fighting going on; bullets crackling, people shouting loudly back and forth at each other. Eventually we switched over to the main CP frequency, the one which the battalions were on. That way we would know in advance if there was any serious trouble and if we were going to be committed.

Night fell. We knew there wouldn't be any action that night. Things dropped off then. Besides, it would be impossible for the helicopters to land us in the jungle at night. So Dai Uy and I took a jeep and went downtown. We drove along the beach. Lots of seafood restaurants there, each one with a porch out front. We picked one, sat outside and ordered a fish meal. While we ate we could look out across the South China Sea. It was so peaceful. It was hard to believe that I was sitting there safe enjoying a delicious meal while a few miles away, fellow Advisors and Vietnamese were fighting for their lives.

The next day Captain Sommerfield joined the battalion. He arrived about 10:00 a.m. My transfer would be effective that day. The helicopter that brought him in would also be the one to take me out. I asked the pilot if he would take me by the "jump" CP up in the rubber, so I could say good-bye to Colonel Wilson. He said he would. So I hopped on. I admired the pilot for this. He didn't have to take me up there. It was a dangerous area. It was just one more chance he had to take, but away we went. When

241

we arrived over the area of the command post, I saw a large clearing in front of an old French plantation house. We landed there and I got out and walked toward the house. As I looked up ahead I could see Colonel Wilson, standing on the porch with about six of his Staff Officers and a few Vietnamese around him. As I got closer, he recognized me and became very angry and shouted at me across the lawn. "You dumb bastard! I told you not to come out here. God damn it, I gave you a direct order not to go on this operation. Those were my specific orders when we had the briefing!"

When I reached him I replied, "Sir, it's true you told me not to go on the operation but you didn't say that I couldn't come out to the CP."

"God damn it, Behnke," he shouted back, "that's not what I told you. I told you—you were not to come out here at all." Then he turned to one of the staff officers who was standing next to him and said, "Didn't I tell Behnke he was not to come out here at all?"

The obsequious officer gave a sheepish grin, and said, "Yes, Sir, that's what you said."

Colonel Wilson turned and shouted at me, "Get your ass inside!"

We walked through two large doors and he slammed both of them shut behind us. We moved to the other side of the room where he had a portable field desk set up. Suddenly his mood changed. He turned toward me and looked at me in a very kindly way. I thought I could almost see tears in his eyes. "Jim," he said, "I know you have been through a hell of a lot. I know you have suffered a lot. You're lucky to be alive. That's why I didn't want you to go on this last operation. You've done a damn fine job and I'll never forget that. I appreciate everything you've done for the battalion. Now go over to the Infantry School and stay out of trouble."

Then he put his arm around my shoulder and walked me back to the door. As we approached the door he took his arm off my shoulder and opened it. As we walked outside his mood changed instantly and began to rant and rave again, but I could tell he was just "putting on the dog." "Get out of here you dumb bastard!" he yelled, "I told you not to come out here and that's what I meant. Now get on that God damned helicopter and don't come back."

I strode off across the grass to the waiting chopper with its blades turning. Once I got past the group of Staff Officers I broke out into a smile. "What a guy," I thought to myself.

I hopped on board and sat on the floor facing back toward the plantation house. Everybody was standing there looking back at me, waiting for the chopper to take off. As we lifted skyward, I brought my arm up in a slow, meaningful salute. Colonel Wilson brought his arm up, too. We both held salutes until I was out of sight. I would miss him.

CHAPTER 18

We rose high above the jungle, banked left and headed west toward Saigon and the Infantry School and my new job. After about a half hour I could recognize the area; the highway, the Rung-Sat Swamps. And then there it was, the Infantry School, located halfway between Saigon and Binh Hoa in a very safe area, just off the super highway. Our chopper started its slow descent, circling the school and then landed in a large grassy area near the parade field. I got off, took my duffel bag with me and walked up to the Advisors house. Here I met an Army Major by the name of Smith. He was my new boss. He was prematurely grey around the temples, and old for a Major, maybe forty-five but a very friendly guy, and very tough and experienced. He welcomed me to the Infantry School and took me to my quarters.

I noticed that the Infantry School was a large place and was laid out just like a Military Academy (which, of course, it was). But this school was not for their "West Pointers." It was their Officer Candidates School for men who came from the ranks or from college. A large parade field was located in the middle of the Academy. Next to the parade field was a tennis court, where the Vietnamese officers played tennis, and across from that the Advisors House where we had our headquarters and took our meals. Down the street from the house was our quarters. They were located in a long white concrete building which had a red tile roof on it. Inside this building was lots of little one room cubicles, each one facing the street. I

244

looked inside my new room. It had an iron cot, a small closet and a bathroom with a shower. Very nice! We returned to the house to meet the other Advisors who were there. Most of them were former Ranger Advisors who have done their time in the field. I learned that the Infantry School had become a sort of rest home for "old Rangers," a place where they could finish out their tour in safety before they went home. I was happy to be with them.

One of the first things that happened to me at Thu Duc was that I got to go on R&R (five days of rest and recuperation). There were many places to choose from; Bangkok, Hong Kong, Tokyo. I chose Hong Kong. Those five days would not be counted against my annual leave (annual vacation). Finally my orders came through. I was to catch an airplane out of Tan San Nhut Airport in Saigon. Before leaving, I learned that our Chinese cook wanted to talk with me. He worked in our kitchen and provided the meals. He was a very friendly guy, and I got to know him well during the first week that I was there.

When he found out that I was going to Hong Kong, he asked to talk to me privately in his kitchen. I walked back into the kitchen to see him. It was all very suspicious. He asked me if I would take a package to Hong Kong for him, a small, book size package wrapped in a plain brown paper bag. I would not be told what was in it and he would pay me $1000 in cash just to do it. I immediately told him no. I just didn't like the idea. I didn't like not knowing what was in the package. I knew, of course, it wasn't drugs, although it could have been, because there was a lot of drugs moving throughout Far East Asia. But he wasn't into drugs. I knew that for sure. It was money. Probably U.S. dollars. He changed a lot of money for the Advisors. If he could get these dollars back to Hong Kong he could get a rate ten times better than in Vietnam. He was probably just setting up a nest egg for himself in Hong Kong in case things went bad in Vietnam and I didn't blame him for that, but it was smuggling and I wasn't going to get involved.

The day came for the flight. The plane was an old four engine prop job. I sat next to a Navy chaplain and a Navy nurse. She was in Vietnam because all the support in Saigon in those days (including medical) was being provided by the U.S. Navy. The Advisors in the field were Army but the Navy was running everything else. The nurse was attractive, so I started talking to her. I found out that she was the girl I had read about in the newspaper. She had been wounded in a terrorist bomb explosion. The bomb had gone off near her hotel in Saigon, a hotel where all the nurses lived. She was the only one that got cut by the flying glass, and became an instant heroine overnight. "The first nurse to get wounded in Vietnam." We had a nice conversation enroute to Hong Kong and agreed to go out to dinner that night.

Upon arrival, we were met by a really neat team of Chinese who worked for the American Army R&R program. They put us on busses, oriented us on the city, told us about sightseeing and got us to our hotels. The whole operation was extremely well run. They wore red blazers with a large gold R&R emblem on it. I decided to split a double room with the Chaplain. That way we could cut our hotel bill in half.

Later it was time for this date with the nurse so I went over to her room and knocked on the door. She let me in and offered me a drink. We went over to a window overlooking the city and talked. As I stood there talking and sipping a drink, I couldn't help but think how ludicrous this all was, of how up to now people had been trying to kill me every day, of how I had actually been under a death sentence, with little chance of survival and now, in an instant, by the magic of aviation, I had been transported to a city like this, a place of safety with millions of electric lights. It all seemed so strange. I began to talk to her about my experiences in the war, and of what I had been going through. I talked on and on. I had to talk to somebody. I had never expressed my feelings to anyone before. And there she was, a girl, very pretty, and someone so very nice to talk to. But it didn't go over. I could tell it was the wrong conversation. It was just something you didn't discuss on a date. Even though we were in the same army, and lived in the same country, I could tell we were miles apart. She just didn't understand what was going on, nor did I expect her to. There was just too vast a distance between her job in Saigon and mine in the field. It was, of course, the wrong conversation so we changed the subject. We had a wonderful time later on with dinner and wine. It was a nice date and she was a wonderful person.

One night, the Chaplain and I decided to venture out and visit the "Susie Wong" area of Hong Kong. Since we were staying on the mainland in an area called Kowloon, we took the ferry across to the island of Hong Kong and then hopped a streetcar down to the "Susie Wong District." The actual Chinese name of the district is Wan Chai but the GI's call it the "Susie Wong District" after the movie of the same title. That's where all the night life was, the young Chinese girls, the prostitutes, the bars, and the U.S. Fleet. The Chaplain wanted to see it for himself, so off we went. Upon arrival, we walked from bar to bar to get to know what the area was like. Every bar had a Madam, lots of beautiful girls, lights, music, dancing, and sailors. Later on we stopped in front of one bar, went in and sat down. The Madam came over and said, "You want girl?"

We said "No, we just came in to watch and have a beer."

Nevertheless, she sat down with us and began to persuade us to have a girl. She was very persistent, so after a while, I decided to have a little fun with her. I told her I didn't like any of the girls. I just liked her. I wanted her. Mamasan. She was "number one." She was the beautiful one. (She was twice the age of the other girls but very good looking.) But I knew she wasn't available so I kept pressing my point. Each time she would laugh and say, "No, no, not me. I Mamasan. You take young girl."

And I would keep saying, "No, no, I want you Mamasan."

We played this game for a while and eventually she left. She walked away still saying, "Me Mamasan. You take young girl." We all laughed.

After checking out a couple of other bars, we decided to go home. It was about 11:30 p.m. We took off walking down a dark narrow street headed back for the main boulevard and the trolley tracks. It was about this time that I noticed we were being followed by three men. I knew

247

right away who they were. Muggers. We were going to be robbed. I then told the Chaplain not to look back and that we were being followed. I told him that when we got up to the next corner, we would just casually turn left, but as soon as the corner blocked the view of those who were stalking us, we would take off in a dead run. So when we got to the next corner, we turned left at a natural pace, and then took off running as fast as we could. We ran up that street at top speed and then turned right. Then we raced down that block and turned left again, zig zagging our way back to the main drag. We lost them. I was sure glad I spotted them. Guys on R&R carry a lot of money (for shopping and spending) and are easy prey to scum like that, particularly if they are coming out of the Susie Wong area drunk (which we weren't).

The rest of My R&R went without incident. I did all the usual things; visited the tourist attractions and shopped my heart out. What a city. The most exciting in the world!

My last day in Hong Kong proved to be quite humorous, in fact a real riot. It centered around my catching the plane home. I got out to the airport early all right and checked in. That part was simple. The R&R people were all waiting for us. We even had our own "check in" counter. The R&R guys were all over the airport in their red jackets so we couldn't miss them. After checking in, we had to wait for the plane to arrive, so I decided to use the restroom. Surely, I told myself, they have a loud speaker in there to call the flight when it was ready. So I took my newspaper along to "while away" the time as I sat on the "throne." When I came out, to my amazement, I found all the guys were gone. The flight had been called, the desk was closed and I was alone. I had missed the plane.

I ran frantically down the row of counters looking for those Chinese R&R guys. Finally, I spotted several of them in their red blazers leaving the building. I ran up to them and told them my predicament. They said they would try to stop the flight. Then they ran over to a telephone on the wall and made a quick call. We ran back to the gate where they had originally called the flight and then they took me outside to a ramp. The plane, which had almost made it to the runway turned around and came back to pick me up. They kept the engines running while I scampered up the ramp and inside the aircraft.

Once I walked inside the plane, pandemonium broke out. All the Advisors started shouting and clapping and cheering. They all naturally assumed that I had been in the arms of some Chinese whore the whole week, and just couldn't break away until the last minute. It made no difference what I said as I walked down the aisle defending myself. They all just kept saying, "Sure, Behnke, sure," and kept on cheering.

Red faced and wearing an embarrassing grin I finally, and gratefully, found my seat.

When I got back to Thu Duc I found out that the Army wasn't going to pay me for five months. It was a long story and went like this. When I was back at Ft. Bragg going through Advisors School, a girlfriend of mine who worked in finance, converted my Army pay over to the Navy system. The reason for this was that the Navy was running all support in Saigon and could handle my pay better when I got there. Enroute to Vietnam however, and on vacation in St. Louis, I walked into an Air Force Base and asked for the month of June's pay because I was broke. Then six months later, with me in Vietnam, the Air Force sent a bill to the Navy saying I owed them $500, which they said they paid me last June. There would have been no problem about this at all if the Navy had kept my pay record going back to last June, because it would have showed that they (the Navy) hadn't paid me, and the Air Force had, and that I wasn't paid double. But they didn't keep that record. For some unknown reason, they closed out my record on 30 June, put it on microfilm and shipped it all to the States, and then started up a new pay card on me effective 1 July. So the proof I needed to show that I was never paid by the Navy, for the month of June, was now in some Navy Archive back on the East Coast. Meanwhile, the United States Air force claimed I owed them $500. Since I could only receive $100 a month in cash from the Navy while in Vietnam (a Navy rule designed to combat black marketeering) the Navy decided they would not take $100 a month out of my pay for the next five months, and give it back to the Air force to repay my debt to them, thus leaving me broke for the next five months. I couldn't believe they wouldn't pay me for the next five months.

Fortunately, I found a friend who ran a hotel in Saigon, who would cash personal checks for me from my stateside bank. But, if it had been up to the Navy I would have starved to death. It taught me an important lesson. An Army man should never take a Navy pay record into an Air Force finance office to get paid while on vacation.

One day at the Infantry School, we had a graduation parade. All the officers and students were dressed in white uniforms. As a part of the ceremony, the officer candidates bent down on one knee, and took their oath of office as Commissioned Officers in the Vietnamese Army. While there, I spotted a beautiful girl in the stands. She was half French and half Vietnamese and an absolute knock out. She had been invited there by one of the Vietnamese officers on the school staff, who was a friend of her family.

I introduced myself and talked to her. She was absolutely beautiful. Since I knew the officer, who invited her, quite well, a Captain on the tactics committee, I asked him if he would get me a date with her and he did. She and I agreed to meet the next Saturday night. I took my jeep and parked it near her house. After picking her up we went out for dinner in a beautiful restaurant in Saigon. We had French onion soup, steak, salad and a glass of wine. I really enjoyed that evening. Later I took her home. She lived on what was an alley but that's the way many homes are in the city, no yards, no front porches, nothing but an alley lined with one solid concrete building and a door spaced every so often serving as an entrance to the various homes. I told the taxi to wait, and then walked her to her door and asked her for another date. She accepted.

I dated her a lot after that. It was really fun. I felt like a character out of a war novel, driving my jeep into town, running around an exciting Far East city with a beautiful Oriental girl on my arm. Yes, life at the good old Infantry School was great.

I met another girl, too. She worked in a bar frequented

by American Advisors. I went there occasionally for a beer. She was a "Saigon tea girl." She too, was very beautiful. I asked her out one night. I wanted to take her to dinner, but she said she couldn't go. I asked her why. She said that as an employee of the bar, she couldn't leave until the minimum number of drinks had been bought on her behalf. I asked her how many that was and she told me ten. (It amounted to about ten dollars.) So, I went over to the Mamasan who ran the place and asked her if I could "buy" her out. "What if I just paid for all the drinks up front," I asked, "could I take her out then?"

She said, "Yes." And so I did.

We caught a taxi and went out to eat. She came from a very poor family in the south of Vietnam and worked as a tea girl to support her mother, father, brothers and sisters. It was easy money and big money for a farm girl. Most of the girls involved in the "Saigon tea" stuff were good girls, who did it just for the money. All they provided was conversation and nothing more. I never saw a hint of prostitution connected with it. Of course, there were bars in Saigon that specialized in pornography and prostitution, but I didn't go to them and neither did most of the other Advisors. All the Advisors I knew were professionals and married men and not about to screw up their lives with unfaithfulness and some rare Oriental disease. Anyway, I dated this girl quite often. I really liked her. Maybe it was because she was so poor, or maybe it was because she was so beautiful, or maybe it was because she was such a sweet person. But one day, many weeks later, she disappeared without a word. I went to the bar to see her one night and Mamasan said she had "gone home." I guess maybe her family had something to do with that. Her father probably permitted her to be a "Saigon tea girl" against his own best wishes in order to meet some extreme financial emergency. Once that was met, it was time for her to come back.

Things were changing in Saigon. More and more Americans were arriving and prostitution was on the increase. The possibility existed that a girl could slip from "tea girl" to something worse. I'm sure that played a part in her decision too, but I'll never know. You have to remember the country was at war. Anything could have happened to cause her to pull up and go back home, but I'm glad she did.

Later in my tour, I dated another girl, an American redhead. I met her at the Rex Hotel dining room and bar, the social club in Saigon for American Advisors. I introduced myself, got to talking with her and asked her for a date. She worked as a secretary for the State Department. I enjoyed going out with her. She was a real nice kid and there were so many nice restaurants in Saigon to visit. We did them all. All the while it was impossible for me to believe that I was in a country torn by war. We could take a taxi around town in perfect safety, go on dates and visit nice restaurants, or just walk the streets, but the war was still there.

I was reminded of that every time I took her home. She lived in a very tall apartment that had a flat roof on top with a patio and we used to go up there after dates and have a drink and look out over the city. Since she lived on the edge of town, you could see where the lights of the city stopped and the Rung Sat swamp area began. Rung Sat was an area full of mangrove trees, mud and canals, and was impossible to control. The VC often moved into this area at night and caused problems for the Vietnamese Army, so they set up ambushes all over the place, hoping to catch them. As we looked out over that dark area, cognac glass in hand, it was like watching a show. Flares hung in the air illuminating the swamp. Occasionally tracer rounds would arch skyward into the inky darkness, indication an ambush had gone off. The country was still at war. And I was a spectator.

Saigon Scenes

Saigon was a fascinating city with immense boulevards, like those in Paris. The architecture was like that of France, with tall concrete structures lining the streets. Of course, all this was easy to understand. The French had been a colonial power there for many, many years. So why shouldn't the architecture and buildings exude the flavor of France? Restaurants, banks, streets, automobiles, all were French. Everything reflected a century of French rule.

The Hotel Continental was a nice place to go, when in town on a Sunday morning. It had a large outdoor coffee area surrounded by huge arches. From my table I could look directly out into the street, or back the other way into a garden. The waiters wore white jackets. The tables were massive with huge stuffed chairs. I loved to eat there. It was plush! I would order a cup of French coffee and a croissant roll for breakfast. Even the butter was wrapped in tin foil just like in the States. All very elegant and all very continental. I would sit there for hours and read my Sunday paper. Occasionally, I would glance up and watch people walk by. No one seemed to know there was a war going on.

One Sunday morning as Sergeant Hieu, my new driver, was driving me to Saigon for my usual Sunday morning breakfast and newspaper, we were suddenly passed by a long line of jeeps and trucks coming up from behind us at a speed of around 40 miles per hour. The trucks were loaded with hundreds of Vietnamese soldiers. We checked their patch. Sure enough they were wearing the shoulder patch of the 9th Division. The 9th Infantry Division was responsible for the area south of Saigon, all the way down to the South China Sea and west to the Cambodian border. They were known as the "coup division," because they always took part in coups. No coup could be successful without them, because of their strategic location next to the capital.

Hieu and I looked at each other and both said, "coup" at the same time. And it was. Another coup was taking place at that very moment and we were caught up in it. It was a good thing that there was no fighting or resistance or we could have been shot by accident. They roared right by us and took over the radio station, the government buildings, and Vietnamese Army Headquarters. They were now in control. A new coup, a new government. This coup would bring into power two men by the names of Hieu and Ky. When I first came to Vietnam, General Khanh was in charge. (He was the one who had that goatee and had overthrown the Diem Regime.) Then he was replaced by a civilian named Hoang. Hoang turned out to be a weak leader so the young officers tried to take

253

over the country but didn't make it. Now it looked like some guys named Thiu and Ky would run the government. (I'm sure I missed somebody in between, but I didn't have time to read the newspapers every day.)

CHAPTER 19

One Sunday I went to the Rex Hotel. It was a very tall building in the heart of Saigon. The top of the building was flat and had a guard rail all the way around it. You could walk over to the edge of the building and look straight down, ten stories. Little Peugot taxi cabs moved around below like crawling bugs, weaving their way around corners and down the streets and alleys. It had a fantastic view of the city. The whole top floor had been converted into a restaurant. The hotel space below was run by the American Government. (It was a place where visiting officers and VIPs came to get a room.) The hotel turned out to be the social hub for all the American Advisors in Saigon. They had a small PX there too, a place where you could buy a toothbrush, toothpaste, or whatever. It was always a thrill for me to put on civilian clothes on a Sunday morning, go to church and then head for the Rex Hotel. I always considered it an extremely safe place, because it was all the way up on the top floor and away from any ground attack. It was also the only place in town where you could get a glass of fresh milk. Genuine fresh milk! How delicious it was. It's funny how you can miss something like that in a foreign country. And of course there was the *Stars and Stripes*, the Army newspaper, complete with funny papers and a sports page. So I would just sit there for hours, enjoying a good stateside breakfast, reading my Sunday paper.

Later after coffee, I would walk to the edge of the roof and look down at the broad expanse of the city below.

After that I would visit the market a few blocks away. This market was huge, encompassing one entire city block, and it had hundreds of booths in it. Each booth sold something different. There was cloth for sale, pecans, pliers, screwdrivers, you name it. The list was endless. It was just like one gigantic department store, broken down into hundreds of little square booths. I ran across one booth that sold brass table tops. They were oval in shape and sat on a wooden stand. Each one had an Oriental design on it, etched by hand. They sold for $15 each, an amazing bargain. So I bought six, one for myself, one for my parents, and one for each of my sisters and brother.

Hieu loaded my purchases into the jeep, and we whipped out onto the main drag, mingling with the seemingly endless, smoky maze of Saigon traffic. I was always amused, and amazed at the same time, by the three wheel motorcycle taxis, (the one with the seat mounted up front over the front wheels were "you're the bumper"). It was a real thrill to ride the motorcycle in 40 mile an hour rush hour traffic. You could almost reach out and touch the back of the car in front of you. Of course, you knew if the guy in front of you slammed on his brakes you were dead.

Just past the Tan Son Nhut Airport, I spotted some ceramic elephants sitting out in front of a store. We spun the jeep around and headed back to talk to the man. He wanted $10 a piece for them, another fantastic bargain. The ceramic elephants were three feet high, and about two feet wide, and were flat on top. The Vietnamese placed them in their gardens and sometimes sat on them. Americans bought them to ship home to put flower pots or vases on top. They were absolutely beautiful. Some were white, others green. Some had painted tusks and feet. Others were just one solid color.

It was a weekday. I took the afternoon off to visit Trinh in the hospital. I drove out of Thu Duc and headed left down the four lane super highway for Saigon. Later I crossed the broad, expansive, American built, concrete bridge that spanned the Saigon River. Then into Saigon itself. I meandered through traffic for a while and finally, ended up at in front of Cong Hoa Hospital. This time I knew where to go. Again, it was a pitiful sight walking toward Trinh's room. Men standing on crutches with a leg gone, others smoking a cigarette, an arm missing. Just row after row of amputees.

I reached Trinh's room. I went inside and stood near his bed. He gave me one of his famous Trinh smiles. Then he told me that he now knew he was a paraplegic, that he was paralyzed from the waist down, and that he would never walk again. He also told me that his beautiful girlfriend had left him. She had to. She had to marry someone who could provide for her. Life was difficult enough in the Orient, trying to scratch out a living, even if you had two arms and two legs. But when you lose one, or all of them, you are really out of luck. There was no Social Security, no pensions, no nothing. So she had to leave. It was a sad day. We talked for a while. I told him about Dai Uy Doung and the battalion, about what I was doing at the Infantry School, about old friends and that I had heard from. After a while it was time to say good-bye. But it wouldn't be good-bye forever. I planned to visit him often and to stay in touch with him.

I closed the door behind me and walked along the porch outside the hospital. I was walking down some steps and turning to the right when I heard a voice behind me call out "Dai Uy, Dai Uy."

I looked back and immediately recognized that thin figure. It was Cowboy. I hadn't seen him in months. The last time I saw him was in Tay Ninh when he had been shot through both arms and was wearing those bloody casts. I remember arguing with that incredibly stupid Vietnamese doctor, who would do nothing to correct the situation. As I approached him, I noticed something wrong about him. He was holding his arms in an unusual position. The lower portion of both arms were sticking straight out from the elbows. I asked him in Vietnamese how he was doing. He told me "sau lam" (very bad). He said that he had been treated by a "bac si sau lam" (really bad Doctor).

I understood what he meant as he showed me the problem. His arms were locked in place, frozen at the elbows. The doctor hadn't had the time, the concern or the skill to do a better job. Cowboy would never be able to

257

bend his arms again. I was very bitter about that. But there was nothing I could do. It was all too late. His arms were frozen in place now. He would soon be discharged from the Army with six children to feed, and there was no pension for him and he couldn't work. I didn't know what he was going to do. I wanted to say "this God damn war," but profanity was not a part of my vocabulary.

While at the Infantry School one of the officers on the staff, with whom I had a passing acquaintance, was killed riding a motorcycle. This was not an unusual occurrence in Vietnam. They all drove at 70 miles an hour and eventually, wound up underneath a truck or over the hood of a car. I was invited to go to the funeral, because I was the Advisor to the section in which he worked. Of course, I wanted to go and pay my respects. I caught a ride with one of the staff officers from the school. Later we arrived at the cemetery, and filed into a one room chapel. The casket was up front draped in the yellow and red striped flag of South Vietnam. The casket was closed. Some people were standing, most were sitting on benches. No matter where they were, sitting or standing, the women cried out and threw their arms into the air, wailing away in that haunting voice. Others lit incense sticks. The whole room smelled of incense.

After a short time the body was transported to the grave. The casket was then placed on ropes and suspended over the grave (just like we do in the States). People cried. Some women throw themselves over the casket. Two of them prostrated themselves over the casket, wailing all the while. All were dressed in white clothes, the traditional mourning color of the Vietnam. There was a constant, sad wailing pitch in the air, rising and falling, sometimes softly, sometimes loudly. Finally, they started lowering the casket into the ground, and then the shrieking really began. It was unbearable to watch. Since it was permissible for all but the family to leave, we did so. Coming back from Saigon we passed another accident. A large cement truck had run over a child on the super highway. A horrible scene. The child had gotten caught up in the dual rear wheels in back and was turned into a mass of hamburger and blood. There was not one part of the body I could recognize. It was just one big gory mess. I had to turn away. We sped home.

It was mid-afternoon. Everybody was taking their normal siesta from 1:00 p.m. to 3:00 p.m. Some slept, others played tennis. I decided to get in my jeep and go for a drive by myself. I headed East across the parade ground, and then downhill past the many buildings, toward the training sites. At the end of this road I got to the so called "safety limit." There was a deep stream there which marked the boundary between the "controlled" and "uncontrolled" areas. The VC did operate beyond that point at night. But there were no problems there during the day. At the stream crossing, just before you passed over an old wooden bridge, was a Vietnamese Army outpost. It was nothing more than some sand bags piled 12 feet high to form a room. The walls had holes in them through which they could stick their rifles to fire back at the enemy. A corrugated metal sheet lay on top to ward off the rain. Three men lived there. They lived there 24 hours a day. Hammocks were strung up. Their job was to guard the bridge. It was located at a very beautiful and idyllic spot. Clear cold water ran by directly in front of them. To their right were bright green rice paddies and across the stream on the other side was the dark, verdant and foreboding jungle.

These three men served little purpose in the war. If the Viet Cong had it in their mind to attack the Infantry School they would simply overrun them and continue straight on up the hill. But in all probability, in a real attack, they would simple bypass them, cross secretly down stream at another spot, attack the school by surprise, and then take them out on the way back. These "mini-monuments to stupidity" existed all over Vietnam. This form of warfare, which we were forced to fight, gave the guerrilla such a distinct advantage over the government. The government had to protect that bridge, (or road, or transformers or whatever) 24 hours a day, and that took an immense amount of men. Conversely, all the guerrilla had to do was choose one night of the month in which to attack and blow it up. If the government was not there on that particular night, then it was gone. Meanwhile the government was forced to deploy huge numbers of men to protect all these places at the same time. It cost the government ten times more in men and manpower than it did the guerrilla. So the odds were against them.

I crossed over the bridge and headed out into the jungle. It was not really "good" jungle, just thick brush. After driving down the road for about 15 minutes, I got out of the jeep and walked over to the edge of the bush. Was there anybody out there in that stuff? Could this be a place where a few VC hid out during the day? Certainly no one ever came around checking and it was too far away from the Infantry School for our security patrols. I pulled out my .38 caliber pistol, cocked it and walked into the brush. It was about shoulder high. I walked in a few steps, paused and listened, and then checked behind me. No one was there. Again I moved forward, carefully and quietly, like a cat, taking two or three steps at a time, pistol cocked, listening. I continued to move forward through the brush in the same rhythmic, pattern. Walk. Stop. Listen. I heard nothing. Was anyone out there? I didn't know but I knew in my own heart what I was doing. I was hunting, hunting one or two Viet Cong. And then I asked myself, "Why? Why was I doing this? Was it because I knew it was safe or relatively safe? Was it because I had been outnumbered in jungle so many times, with so many hundreds of the enemy against me, that I now liked this new and unusual thrill? Or did I just like to stalk people, one on one, when it was 'even steven?'"

It was a welcome change to the senseless slaughter I had witnessed. I squatted down and listened. Beads of perspiration formed on my forehead, but they were not from fear. It was simply hot. Steamy hot. I was not afraid. In fact I was enjoying it, being there, hiding, listening. After about 20 minutes of "stalking," I moved back to my jeep, cranked it over and headed back to the Infantry School. Along the way I thought out loud to myself. "You know you're a coward Behnke. You know you're not brave. You fear the jungle, and the thousands of enemy, and the bullets, and death around every corner. You're not John Wayne." Yet there I was experiencing a feeling of exhilaration in the brush. I was the hunter and they were the hunted. The tables were turned. I was the one who had the element of surprise on my side. I was the one doing the stalking. And I liked it.

During another afternoon siesta, I got in my jeep and went for another drive, this time to the Buddhist Temple located about a half a mile beyond the school fence. It was situated in the middle of an open pasture. I took Sgt. Hieu with me. Sgt. Hieu was an interpreter at the Infantry School and a good friend of mine, as well as a part time driver. We talked a lot together. He was also a leader in the Thu Duc Protestant Church and a great Christian. So we decided to visit this Buddhist Temple together. I had never seen one before.

We parked the jeep in the grass field outside and walked in. Even though I had lived in the Orient for what seemed to be a long time, a very strange and eerie feeling came over me as I entered the building. It was dark inside. As my eyes focused and I could see tapestries hanging on the walls. There was also the strong, pungent odor of incense burning. Off to the side I spotted a large gong which they struck every hour or so. Sgt. Hieu motioned for me to take off my shoes and to leave my carbine at the door. I didn't feel like doing it but of course I couldn't offend the Buddhist Monks who were in the Temple. Two of them gazed at me impassively. They seemed to understand that we just wanted to look around. They didn't act like they were happy to see us but they didn't act unfriendly either. They seemed detached.

I left my weapon with the clip and bullets in it at the door along with my boots. We walked around. One of the Buddhist Monks spoke with Sgt. Hieu and answered questions from time to time. I wondered if these particular Monks were sympathetic to the VC. Word had it that the Buddhist and the VC had been talking to each other and that they were on the same side and that the Monks wanted to cause trouble for the government. We would never know about these two guys. After a tour of the Temple, I put my boots back on, grabbed my weapon and walked out into the bright sunshine. We hopped into the jeep and roared back over the green grass to the school.

One of my jobs at the Infantry School was to go around and check the perimeter at night. The perimeter was a

261

security fence that ran around the outside of the Infantry School. It was quite large. At various spots along the fence, the cadets set up outposts consisting of twenty or so men. My job was to go around and check these outposts to make sure the cadets were on the ball and had not fallen asleep. Since I was the Duty Officer, it was my turn to go out and check the troops. We chose an outpost to inspect, then parked some distance away from it and walked toward it in the dark. Suddenly one of the Vietnamese cadets screamed, "Ai." ("Ai" means "who" or "who is there?") The Vietnamese duty driver replied in Vietnamese that the American Advisor was there to check the outpost. He ordered us to come forward. Once he recognized me he relaxed a little bit. We talked for a while and I looked around. Some of the men were awake but most were sleeping.

I looked out across the barbed wire fence that marked the ring around the school and peered out in the darkness. Anything moving beyond this point at night could be shot dead on the spot without question. Nothing moved at night in Vietnam, (except the enemy). The people were very strictly warned about this to prevent innocent casualties. It was all fair and square. They knew anyone who did move at night would be killed so they stayed at home.

Since it was just about daylight I decided to stay and watch the sun come up, before I headed back for breakfast. As the first light of day started to illuminate the fields to our front, the world became alive. Dogs come out into the fields and barked and looked around. Later a farmer with a hoe walked past. Then an oxcart with a driver perched on top rolled by, wheels creaking. Later a farm woman, wearing black pajamas and a conical hat, sauntered past with a long pole balanced on her shoulders. Hanging from each end of the pole were two baskets loaded with vegetables. She was on her way to market. I found all this very odd. A few minutes ago it was darkness and death, now it was light and life.

One day, about 3 p.m. in the afternoon, as I was taking a short cut back to the Advisors House, past a series of gas pumps where they fueled up the vehicles, I heard a voice call out to me, "Dai Uy, Dai Uy."

I stopped and turned around. It was one of the

Sergeants from the battalion, the 33rd Rangers. I recognized him immediately. I remembered his as a real friendly guy. He was wearing the stripes of a Senior Master Sergeant. I noticed that he was all crippled up now. He shuffled toward me like the Hunchback of Notre Dame. He must have caught a mortar round somewhere out there that blew him halfway to kingdom come. Despite his scars and hunchbacked condition he came up to me and gave me a big smile and said, "Dai Uy met qua?" (The old traditional greeting used so many times along the trail in the past, "Is the Captain tired?")

Tears welded up in my eyes as I told him, "No, Dai Uy khong met." ("No, the Dai Uy is not tired.")

What a soldier, to be able to smile through all those wounds and scars. I held his hand tightly, but I couldn't speak. I was all choked up. He was so badly wounded. But he understood. There was a communication there, a respect, words didn't need to be spoken. After clasping his hand for a long time I turned and walked away. Bitterness overwhelmed me.

It was Sunday, time to go to church with Mr. Hieu. We got together quite often. When I found out that he was a Christian I started worshiping in his church in Thu Duc. They were affiliated with the Christian Missionary Alliance back in the states. Their chapel was a very simple building, plain and white, made out of concrete, with a slanted roof, and a steeple with a cross on top. I always sat next to Mr. Hieu and his family. His kids were so cute and they would always smile at me. Everybody dressed so nicely. The women wore the traditional Ao-Dai clothing and the men bright colored shirts. Some even wore a white shirt with a tie. I really enjoyed the service with them, even though I didn't know what they were saying. They sang their hearts out. It was very much like a service back home; some readings, the pastor's message, and hymns. After worship, I met the Pastor. He was an older man, maybe 60 years old. He gave me a huge Vietnamese grin. It was a great day. It was good to see the Gospel at work.

We had a Captain Bradley at the Infantry School, who wanted to leave the school and become an advisor to a battalion. When he arrived in Vietnam he was immediately assigned to the Infantry School, so he never had a chance to join a unit in combat. But now he wanted to go. He kept saying, "I gotta go. I gotta get out of here. I gotta get a battalion. I gotta get a CIB."

And we kept saying, "No, don't go. You don't need it. You've done a good job here. You'll get killed out there."

But he wouldn't listen. The day came and he finally got his battalion. He was assigned as an Advisor to an Infantry Battalion in the Delta. We all wished him the best. But I had a strange feeling as I shook his hand and watched him leave for his new assignment.

Lunch time. I walked into the dining room of the Advisors House. The guys were standing around waiting for chow to be put on the table. They were talking about some Captain who got killed down south. Seems like he was on an operation on an LCN. (A Navy boat shaped like a floating cheese box.) They were riding up river when they ran over a 55 gallon barrel full of C4 (dynamite). They didn't know whether it had been set to go off automatically, or had been fired from the shore with wires, but the whole LCN was blown to bits and they couldn't find the Advisor's body.

They found him two days later floating in the water. They also said this Advisor only had two weeks left in the country. I asked somebody if they knew who he was, because I only had two weeks to go too. It had to be somebody I knew. Then they told me it was Clay Mansfield. What a shock. Clay, my best friend from the career course, married to a pretty blond girl, who always had me over for supper and a glass of port wine and a cigar, who always said that nothing would ever happen to him. Clay, dead. I didn't know what to think. I immediately thought of his wife, of someone going to the door and giving her the telegram. Clay gone. I was dumbfounded.

It was Friday. Mirth 6 called me and offered me a free flight to Vung Tau for the weekend. The helicopter pilots had a villa down there, where they vacationed on weekends. I packed my gym bag and walked out to the big flat parade field to wait for the "bird." It circled and came in. I hopped on and we were on our way.

It was a beautiful flight down. Once we got altitude I

could see a long way off. To my left was the highway from Binh Hoa down to Vung Tau and "ambush alley." Directly below was the Rung Sat Swamp stretching for miles. (The Rung Sat can best be described as a low jungle area flooded with ocean water. It has hundreds of thousands of acres of swamp, canals, mangrove and you name it. Anything and anybody could be down there.) Eventually, we saw the blue of the ocean and Vung Tau ahead. We landed and got in a jeep and headed for the villa.

Later that night, we all went down to the beach where all the nice restaurants were located. (The same spot where I had supper with Dai Uy that night when we were in Corp Reserve.) We sat outside on a large porch and had a wonderful seafood meal. The water lapped peacefully against the beach. Again it was hard for me to believe that I was in Vietnam and there were people being killed right up the road.

I also came to Vung Tau for a purpose. I had heard that LT Trinh was there. He had been moved from Cong Hoa Hospital to the rehabilitation hospital in Vung Tau. I would try to find him. So I caught a little Peugot cab and took it over to the outskirts of town where the hospital was located. I got out and walked around the grounds. Lots of people there were on crutches and amputees sunning themselves in chairs. I couldn't find the main office so I walked around from ward to ward, asking questions in Vietnamese looking for my friend. After about 20 minutes, someone pointed to an area in back of one of the wards. It looked like the entrance to what we would call a storm cellar. It had steps going down into it. The man pointed there. "There is where you should go," he said.

So I did. I walked down some large cement steps that led to an underground room. At the bottom were large wooden doors, so I pushed them open and walked inside. It was dark. I stood there for a few moments trying to get my eyes accustomed to the blackness of the room. The longer I stood there, the more I could see. Gradually a horrible scene presented itself. The room was full of burn victims, men burned beyond recognition. They were sitting in their beds staring at me. All of their faces were gone. They had no lips, no ears, no eyes, nothing, just

265

holes. Their fingers had been burnt off too and there was nothing left but stubs. I could hear their voices gurgle as they tried to talk to me. It was all so horrible. I tried not to show my fear. I mumbled something about looking for a friend and then closed the door behind me.

It was absolutely unbelievable, like something out of some macabre movie. I walked back into the brilliant sunlight. I thanked God that I was still alive and well. (I later learned that Trinh was not in Vung Tau at all.)

The weekend was over. It was time to fly back to the Infantry School. I got on the chopper and we headed back toward Thu Duc. After getting airborne Major Stewart (Mirth 6) asked, "How would you like to drop by Binh Gia and say hello to the family you stayed with?"

I told him, "I'd love it."

So we banked right and followed the blacktop out toward Binh Gia. We circled the village and then landed in front of the large stone Catholic Church. I hopped out and ran over to the house where I used to stay. The little girl was there along with her dad. It was like coming home again. Soon Major Stewart joined us and asked me to follow him back to the market place. He said there was something he wanted to show me. Upon arrival he pointed to a Vietnamese boy in an Army uniform carrying a carbine and asked, "Do you know who this is?"

I said, "No, I don't."

He replied, "This is the little boy you shot, the one that you called that helicopter strike in on, he's alive."

I ran up to the kid. He was about 14 years old. I gave him a great big hug. He was alive. I couldn't believe it. I pushed him back at arms length and looked at him. Tears came to my eyes. He was healthy and alive. It made my year.

Monday morning. After watching the troops work out on tactical maneuvers in the field, I came back for lunch. I could tell something was wrong by all the somber looks on the Advisors' faces. It didn't take them long to tell me. Captain Bradley had been killed. He was with us just a few days ago, and now he was dead. They said he got it on his first combat patrol, walking down a dike when a machine gun opened fire and caught him. I told him not to go. I told him.

CHAPTER 20

It was Monday night. I was the Duty Officer. It was about 1:00 a.m. when I got a call to go up to the main gate. The Vietnamese were having a problem with some drunk who was giving them trouble. He was a "Co Van My" (American Advisor). I drove up. Upon arrival I saw a jeep stopped on the other side of the entrance gate. It had three Americans in it. They had been drinking. I recognized the Senior man as a Major from the Armor School. He was very, very drunk. He was so drunk that he could barely sit up in his jeep. The Vietnamese guards opened up the gate to let me go through to check things out. Evidently, these three had been out drinking all night and had gotten back too late, as the gate was locked for the evening.

As I pulled my jeep up along side the Major's I could see he was slobbering drunk and wobbling. It was then that I noticed he had a .45 caliber automatic pistol resting in his lap. He picked up the pistol and slowly moved it until it was pointing smack dab in my face. I didn't say a word. I didn't dare argue with him. One drunken twitch and I was dead. I said, "You go on through."

Then I motioned for the Vietnamese to let them pass. They drove back to the Advisors Building and went into the Major's hootch and didn't come out. Satisfied that they had turned in for the evening I went back to the Advisors House. I had to file an "incident report" the next day. I knew it would get the Major in trouble, but I had to do it. A Duty Officer is duty bound to report the truth. I printed it up in ball point pen and gave it to the Colonel. The Major was gone in 24 hours. I later heard he was shipped back to the United States, a short of "Persona Non Grata" by Army standards.

A typical day for me at the Infantry School was to get up in the morning, take a shower, shave, put on my jungle fatigues and boots and walk over to the Advisors House for coffee, eggs, and toast. Then my job took me out to the field, to check training to see how they were doing; to see if they were doing anything wrong, if they were well organized, and to give them advice on how to improve the situation. They had been very well organized lately. For example, they no longer had two units showing up in the same site for training any more. That used to be a problem before Captain Bradley showed up. He had been a "training schedule" specialist. He had shown them how to block out each hour of training on one gigantic board so that there would be no duplication of hours. This system put the right number of men at the right site on the right day.

I was not super impressed with their tactical instruction, however. (The subject that taught them how to fight in the field.) I didn't think that the men, who were doing the instructing, knew very much about what they were talking about. The problem was, most of them had never been in combat. They were very sharp of course. Most of them had gone through training at our own Infantry School at Ft. Benning. But, they taught everything right out of the book. Another problem was that they were teaching "conventional tactics." That's great if you're fighting a conventional war, but we weren't. We were fighting a guerrilla war and the guerrillas didn't go by the book. So I figured if the enemy didn't go by the book, then neither should we. We needed to fight fire with fire. So one of my goals was to change the tactical instruction to fit the unconventional situation we faced in the field. But it was like pushing wet spaghetti uphill.

The ambush training for example was ridiculous. The men would lie out in the open and were not camouflaged. You could plainly see them with your own eyes. (An ambush is supposed to be a surprise attack on a moving

268

enemy from a hidden position.) It was obvious they weren't going to surprise anybody. And they didn't employ an early warning system either, to tell them when the enemy was coming down the trail. If they pulled this sort of stuff out in the field, they would be the ones who ended up ambushed. There was just all sorts of things that needed to be done. So I had to train them to be guerrillas and soldiers at the same time and it wasn't an easy job.

About a half an hour before lunch every day, I got together with the Vietnamese instructors, to talk tactics and how to improve the training. Then came lunch, and there was nothing to do after that, but take a siesta. Usually, however, I played tennis during that time (from about 12:30 until 2:30). The Vietnamese thought we were crazy to be out in the hot sun playing tennis when we should be resting. It reminded me of that old phrase, "mad dogs and Englishmen go out in the noon day sun." It was extremely hot, but we loved it. We got sun tans, lost weight, and stayed in shape. At 2:30 p.m. it was shower time and then back out to the field. They usually held live fire exercises in the afternoon (exercises in which the Cadets shot real bullets instead of blank ammunition). It was funny but before I came to Vietnam firing "blanks" didn't bother me. But now when I heard one of those guns going off...it sounded like someone was really shooting at me and it put fear in me.

After training it was time for supper. The meals were fantastic and the Chinese chef a whiz. We all chipped in each month to pay him. After supper we just sat out on the porch and had a beer and then later walked inside to watch a movie. We got first run films brought over free by the Army. At night our counterparts, the Vietnamese officers played tennis across the street. The courts were lighted. They really dressed up for the occasion. I guess they learned that from the French. They wore white tennis shoes, white over the calf length socks, white shorts and white shirts. It was really a big thing. They had tournaments and played every night. After the movie, I usually went back to my room, turned on the lamp and stayed up until about 11:00 p.m. writing letters to my family. And that was a typical day at the Infantry School.

One day I decided that the officer candidates needed a class in "dustoff" procedures (aerial medevac). Dustoff was the call sign we used for the helicopter ambulance that flew the wounded out of the jungle. There were lots of problems associated with this in the field. First of all, the pilot had to find the infantry down there in that mass of green jungle, and many times he had to do it in the dark. So, you needed to know how to orient the pilot to your general location, and how to talk him down to your actual spot on the ground. This included the importance of bringing them in over friendly areas, and not over the enemy so as not to get them shot down while coming in for the pickup. Also, once he was on the ground he was very vulnerable to mortar attack, so the wounded needed to be loaded on board as fast as possible.

The Vietnamese were very poor on all of this so I decided to give them a class on the subject. I picked a real sharp Vietnamese Infantry Captain to teach the class. He spoke fluent English so we were able to go over the procedures one by one. We covered how to locate the chopper in the sky, how to vector him in, how to bring him down, how to use the approach of least danger, and most importantly, how to organize the landing zone so that people weren't in the way of each other, and that the "carrying parties" were ready to shove the wounded on board as fast as possible. We went over all of this in minute detail. Then came the night for the class. I had ordered a real helicopter to come out and to land right in front of the Cadets in the bleachers so that everybody could see exactly how it was supposed to be done. I was really looking forward to this. Finally, we were going to do something the right way.

The Captain proceeded to spend the first two hours before darkness teaching them the importance of proper medevac procedures. Then he organized some of the students into a landing zone party. All was ready. We called in the helicopter and vectored him in using a strobe light. That part went well. But once he landed, it literally turned into a "Chinese fire drill." Even though they had been trained on it, even though they had gone over it step by step, even though they had practiced it, it turned out to be a real mess. The "wounded" who could walk jumped on the helicopter first, leaving the stretcher patients lying on the ground. (Just like they do in combat I might add.) The crew members had to hop out of the helicopter and load the stretchers because the carrying parties didn't seem to know what to do. I don't know what went wrong, but I remembered the saying, "the best laid plans of mice and men." In any event, I hoped they had learned something from it. Prior to that time they had received no training at all in aerial medevac.

The Infantry School decided to conduct training on the Infantry Battalion in the day and night attack in a conventional environment. Why they did this, I'll never know. They would never get a chance to attack the VC on line. Perhaps there might be some remote place in this war where it might apply, but for the most part it would be wasted training. Of course as a by-product it would teach them organization and control and that couldn't hurt.

So the day came. They put two student companies on line, a third company in reserve, and moved out through the brush to assault a hill. They learned how to maneuver and how to use supporting fires, and that was good. Also, one value of the exercise, was that we were able to walk every inch of terrain that we were going to use that night to insure that no VC would be in it. After the day problem was over we moved back to the same starting line to prepare for the night attack. But first we ate supper, then the Cadets were briefed. They were shown how to conduct a night attack (a very complicated maneuver). To assist the students to see where they were in the dark, an 81mm mortar was going to fire flares into the sky to illuminate the area. The area would be as bright as daylight with those parachute flares hanging up there. Of course you couldn't do that in combat. The instructors were only doing it to assist the Cadets as a part of their training.

The correct methods (in combat) was to sneak up to within 100 feet or so of the enemy in the darkness, and then charge him quickly on a common signal so as to catch him in his sleep. If you did use flares, you were supposed to drop them behind the enemy so that they

271

would be silhouetted against the sky and you could spot them.

There was usually no problem associated with the use of parachute flares. If fired properly, by the time they hit the ground, they were all burned out and wouldn't start a fire. The entire shell was fired from an 81mm mortar tube, and then climbed up to about 1000 feet, where it exploded. The shell then separated into two pieces. One part became the floating parachute. The other, the container that got it up there, would fall back to earth. That container (called a sabot) was quite heavy and was shaped like a wine bottle. The trick was to fire the mortar so that the sabot would land off to the side of the troops, and the parachute itself would drift over the troops.

As I moved along with the students later in the night I could hear the sabots falling in among us. (They made a whistling sound as they turned end over end.) It didn't take me long to figure out that somebody was going to get hit on the head and killed, so I quickly radioed back to the Advisors at the firing position, and told them that the sabots were falling among the troops, and that they should shift their fire immediately, so that they might fall to the side. Then I continued to follow the students. However, sabots continued to fall among us. Then after a few minutes, I heard a tremendous commotion; shouting, Vietnamese jabbering, flashlights being turned on. Someone shouted that a student had been shot in the back.

The Captain in charge of the problem immediately called off the exercise. We picked up the wounded officer candidate by his arms and legs, and carried him over to a little bamboo hootch and laid him down. The medics put him on his stomach. Everybody shined their flashlights on him. Then they took scissors and cut away his shirt. There, just to the right of his spine and a little above the buttocks was a large hole, about four inches wide. No blood was gushing out. It just looked like somebody had taken a very sharp knife and cut a big hole in his back, lifted off the skin and threw it away. As I looked into the cavity, I could see blood pulsating up and down but it didn't run out of the wound. It was almost like watching a surgical movie. I could see what appeared to be organs or parts of his body inside.

I looked up at the Captain and he looked back at me. Both our fingers went to the triggers of our carbines at the same time. We had the same thought. Somehow or another a VC sniper had slipped in among us. We switched off all but one of the flashlights. The medic continued to work in low light. Then we fanned out. We looked around. Was there somebody out there? No one seemed to act like it. I could hear the students continue to talk back and forth. Eventually the wounded man was put on a stretcher and taken out. We called off the problem and went home for the night.

The next day we learned what really happened. A sabot had fallen from the sky and struck this Cadet in the back just above the buttocks and then passed down through his stomach cavity. The shell actually plunged down through the flesh of his back, through his groin and lodged partially down his leg with the rest of it sticking up in his lower intestines. It was completely hidden inside his body so we couldn't see it the night before. He died, of course.

CHAPTER 21

One day my boss, Major Smith, wanted to know if I wanted to go with him on R&R. I told him "Yes, of course. But I can't. I've already had an R&R to Hong Kong."

But he said, "That will be no problem. I can arrange another one for you." (He wanted to go to Bangkok and he didn't want to go alone.)

So I said, "Great!"

The day arrived and we flew to Thailand. What a beautiful city! We stayed at the American run R&R hotel, complete with its own swimming pool. The hotel was used mainly by Army and Air Force pilots that flew into the country on TDY and needed a place to rest. That night we went out to eat. We picked one of the places listed on the bulletin board. It turned out to be a combination restaurant/night club. When we arrived, I noticed lots of GIs out on the dance floor dancing with Thai girls.

After dinner, as I worked my way down a hall towards the restroom, I passed by a room chock full of beautiful Thai Women. They were all seated around in a circle on folding chairs facing the door. The door had a square glass window in it so you could look inside. I learned that these were dance girls who were available for hire by the hour. All you had to do was go up to the window, pick out the one you wanted, point her out to the Maitre'd and they would bring her over to your table. You could buy her dinner or pay for her conversation and dance by the hour.

Major Smith and I decided to pick out two girls to dance with that night. It was all sort of humorous. We went up to the window. There I spotted a beautiful Thai girl. I pointed her out to the Maitre'd and they brought her over to me. She spoke English. Major Smith picked out a girl, too. Then we took them over to our table. We had no thought of taking these girls home because Major Smith was a very happily married man. (In fact, that's why he asked me to go with him on his R&R because he wasn't going to run all over the place getting into trouble. He just wanted to have a good time.) It was so much fun to talk to these girls and to dance with them and laugh and have a beer.

At 11:00 the place closed and the girls went home. They thanked us for a good time and left. I noticed that they all left together. I guess they did this kind of work for meals and money. That's not to say that there are no prostitutes in Thailand. There are literally thousands! You can buy a girl to live with by the hour, the day or the week and many Americans did this. But this night club, was evidently not that kind of place. It was just a "talk and dance" place.

While I was in the club, I saw General Minh seated at a table. He was the leader of the first coup in Vietnam, the one that had toppled General Diems' regime. But "Big Minh" was later overthrown by General Khanh. He was now living in exile in Bangkok. What an important figure in history.

The next day we decided to go down to the beach at Pattaya (about a hundred miles from Bangkok). We talked to some of the people at the hotel about the best way of getting there. They said the cheapest way was to hire a taxi. (Taxis were extremely cheap in Thailand.) So we went out the front door, found a very friendly taxi driver, who spoke excellent English, agreed on a price and away we went. He owned a large, old, beat up, Chevrolet. After winding our way through the heavy, choking, fuming, impossible traffic of Bangkok, we finally got out on a two lane blacktop road and sped South.

As we drove along, I noticed canals to the left and the right of the road. Thailand had hundreds and thousands of canals all teeming with small boat traffic. These small boats seemed to be the taxis of Thailand. Their boats don't use outboard engines like ours. Instead, they have a gasoline engine mounted on the back deck with a big long propeller shaft sticking out the back of it. The whole thing was balanced with a handle and the motor was always running. When the driver wanted to make the boat move, he simply dropped the whirling propeller down into the water and away they zipped. They traveled at phenomenal speeds. When he wanted to stop, he simply cut the engine, lifted the shaft out of the water and glided to the next dock along the river. It was a very unique system.

Later, our route started to pick up large rice paddy fields and occasional jungle. It reminded me so much of Vietnam. As we headed southeast we could see more and more jungle and fewer villages. As we crossed one extremely large rice paddy with a jungle line ahead, I tensed up. I couldn't help it. I kept asking myself, "Is anybody over there? Are they going to try to kill us? Has this road been cleared?" I couldn't get Vietnam out of my mind. But of course, it was all very safe.

After a successful beach trip and a wonderful R&R, we flew back to Vietnam. Driving back to Thu Duc I saw a sight that I couldn't believe. It was truck after truck after truck loaded with American Soldiers. And these were not Advisors. They were combat troops. I could see privates and corporals and sergeants sitting on those trucks. They looked real sharp and there was a precise 50 yard distance between each truck, (just like it called for in "the manual"). And the men were very alert. Everybody was wearing their "steel pot" and there was no joking around. Weapons were cocked and at the ready. A machine gun sat on top of each cab and it was pointed outward ready to fire. They looked good, *really good*. These were professional soldiers. I noticed that they were all wearing a brown patch on their shoulder with a big red "1" emblazoned on it. These were the men of the famous U.S. First Infantry Division. They were now the first American Combat Division to arrive in Vietnam. It sure was a surprise to me! Since we were on a super highway, we simply sped past them and headed for home.

As soon as I arrived back at Thu Duc, I told all the other Advisors that the Americans had landed. They couldn't believe it either. We later learn that these troops would be setting up at the corner of the Binh Hoa/Vung Tau highway, a relatively safe area. But we all knew what was going to happen that night. We talked about it over supper. We all agreed that the VC would probably send over one or two men to harass the new arrivals and then all hell would break loose. All those scared, 18 year old, inexperienced privates would let loose with everything they had. It would be quite a show. And we would be able to watch it from our front porch.

After supper we all drifted out onto the porch to watch what would happen. Sitting there at 9:00 p.m. with a beer in our hands we suddenly saw a parachute flare far, far away, hanging in the sky. Then, in the extreme far distance tracers streaming heavenward. The war had begun. We were too far away to hear the gun fire of course, but we could see the fireworks. All of us realized that they were not under any serious attack. It was probably just a couple of locals harassing them. So we sat there and laughed about it. But deep down in our hearts we felt sorry for them. Most of them would not be coming home in a year.

The next morning when we all gathered together for breakfast, we learned that a First Sergeant from the 16th Infantry had been killed the previous night. It was a real shame too because it didn't have to had happened. He was probably accidentally killed by one of our own panicky soldiers. Of course the report will read "killed in action by enemy fire." And that's the way it should be.

It was getting time for me to go home to the States. I only had two weeks left in country, so I decided to throw a farewell party and invite all my Vietnamese friends and fellow officers of the Tactics Department at the Infantry School. As a matter of protocol, I also invited the School Commandant, a full Colonel. I headed up the road and picked a restaurant near the school which I knew would be safe. I went over the menu with the owner. I picked pigeon soup, salad, rice, and two different meat dishes (pork and beef strips prepared Chinese style). I also talked to the Infantry School about security. They agreed to station a squad of men around the place that night,

277

armed with sub machine guns. That would insure that a grenade wouldn't come flying through the window and land in our soup.

The night of the dinner arrived. There were about thirty of us sitting around a "U" shaped table. The School Commandant was in the exact center and place of honor. I was to his left. The first course to be served was a bowl of pigeon soup and they served me first. As I looked down into the bowl I immediately became a little bit disconcerted. There, floating in my bowl of soup, was a pigeon's head; beak, eyeballs, and feathers and all. It really was disgusting looking. I then recalled from my MATA training, that the guest of honor was supposed to get the head. It always went to the Senior man or the guest of honor. I surmised that they had given it to me because they considered me the head man, since it was my party and I was paying for it. Suddenly I got an idea. The Commandant was sitting next to me and he was a Colonel. I knew he would enjoy eating the pigeon head. (After all the Vietnamese considered it a delicacy.) So turning to the Colonel I said, "Colonel, I understand that in your country the head man always gets the pigeon's head in his soup. Sir, I am only a Captain. You are a Colonel. You must have the head."

He smiled broadly and exchanged his soup with me with the greatest of pleasure. Suddenly everybody around the table nodded their heads in approval and smiled. They all thought it was the most respectful thing they had ever seen. Then the Vietnamese Colonel reached down into his soup, grasped the pigeon head by his two fingers, stuck the whole thing in his mouth, and bit it off at the beak. I could hear him crunch right through the bone, yuk!

Later we got the word that the Infantry School was planning to take all the Cadets out on a "real live," combat operation. Up until then, the areas that they had been training in had all been very secure. But the Commandant now felt, that before they went out to the field as commissioned officers, they ought to load up their rifles and head out after some real VC, at least once. So, he planned an operation departing directly from the School, sweeping across some farmland and rice paddies, and then eventually, patrolling into a jungle area before breaking out on the Bear Cat Highway, between Binh Hoa and Vung Tau. It would be a two day operation with one overnight. However, to be on the safe side, one RVN Infantry Battalion would sweep the area in advance of us just to make sure there were no large size enemy force in it. But that didn't mean that some local force might not slip back in after they had passed, so live ammunition would be handed out.

The next morning we moved out. It was real disorder, a "Chinese fire drill." People just didn't know what they were doing. You would have thought that after all the hours of training they had received, they could at least fan out and get organized. But they couldn't. I was very discouraged about it. These were the future leaders of the country, the future combat officers of the infantry battalions, and I didn't like what I saw. As I walked along with the troops, I could see fear in their eyes, even though they were in a very secure area. Of course, it was easy for me not to be afraid because I knew when to fear and when not to fear. But it was just ridiculous for anyone to act that scared that close to home. We were only a couple of miles out and yet I could read fear in their faces. They were scared to death to leave the safety of Saigon, rich city boys and absolute cowards, men who would not fight for their country.

As we moved along, one man fell out from heat exhaustion. They loaded him up on a stretcher and carted him away back towards a road where he could be put in an ambulance. Ridiculous. If you fell out that soon with a regular Infantry Battalion, they would probably leave you behind.

After an uneventful day of crossing fields, and vegetable farms, and a little bit of brush, we ended up on top of a big hill in the middle of a bunch of rice paddies. They had decided to put the class in a circle on top of this hill for the night. Unfortunately, there was no water on top of the hill. However, the abandoned rice paddies below did have stagnant water in them. There was green slime floating on top of it but it was the only water available. We were completely out and it was hot. So I took my hand, scraped away the green slime, held my canteen down and let the water juggle in. When it was all filled up I threw in double the amount of purification tablets for good measure. Then I let it set for an extra long time to make sure the capsules had done their work before I drank it. Later the Infantry School flew in a helicopter loaded with fresh water cans. Pandemonium broke out among the Cadets. Most of them had not drank the water from the paddy and were now thirsty beyond belief. Their physical needs preempted any form of security. They all gathered around the chopper like a bunch of little kids pushing, shoving, and begging. There was absolutely no order or discipline. It was all very disgusting.

The next day we moved out. This time it was through more brush and jungle. Eventually, we hit the road near Bear Cat. We loaded on the trucks and headed North. I could tell the road was very well protected all the way up to the Binh Hoa junction. We roared home. The training operation was over.

The next day, right after lunch at the Advisors Compound, the guys were getting up from the table, scooting their chairs back and heading for their rooms to change clothes and play a little tennis, when the Senior Advisor came up to me and told me that he had been in contact with the First Infantry Division, and that they were looking for someone with a little field experience, who might go along with them as an Advisor of sorts, on their first combat operation. The person they were looking for was an "old Indian scout," someone who knew the area and could show them a few tricks and what the jungle was all about.

Then the Colonel informed me that he had selected me to go. Of course, I was flattered. But I really didn't want to go either. I didn't want to go because it seemed like everybody in Vietnam was either getting killed their first two weeks in country or their last two weeks and I didn't want that to happen to me. It was just an incredibly weird thing, but, helicopter pilots, advisors, whomever, were either shot dead their first two weeks or their last two. In fact, it was so bad in some units that they had a rule that you couldn't go out on an operation your last two weeks in country because things like that were happening. And now, here was my own boss, volunteering me to go. I hemmed and hawed about it and didn't act super interested. I felt sorry for the American infantry of course and wanted to help them but I was torn between two worlds; the world of wanting to go home alive...and the world of being killed. But I knew in my heart that I should go and that I would go. Besides, he had already nominated me. I couldn't back out. So I "volunteered."

The next day, with a heavy heart, I grabbed my pack, carbine, ammunition, smoke grenades, and hand grenades and hopped into my jeep and headed for the Binh Hoa/Vung Tau road junction where I had agreed to meet them. It turned out to be an infantry platoon, forty men, commanded by a Second Lieutenant. It was unbelievable. I had never seen more than two or three Americans together at any one time in Vietnam and now here they were, a whole bunch staring right at me. I was use to seeing little Vietnamese soldiers with grins on their faces, not tall, somber faced Americans.

I got together with the Lieutenant. We looked at the map. He seemed to know where to go and what to do, so it looked like I would just be tagging along. He had selected a pretty good route. Away we went. I was immediately impressed with the platoon. All the while that I had been talking to the Lieutenant his men had spread out in a circle, weapons at the ready, and were not talking. Using only hand and arm signals they moved out silently into the jungle. They moved like a real military machine. The sun was shining. It looked like it was going to be a good day. As we moved through the jungle the platoon automatically tightened up a bit. Then later, as we came out of the jungle and into an open area, his men spread out and posted scouts and flankers. One thing was certain, these guys weren't going to be surprised. Of course, the scouts might get surprised but that's the way it was supposed to be. It was their job to protect the main body. These guys were really doing it right.

Later we crossed a rice paddy and then into some brush again. As we moved south, I looked off to my left and saw those hills where I was pinned down that day (the day when I had no radio support, no artillery, no Air Force, and no helicopter medevac and no nothing). I remembered that day very clearly, lying there, having all those bullets cutting down the leaves above my head. It all seemed like a dream now.

We continued moving south. To our front appeared a large open field with a hill and jungle behind it. Again, everything was done according to the book. He sent scouts across first. They used the Tonto and Lone Ranger method; one ran across the open area while the other hid behind a dike covering him. The scouts "leap frogged" across without incident and then disappeared into the jungle to our front. Minutes passed. It was all quiet. We looked at each other apprehensively. Then the scouts emerged back from the jungle and signaled an "all clear." It was now okay to cross. Again, the Lieutenant took no chances. He put out flankers. We moved across in a very spread out formation.

When we arrived at the jungle, to my surprise, I found fighting positions there, foxholes and trenches, all freshly dug. The dirt had only recently been piled up. I could tell that somebody had just been there. How long ago, I didn't know. I thought to myself, did the Lord cause them to move at some earlier time in order to spare my life, or had they been there just a few minutes ago, and had cleared out when they saw things were being done right, and didn't want to take on the First Infantry Division. I would never know. In any event, God had spared my life another day. I knew he had. And I was grateful. We moved up the hill and then further south without incident. Eventually we cut left, and then headed back to the highway.

While waiting for the trucks, I got to talking to the Lieutenant. He had taken a liking to my carbine. (It had the barrel sawed off and utilized a folding metal paratrooper stock. When folded, it was only about a foot and a half long and very easy to carry. Yet, when snapped out, it became a very fast bursting, accurate submachine gun.) I could tell that he wanted it. On sudden impulse, I tossed him the weapon and said, "Here, take it. It's yours, I won't be needing it anymore, I'm going home."

I looked at him. He was so clean cut, like a West Point Cadet right off the poster. He had 360 days to go. I wondered if he would make it!

It was time to go home, home from my last combat operation. As my jeep sped northward toward Binh Hoa, I thought about my tour. This was the last operation. Now I was safe, I was going home. But something warned me, too. You're not on the plane yet. "Pride cometh before the fall." You can never let your guard down. You can never be totally sure. You're not home...until you're home.

The time came for me to drive to Saigon for my final medical examination. Every Advisor had to get one last physical exam before he went home, to make sure he wasn't taking some rare disease back with him. The two most common problems were yellow jaundice and malaria. A full thirty percent of all Advisors were lost to these two diseases. They usually knocked a guy out for four months, and most of the afflicted had to be medically evacuated back to Japan, and sometimes all the way back to the States. Some never got to complete a full tour due to sickness. So it was my turn to see the Navy medics. They worked out of a large building located in Cholon. The war was still being run by the Navy, but the Army would be taking over soon. The name would be changed from MAAG to MAC-V. The Navy medics did the usual thing; chest x-rays, blood sample, stool sample, etc. After turning everything into the medics, they then asked me to sit out in the lounge and wait. After about a half an hour a corpsman came out and said, "Where do you eat?"

"Why?" I asked.

"Because I don't want to eat there," he responded.

He then told me that I had amoebic dysentery. I knew there had been something wrong with my stomach the whole time I had been in Vietnam, but I didn't know what. It was just impossible to live out in the bush, eat off plates washed in cold water and not get something. Even if you did figure out that you had amoebic dysentery and took medicine for it, the next time you went out to a village and ate with the Vietnamese, you'd have it again. He gave me a big bottle full of large white pills and told me to take them faithfully for two weeks and it would clear up my problem. I was not to eat anymore Vietnamese food whether in a nice restaurant or not.

I promised him I would eat only American food at the Advisors House or canned C rations. He said, "Good."

I later found out that amoebic dysentery was another big "crippler" too, and it sent a lot of good men home. But in my case, I guess my system just learned to live with it. I was thankful that I didn't have to go home on account of any illness. One of the problems with being "medevaced" out early is, that unless you complete a full six months "in country" before you leave, you don't get credit for a full tour. It simply meant that they would send you back to Vietnam again and you would have to start over from scratch. And I didn't want that to happen to me.

It was noon, the day before I was to go home. We were listening to the news at the Advisors House. AFN radio announced that the airport had just been bombed. Somehow or another the VC had sneaked into the building and planted an extremely large bomb. It blew out one of the walls and all of the glass. My heart sank. I was flying out tomorrow. Would the airport be closed? Would my flight be delayed? I wondered.

My last night in Vietnam. Wouldn't you know, I got assigned as the Duty Officer. As usual I would have to get up at various times during the night and check the perimeter. No danger there. It was the easiest job in the world. But I wouldn't be able to get a full night's sleep. About 3:00 a.m. I got up with the interpreter, grabbed my carbine, piled into the jeep and headed out, lights off, down the perimeter road. The bunker I decided to inspect was the one furtherest down the ridge. It looked out over a rice paddy and the Rung Sat area below. It was our most dangerous approach. If the VC did attack, it would be from this direction.

I stopped way short of the position, turned off my motor and walked quietly towards the bunker. When I got there I was not challenged. They were all asleep. All of them. So I started rousting them up. The Vietnamese interpreter shouted at them in Vietnamese. I watched in the glow of the moonlight. Every single one of them had been bagged out. They stumbled to life. Rich kids from

Saigon, used to luxury, well educated. None of them wanted to be there and none of them wanted to fight for their country. They were taking the easy way out...officers school. It beat being drafted as a private.

I was furious with them. They were supposed to be protecting everybody else back at the school. People were counting on them. I started chewing them out using the interpreter. I told him to tell them that they were lazy and that they were not doing their job and that they were a disgrace to their country. He started but I could tell by the sheepish look on his face and my knowledge of the Vietnamese language that my message was not getting through. I grabbed the interpreter and told him, "You tell them exactly what I tell you. Don't mince words. Don't save any face. This is my last night in Vietnam and I want them to hear it the way it is."

Then I let them have it with both barrels. It was something the Cadets weren't used to. In their culture, you didn't talk to their face, you didn't shout at them, and didn't tell it like it was. You always let them "get by" a little. But this was my last night in Vietnam and I was going to let them have it all. One year of pent up emotion and frustration poured out of my heart and fell on them. At the end I told them, "It's your country. You are going to have to fight for it, and if you don't, it's going to go down the tubes. It's going to fall to the Communists. It's all up to you," and then I stalked off.

It was my last day in Vietnam. I had made arrangements earlier to meet Dai Uy Duong for lunch and to say good-bye. We would be having an early lunch, about 11:00 a.m., so I could catch my afternoon flight. I pulled up in front of the French restaurant on Thu Do Street where we agreed to meet. There was Dai Uy grinning as usual. It was good to see him. We went inside while our drivers waited outside with our weapons. We sat down at a small table on the porch overlooking the sidewalk. He ordered some wine and paté followed by sausage and french bread. Then we talked. He told me that he was not on the Ranger staff in Saigon and that he was being promoted to Major. He also told me of a new concept that they had for the employment of the Ranger Battalions. No longer would they be "piece mealed" out to the Districts. From now on out they would work directly for a newly formed Ranger Command and they would be employed in regimental strength only (three battalions at a time).

I liked this plan because the Rangers would now be their own boss and could supervise their own operations. In this manner they could also achieve an element of surprise. Not working for the locals meant that they would have better food, better equipment and better support. It was a great idea. The old concept of shoving them around from District to District was a bad one because of the poor manner in which the Districts employed them. Every District had its own hornet's nest in which they were afraid to go, so they just waited until they got a Ranger Battalion to clean it up. They didn't care about the Ranger casualties because the Rangers didn't belong to them. They were a gift. Conversely, their own local replacements were impossible to come by, so the District Chief reasoned that it was better to lose Rangers than his own men. Also, Rangers were the elite. All volunteers. They were supposed to fight hard. Why not give them the dirtiest jobs. But this practice was decimating the Ranger Battalions and this new concept would be a vast improvement.

Finally, it was time to say good-bye. Lunch was over. We walked outside. We stood by the jeeps looking at each other. It was an emotional moment. Neither one of us could talk. Finally I spoke, the words blurted out, "Take it easy Dai Uy. Don't push too hard. Don't get killed. the U.S. Troops are here now. Be careful. I'll miss you."

Tears welled up in my eyes. He nodded. We stood there silently for a moment. Then he walked away. He climbed into his jeep and turned around for one last look. He smiled as the jeep pulled away. I wondered if I would ever see him again.

I was time to leave...my plane was waiting. I received word earlier that day, that the airport would be open for business even though it had been bombed, so I drove over. Security was tight, very tight. There were soldiers with guns all over the place. As I pulled up into the main terminal I could see what they were talking about. All the windows had been blown out and glass was everywhere. I lifted my duffel bag to my shoulder and worked my way through the broken pieces to the "check in" counter. The terminal was a sea of khaki clad Advisors waiting to go home.

Outside a World Airways 707 jet stood ready to take us back to the States, the "Freedom Bird" they called it. Processing was relatively simple. Then we all moved out to the plane. I walked up the ramp, sat down, and buckled in. The engines came to life in their usual slow, whining fashion. Then the plane taxied down to the end of the runway and turned around, poised for take off. The pilot gave it maximum power, and we roared off into the sky. I thought maybe all the Advisors on the plane would let out some tremendous cheer when our wheels lifted off the runway, but there was nothing. Everybody just sat there silently, staring straight ahead or looking out the window. Too much had happened. Too many friends had been killed. Too many Vietnamese had died. We had seen too much. There was nothing to cheer about. I looked out the window. The plane banked left and I got a good view of the Rung Sat area south of the Infantry School. I looked down at the dark jungle below and told myself, "I'll never be back."

The plane leveled out and headed for cruising altitude. Later in the flight, the stewardess slid back a panel exposing a movie screen and turned on a projector. Wouldn't you know it, a war movie. Lots of submachine gun fire, grenades, and bombs. What a way to fly home from Vietnam...watching a war movie.

The jet engines whined as we began our descent into Travis Air Force Base, California. The plane touched down and we were safe. We all filed out and caught the bus to San Francisco for connecting flights at the commercial airport. When I arrived in San Francisco, I called Clay Mansfield's widow on the phone. I had written her a letter earlier, before I had left Vietnam. I wanted to see her and she wanted to see me so we agreed to go out to dinner. We were old friends from our days at Fort Benning. I had time to do this. My flight to St. Louis wasn't until much later in the evening. She picked me up in her car and we drove over to Fisherman's Wharf where all the good restaurants were located. As we drove along I looked out the car window. I could see lights, traffic, a country at peace.

It was so hard to believe that I was home. It was just as if there were no war at all. You just get off a plane and you're in another world. But as I glanced over at her I knew there had been a war because her husband had been killed in it and he was now buried.

We ate supper at Alioto's Restaurant. We got a table on the second floor. It had a nice view of the boats docked peacefully at the wharf below. While eating, I heard a loud boisterous man across the room from us, half drunk, sounding off about some country called Saigon and American involvement. He didn't even know the name of the country. How stupid. But later things got quiet.

We talked about Clay. She told me about his funeral at West Point. He had been buried there along with his father who had been killed in the Battle of the Bulge in World War II. So now Clayton's mother had lost two; her husband and her only son. She told me how Clay's mother had refused to accept the flag at grave site. It was just too much for her to bear. So Susan accepted the flag for her. Tears streamed down her face as we talked. What could I say? What could I do?

Later she drove me back to the airport. It was time to say good-bye. I looked at her. She was so pretty. It was a very emotional time for both of us. Suddenly we were in each other's arms. I held her tightly for a long time. Then we kissed. I got out of her car and stood there watching as she drove away. When her car was out of sight I walked slowly up into the airport. The words of President Johnson, that I had heard earlier in the day, rang in my ears. "We seek no wider war. American boys will not be sent to fight in Southeast Asia."

Inwardly I responded, "I hear you talking but what do you know, you live in Washington and I lived in the village." I took a deep drag on my cigarette, inhaled, flipped it away and strode into the terminal.

EPILOGUE

Captain Behnke returned to Vietnam three years after the events in this book took place to serve yet another tour in that country, this time with the U.S. First Infantry Division. He was never wounded or injured. He retired from the Army in 1977 as a Lieutenant Colonel and then studied for the Ministry. He is currently a Lutheran pastor in Frankfurt, Germany, serving the American community.

In 1990, he returned to Vietnam as a tourist, along with his son, Michael, his brother, Al, and a friend from college days, Mr. Art Haake. They received a tumultuous welcome in Binh Gia Village. Mr. Sung, the man who's house he stayed in Binh Gia, is still alive, as well as his wife and two daughters. The young priest, Father Thuy, also met him there. (The Communists had imprisoned him for 11 years after they had taken over.) Their wonderful reunion was cut short a half hour later when the communist police arrived and took Behnke and his party to police headquarters in Vund Tau where they were released after five hours of lectures and a warning not to return to Binh Gia without a police escort. The fate of Father Thuy after this reunion is not known.

Dai Uy Duong, Comanding Officer of the 33rd Ranger Battalion, was imprisoned by the Communists for 13 years after their take-over, just for being a Ranger. He miraculously surfaced in California just two weeks before this book was to go to press and two weeks before Captain

Behnke was to go to Germany. A personal reunion was not possible, but they were able to talk on the telephone. Dai Uy Duong, now lives with his daughter (the baby daughter in the book) in Southern California.

Lieutenant Trinh, the paraplegic, died trying to escape Vietnam in a boat.

Captain John Ramsey left Vietnam for ROTC duty at Westminster College. Oddly enough, one year later Captain Behnke was assigned to the same ROTC unit and John ended up being Behnke's boss. They remain the best of friends to this day. Captain Ramsey survived four tours in Vietnam and is currently a retired full Colonel near Ft. Bragg, North Carolina.

Colonel "Jap" Wilson retired to Tucson, Arizona where he later died of cancer.

Tau, the jeep driver, is alive and lives in Saigon.

Sgt. Hieu, the interpreter at the Infantry School and leader of the Duc Protestant Church, disappeared without a trace, after the Communists took over the country.

The Infantry School is now a prison for political re-education.

Captain Johnson, who made the daring helicopter rescue of Captain Behnke at Binh Gia, was later shot through the right arm by a .50 calibre machine gun bullet and was forced to leave flight status due to his wounds. However, he remained on active duty and a few years later attended Captain Behnke's promotion party to Major.